Literary Structures

Edited by JOHN GARDNER

Previously Published Titles in the Series

Construction of Christian Poetry in Old English
by John Gardner

Construction of *Paradise Lost*
by Burton Jasper Weber

Construction of the Wakefield Cycle
by John Gardner

Flamboyant Drama
A Study of *The Castle of Perseverance, Mankind*, and *Wisdom*
by Michael R. Kelley

Forms of Glory
Structure and Sense in Virgil's *Aeneid*
by J. William Hunt

Homer's *Iliad*: The Shield of Memory
by Kenneth John Atchity

Kingship and Common Profit in Gower's *Confessio Amantis*
by Russell A. Peck

Wedges and Wings: The Patterning of *Paradise Regained*
by Burton Jasper Weber

Epic and Romance
in the
Argonautica
of
Apollonius

CHARLES ROWAN BEYE

Foreword by John Gardner

SOUTHERN ILLINOIS UNIVERSITY PRESS
Carbondale and Edwardsville

Copyright © 1982 by the BOARD OF TRUSTEES, Southern Illinois
University

Printed in the United States of America
Designed by DESIGN FOR PUBLISHING, Faith Nance
Production supervised by JOHN DEBACHER

Library of Congress Cataloging in Publication Data
Beye, Charles Rowan.
    Epic and romance in the Argonautica of Apollonius.
    (Literary structures)
    Bibliography: p.
    Includes index.
    1. Apollonius, Rhodius. Argonautica. I. Title. II. Series.
PA3872.Z4B4   883'.01   81–21402
ISBN 0–8093–1020 1   AACR2

For
William Musgrave Calder III

Contents

Foreword ix

Preface xiii

1. The Poet 1

2. The Tradition 39

3. The Heroes 77

4. The Voyage 100

5. Sweet Talk 120

6. Love Affair 143

Bibliographical Essay 169

Notes 179

Index 189

Foreword

The Literary Structures series presents close analyses of literary master-pieces, studies not primarily for specialists but written by specialists for literary generalists—that is, teachers not mainly concerned with ancient poetry, for graduate students, and for anyone interested in increasing his understanding and appreciation of great works of literature. Judging by the professional critical response, the series has proved more avant-garde than it was originally intended to be. Books like Burton Weber's on *Paradise Lost* and *Paradise Regained*, or Russell Peck's on the *Confessio Amantis*, or Kenneth Atchity's on Homer's *Iliad* have been received as not only good introductions to important works of art but convincing statements, overturning received opinions.

There are good reasons, I think, for the extraordinary success of the series. For one thing, or so it seems to me, in the fifties, sixties, and seventies, professional students of literature specialized themselves almost out of reach of the ordinary educated reader. It was bad form to talk about the poem itself; one had to have an angle. One talked about Chaucer and Neoplatonism, or Chaucer and the Patristic tradition, or Chaucer and medieval fashion. One could not simply follow where the poem led. This is not to deny that specialization has its virtues; it is only to say that, once the specialists have come in with their data, it is important to go back to the poem as a whole. That has been the business of the Literary Structures series: to read great poems in a newly informed way.

Another reason for the success of the series, it seems to me, has to do with the temper of the times. Greek, Latin, Old English, and Dante's Italian are no longer widely taught. Yet there are those of us who are hungry to understand the masterpieces of the past. All of us living in the modern world—perhaps all human beings everywhere, from the beginning of time—feel, or have felt, that something is missing, maybe sometime it was better. Perhaps, we think, the great poets had an answer. As we read them, with the help of a good teacher, we realize that indeed they did, an answer (or a multitude of answers) still worth hearing.

Charles Beye's study of the *Argonautica* is one of the most interesting and lively pieces we've published. At one time, the *Argonautica* was thought to be a masterpiece. Virgil made heavy use of it for his *Aeneid*, and medieval mythographers turned to it again and again. Relatively little has been written in English on the *Argonautica*, and none of the available translations is either very accurate or very exciting, mainly because none of them quite bring across for us the symbolic richness, the jokes, or much of the irony. Perhaps it's simply that in the old days, when the *Argonautica* was used mainly as an exercise study in hard Greek, no one seemed to much notice the considerable literary value of the poem.

In any event, the strange fact is that—except, possibly, for a very special group of specialists—for something like twenty-one centuries one of the greatest works of the ancient world lay, for all practical purposes, fast asleep. Why did no one—except Virgil and a few others now forgotten—notice it? The answer, I think, is that history has come around at last to a repetition of the age of Apollonius of Rhodes. In spirit, Apollonius is a brother to John Barth, Donald Barthelme, William Gass, Robert Coover, and others of our moment. In twenty-one centuries almost no one else of that ilk showed up, or at any rate survived in print.

As Charles Beye points out in his first chapter, Apollonius was a member of that special society that supported and served the Library of Alexandria, the greatest library of the ancient world. The library contained thousands and thousands of works, including perhaps hundreds of versions of Homer's epics and many of the Greek plays, odes, hymns, lyrics, and histories now wholly or partly lost. It included, too, what we might describe as a society of scholars. Apollonius could write for the most literate audience the world ever knew until now. It was a culture that had learned, to some extent, the intellectual and emotional power of women, and the limitation of the old "heroic values" of stealing, killing, and raping. Apollonius could understand Homer more clearly than we do, at least in some respects: could see not only his greatness, which we recognize, but also the inhumanity of his age, noble as it was. The more questionable values in Homer's poetry—for instance his view of women as household treasure—are not troublesome to us because we've largely outlived them and hardly notice them. For Apollonius they were close enough to need correction.

Apollonius was what we now call a Deconstructionist. To make clear just how "modern" he is, and to suggest the importance of the work he did— aside from the glory of his poetry—it will be useful to talk about the present, much misunderstood theory of Deconstruction.

The New Critics of the thirties and forties—much maligned of late, for the most part wrongly—took the point of view that a reader's or critic's business was to understand the text line by line, suspending all moral judgments, simply trying to understand precisely what the poem said. The Deconstructionists take the point of view that often we are fooled by language. They claim that often what we say we'd be ashamed to say if we understood the subtle implications of our words. An easy and obvious example is the male chauvinism of our language. When speaking of the painter or musician we say "he," though many painters and musicians are women. The Deconstructionist begins, like the New Critic, by trying to understand what the poem or fiction says, but then he moves further, trying to see how language has tricked the writer into saying things that are not true. He looks at the noblest myths of our culture and suggests ways in which they may mislead us. For instance, he looks at stories of how the extremely rich are in fact miserable—the tale of Midas, for instance—and asks whether the story is "true" or merely a comfort to the poor.

Apollonius looks at Homer with an admiring but critical—Deconstructionist—eye. As a city man, he notices that the great heroes of the mythic early wars (Heracles, for instance) might not function very efficiently in town, where new kinds of heroism are needed. And he notices, of course, that Homer was a trifle male chauvinist. (Charles Beye points out, in his brilliant final chapter, that the "hero" of the *Argonautica* is Medea.) A part of Apollonius' project is the undermining of the old heroic ethic. By one trick after another he makes us look askance at the old-time strong men. He respects the physical power of a Heracles, but he persuades us that the man was, to say the least, a bad model.

In short, Charles Beye's reading of the *Argonautica* shows why it has caught on with contemporary writers—Donald Barthelme's *The Dead Father*, my own *Jason and Medeia*, and so on. Understanding the work as Beye explains it, we can see why it apparently failed with most of the sorrowful, lawful Romans; why only a few passages were allegorically acceptable to the Middle Ages; why the Victorians scarcely noticed it; and why now, in our time, it has resurfaced as an important work. In an age of nihilism and cynicism, it satisfies all our needs, yet it is not finally nihilistic or cynical. If in a sense it undermines the great works on which our civilization stands, poems like the *Iliad* and *Odyssey*, in another sense it adds to them, enlarges our vision, softens the sharp focus, makes ambiguous what once seemed plain and simple. No more old-style heroes, Apollonius says. No more fake nobility. A young woman—a brother-murderer, a father-betrayer, a witch—has more right to heaven than Heracles. The greatness of the poem is that, deconstructing the grand old myths, it seems true and, like those myths, give us a sense of the grandeur of human life.

Binghamton, New York JOHN GARDNER
February 1982

Preface

As the memory of pagan antiquity begins to slip from our grasp because we no longer learn Greek or Latin or study ancient history, literary historians have ceased to acknowledge all but a very few of the writers out of that throng who produced so prodigious a heap of literature over a span of a thousand years or more. Many these days begin with Dante, darting only a backward glance at his pagan antecedents.

Apollonius is a poet universally ignored. But he remains the essential link between Homer and Virgil—remains the poet who showed the Roman the way to translate the oral poetry of heroism into a complicated literary expression freighted with symbol. Apart from Theocritus' slight pastorals the *Argonautica* stands as the one complete and monumental text amid the uncertain fragments of the poetry of Alexandria, there to bear witness to the enormous shift in attitude toward poetry which informed all Roman literature and through it the literature of the West for the next two millenia. Apollonius' epic poem demonstrates, in addition, the inclination to shape narrative in the way novelists will eventually do; it is a poem at the crossroads.

More than anything else, however, the *Argonautica* is entertaining in itself. By turns witty, humorous, perverse, sad, even tragic, the narrative is itself a voyage; the narrator asks us to embark with him to gain not only the Fleece and Medea but a style and a chastened sensibility as well. And then, of course, there is the love story, one of the first in the Western tradition and one of the best.

Studying the *Argonautica* has been, for me, immensely gratifying. The intrinsic worth of the poem and the excellent scholarship inspired by it (of which more later) have made up part of the pleasure; another part derives from my encounter with the creative and provocative ideas of the many students who have worked on the poem with me. My seminars at Boston University and at the American School of Classical Studies remain delightful memories. Over the many years of discussing this poem I should like to recall and thank here especially J. M. Tillotson, T. M. Klein, L. Rissman, D. Staples, R. Elia, M. Fiveash, and M. Margolies. The manuscript has been read and much improved by M. Margolies, M. Fiveash, M. K. Gamel, and W. M. Calder III. This last gentleman has read everything I have written since I was in graduate school and I dedicate this book to him in thanks for his inspiration all these years.

Thanks are due as well to the Managing Committee of the American School of Classical Studies which afforded me the opportunity to pass a highly productive year in the library of the School, and to Nancy A. Winter, its librarian, who was tireless in her efforts to assist my research. I am also grateful to the Office of the Dean of Graduate Studies at Boston University who provided funds for the preparation of the manuscript of this book, and to John Engstrom who prepared the manuscript and improved it in many ways.

Because of their greater familiarity to modern readers than the Greek, Latinized spellings have been used throughout for all proper names. Thus our hero and heroine are Jason and Medea, not Iason and Mēdeia.

All the translations are my own. I have used the Greek text established by H. Fränkel in the Oxford series, but since it is so idiosyncratic, I have paid close attention to F. Vian in the Budé series for books 1 and 2, that of M. C. Seaton in the Loeb series for book 3 and that of E. Livrea for the fourth book. Readers will note that I translate brief bits into prose when I wish to stress the surface sense of the passage only, and longer pieces into a vague approximation of poetry when I wish to remind the reader that Apollonius was, after all, a poet telling his stories in dactylic hexametric lines.

I am particularly indebted to John Gardner, not only for drawing my attention to so many of my stylistic infelicities and introducing numerous improvements, but also for offering valuable questions, comments, and suggestions from which I have constantly benefited.

Boston, Massachusetts   CHARLES ROWAN BEYE
January 1982

Epic and Romance
in the *Argonautica*
of
Apollonius

1

The Poet

We know almost nothing about the life of Apollonius. He was born sometime in the early part of the third century B.C., perhaps at Alexandria. He studied with the poet-scholar Callimachus. His poetic career got off to a shaky start with an initial unfavorable critical reception of his poem *Argonautica*, but he later was much esteemed. He may have spent time on the island of Rhodes; he may have been the royal tutor of the Ptolemy heir as well as director of the Library; he may have quarreled with Callimachus.

This flotsam and jetsam of fact compel us to give up speculating about the poet's life. We can, however, conjure up in more general terms the ambience of Alexandria, the poet's intimacy with Callimachus, his association with the Library and the Museum. The tradition of Apollonius' failure and later success, and his quarrel with Callimachus, establish only that Apollonius was held to be an important poet at Alexandria, and that his work displayed certain tendencies which ran counter to those promoted by Callimachus, the self-appointed spokesman for the avant-garde. Beyond this we cannot go. The persona of the narrator which comes across to us from the poem, startling as it is when set against the resolute self-effacement of the Homeric narrator, is nonetheless a poetic contrivance. We have the poem, therefore, but not Apollonius.

Whether or not Apollonius was a native of Alexandria—Callimachus and Theocritus were not—his poetic career certainly began there. Whether or not he later removed himself to the island of Rhodes, the influence of Alexandria certainly stayed with him wherever he was. Alexandria was the major city of the third century, superior in its cultural vitality to either Athens, which was then commencing its centuries-long slumber as a university town, or Rome, which had yet to realize that *rhomē* in Greek means, prophetically enough, "strength" or "power."

A certain Timon has left us a memorable description of the Alexandrian literary scene, saying "in Egypt, land of diverse tribes, graze many pedants, fenced in, hugely arguing in the Muses' wicker cage." Timon's poem says it all: intellectuals and scholars, fattened for Ptolemy's use, kept apart from the polyglot, cosmopolite new urban experiment which was third-century Alexandria, living in some rancorous intimate college reminiscent of twentieth-century academic life. But clearly enough, this cage liberated while it confined, for the literary production of third-century Alexandria was a great, sudden, and original flowering which, like the earlier classical age of fifth-century Athens, furnished some of the major models in the Western literary tradition.

Timon's "Muses' wicker cage" was in actuality called the Museum. We know relatively little about the Museum, or for that matter the Library which supported its activities, and even less about the actual association of any major author with them; but if any institution were to characterize the age as some say the theater of Dionysus best describes the major literary fact of fifth-century Athens, then it would have to be the Museum and the Library, those monuments to intellectualism which Demetrius of Phalerum brought to the Ptolemies from the school of Aristotle at Athens.

The Museum, a cult center for the worship of the Muses, already had a long history in Greece, where the association of the Muses and literature was as old as Homer and Hesiod. Functioning somewhat like a medieval monastery or a twentieth-century think tank, the Museum provided a workshop and a place of association for men in the service of literature.

The new Alexandrian Museum was certainly different from its predecessors. Scientific inquiry, description, and categorization were major activities. These may have been a legacy of Aristotle, whose preoccupation with natural science was very probably reflected in what Demetrius brought to Alexandria. (Demetrius himself was a student of Theophrastus, who had continued Aristotle's scientific inquiries and compilations.) The Lyceum, as Aristotle's school was called, had emphasized polymathia as an ideal, and favored cooperation in research rather than the eristic psychology which characterizes Socrates' competitive dialectical method. The Library was the embodiment of polymathia, the Museum of the cooperative ideal.

Like monasteries, think tanks, and senior common rooms, the Museum provided collectivity, literary and intellectual intimacy; and that is also the atmosphere in which a coterie with its demands of exclusiveness, loyalty, and obedience often develops. The tradition of the quarrel between Callimachus and Apollonius, their penchant for quoting or referring to each other—a habit shared by their fellow poet Theocritus—betokens the kind of incestuous relationship which is the hallmark of the coterie. It might have been the Alexandrian Bloomsbury.

The Museum was founded upon royal patronage, which seems to have sponsored far more literary scholarship and natural scientific study than pure poesie. What the Ptolemies created seems to have been far less of a public relations office than was the literary circle which the Roman emperors supported. One thinks of Horace's Roman Odes, or Virgil's *Aeneid*, which celebrate enthusiastically—how honestly, or how ironically, one cannot be sure—the triumph of the Augustan Age. The Roman poets' enthusiasm stems from their proximity to and intimacy with the Augustan imperial experiment. The Alexandrian poets had nothing so immediate to cheer about—or cheer to, for that matter. Ptolemaic Alexandria was far less democratic in theory and practice than late Republican or early Imperial Rome. Alien in some ways to each other, the writers of Alexandria were aliens in Egypt, sprung as they were from a variety of city states with diverse traditions. And they all looked back to the Athenian literary experience, which was to them in many ways already foreign. Their utter alienation then from any presumed or potential or actual public made for the kind of introversion which inspires literary research or literature born from literary scholarship.

The poet Callimachus, whose few remaining poetic fragments show a man who was relentlessly experimental, was equally esteemed by his contemporaries for his monumental work of scholarship, the bibliographical compilation known as *Tables of persons eminent in every branch of learning together with a list of their writings*. It stands as an emblem of the Alexandrian Age. Whereas the fourth century Aristotle produced a theory of literature, the Alexandrian Callimachus made a history of literature. The distinction is the typical one of the two ages, the earlier looking to the ideal, the generic, the abstract, the latter immersed in concrete fact. What Hesiod and the successive mythographers had done for myth, what Herodotus and Thucydides had done for war, diplomacy, and heroic saga, what Aristotle had done for government, Callimachus' encyclopedia did for literature, that is, to distance it, objectify it, make it preeminently a matter for study. The encyclopedia was an enormous undertaking which brought to the Greeks' literary past a control, mastery, and self-consciousness which marks a turning point in Western literary history. Nothing was ever the same again. This is obvious from the fact that one cannot approach fifth-century Athenian literature with the same critical positions one employs for not only Alexandrian but all other literature in the Western tradition. Callimachus is the serpent in our departure from innocence.

Callimachus' *Tables* have sometimes been considered to be a *catalogue raisonné* to the Library's collections. This may not have been the case, really, since Callimachus did not in fact ever hold the position of Librarian. More to the point, Callimachus' *Tables* represent the best and most complete expressions of the contemporary manner of apprehending literary production. Because the manuscript is lost, we know of it only through scholiasts' references. These suggest that Callimachus was very particular with his classifications and his verifications of the authenticity of the works he listed. The keys to understanding the literature of the Alexandrian Age are authenticity and classification.

While those considerations were an inheritance from the Aristotelian school, they are also natural preoccupations in an intellectual climate dominated by the problem of gathering, sorting, verifying, and maintaining the first great book collection of the ancient world. Whether the Library was at first one building designed for the purpose or simply a group of storerooms and warehouses taken over, the librarian's typical tasks began early on. In the absence of any system of publishing which could legitimate a text, the librarian's principal task was to establish more or less authentic texts—especially, of course, to establish the text of Homer from the many exemplars which had been collected. Homeric research was already a step on the way to becoming the industry nineteenth- and twentieth-century scholarship has made of it. When Zenodotus, the first Librarian, made his recension of the Homeric texts, he could draw on the work of his teacher Philetas of Cos who had made a glossary of rare words in Homer, the studies of Homer by Aristotle and Demetrius of Phalerum, even perhaps a text by Antimachus of Colophon, the fifth-century poet who anticipated by a century the commonplace Alexandrian practice of combining scholarship with original literary production.

The preeminence of Homeric scholarship was a natural consequence of the vast assemblage of copies of the Homeric poems available in the Library, copies whose variant readings made a reformed text imperative. On the one hand, the poems of Homer were at the center of the Greek literary and cultural tradition; the divine poet dominated every subsequent author. On the other hand, the centuries which had passed since the composition and copying of the *Iliad* and the *Odyssey* had made these two poems remote, giving them a quaintness and strangeness which made them natural objects of study in an institution dedicated to literary history.

The establishment of a genuine text rests immediately upon a sure and intuitive grasp of the Homeric manner—what was true to it, what not. We can only glimpse the preoccupations of the Homeric scholars of the third century through the marginal comments left by subsequent generations on the manuscripts. There it is clear that propriety was the overriding consideration. But then it is not altogether clear whether propriety means what Homer would or would not have been likely to say or what in the opinion of any particular critic ought or ought not to be said in epic poetry. Aristotle had already established the notion (*Poetics* 1447a) that poetry has subspecies, that there are definitions of these that are mandatory for the critic and the poet.[1] It is often as much the propriety of the genre as it is the propriety of the poet which the Alexandrian critics were trying to establish.

Their formulations of criteria are wide-ranging.[2] There is human morality. Zenodotus alters lines in which Achilles indicates that his personal glory is the paramount consideration in Patroclus' return to battle because, it seems, Zenodotus cannot tolerate such naked egoism and cannot fathom a world where such egoism is acceptable and may be freely acknowledged. Aristarchus athetizes Homeric lines in which the action seems to him unduly brutal. Then there are problems in style. Zenodotus, for instance, offers a two-line substitution for a ten-line passage repeated verbatim. The Alexandrian Age did not fancy repetition, and tried to take it out of the Homeric text, probably because it seemed so crude as to be substandard. Likewise, the commonplace Homeric way of describing action in synonymous terms set Alexandrian teeth on edge. Such a characteristic phrase as "sad and grieving" becomes, under Aristarchus, the metrically equivalent "grieving in his heart."

Nor could Alexandrian critics accept the more earthy attributes of Homer's divinities. Aristarchus in one place suppressed a description of divine arrogance in the *Iliad* and at another point removed Homer's depiction of Hera experiencing physical pain. And Zenodotus changed "Dionysus afraid" to the metrically equivalent "Dionysus angry" for the same reason. Aristarchus rejected Thetis' advice to Achilles to get over his grief by sleeping with a woman (*Iliad* 24.129–31) as unseemly. Sometimes there appears a rather sophisticated historical point of view: Aristarchus' objection to Zenodotus' reading of *daita* at *Iliad* 1.5 is a case in point. Would Homer have said "a meal for birds?" The discussion of this recorded by Athenaeus is anthropological, based on a consideration of whether the Homeric mentality was sufficiently socialized to understand that a meal in *portions* (*daita* from *dateomai*, "to distribute") is possible only for humankind.[3] Elsewhere Aristarchus seems less aware of historical change. When Homer speaks of Pandarus as one "to whom Apollo himself gave a bow" (*Iliad* 2.827), Aristarchus interprets the "bow" as skill at archery, not understanding the emphasis upon the concrete and the absence of intellectualist categories in the archaic way of thinking.

More difficult to demonstrate but far more important is the period's scholarly fascination with linguistic usage and etymologies,[4] a fascination which determines the language of Apollonius everywhere as he tries to establish meanings which he seems to imagine are inherent in the Homeric form.[5] Apollonius was a poet, but his scholarship provided him with increased subtlety when it came to recasting the traditional epic language for a contemporary poem. We must not forget that the Greek-speaking peoples of Alexandria were hedged in by Egyptians, hence their obsession with linguistic purity, which is forever the problem with colonials.[6] At the same time, the Greek language was the entrée to a special world, to the educated elite who surrounded the Ptolemies.

Apollonius' vocabulary contains both rare words and words unusual in traditional epic diction. His grammar is often harsh, introducing a kind of prose periodicity where traditionally there would have been shorter, grammatically integral elements punctuated by the pauses of the cola. The tendency to difficult language, begun, as the tradition tells us, by Antimachus of Colophon, blossomed into full flower in the Alexandrian Age. One has only to think of Lycophron whose surviving poem is a monument to the final perversity of this tendency. Perhaps Apollonius' difficulty is no more than mock pedantry and as such an ironic reflection of the great age of scholarship which the Library and Museum ushered in. Nonetheless the difficulty has a way of distancing the unsuspecting reader, making the poem less immediately accessible. It is a Hellenistic attitude foreign to fifth-century public literature, an attitude translated to Rome and memorialized in Horace's famous "Odi profanum vulgus et arceo" ("I hate the public who must wait outside the temple door and cringe from them").

One can only infer from the scholarly emphasis upon the Homeric texts and from the general penchant of the time for creating canons, that the literary circle had *idées très fixes* about epic. It has been argued that the Alexandrian avant-garde dismissed long epic as being hackneyed.[7] Callimachus seems to have done so, and yet our meager information for the period suggests that epics went on being composed.[8] The literary historians of antiquity record a quarrel between Callimachus and Apollonius over the propriety of composing a long narrative poem. The *Argonautica* was derided, we are told. Apollonius was embarrassed, withdrew from Alexandria to Rhodes (hence Rhodius) only to return later in triumph with his masterpiece revised. The literary historians—true to the general ancient Greek tendency to substitute biographical anecdote for abstract discussion—are probably saying no more than that Callimachus cut certain critical patterns, and that Apollonius tried them on and, where they did not exactly fit, reshaped them to his need. Certainly the quotations of Callimachus in the *Argonautica* do not seem to be motivated by hostility.[9] Furthermore, the *Argonautica* is hardly a long poem, a fact often forgotten when critics argue that the Alexandrians would disapprove of an attempt by Apollonius to rival Homer. It is only 5,835 lines long, whereas the *Odyssey* is over 12,000 and the *Iliad* over 15,000 lines. Aristotle says (*Poetics* 1459b) that the successful new-style epic must be far shorter than the typical old epics. It should be fit rather "to the size of tragedies performed for one hearing." Does he mean the time allotted to three tragedies and the subsequent satyr play by the term "one hearing"? If so, the *Argonautica's* four books, each of them approximately the length of a typical tragedy, would satisfy his prescription.

We happen to have a better idea of what Callimachus admired than we have of any other critical position of the age.[10] He wanted pieces made up of only a few lines (*oligostikhos*), a muse who was peeled down to the subtleties of essence (*leptalea*), and wanted a sound that was clear and pure (*ligus*), that is to say apparently not thickened with resonances. It is an idea that fits with his use of the images of the clean path, of the priestesses bringing their water from the clear spring and not the muddied river, of the path untrod by the many, of the narrow path where the carts cannot go.

Homer is *eskhatos*, extreme, probably in the sense of inimitable, and therefore one must not try to mimic him. In any case, Callimachus disdains the long narrative, poems in thousands of lines, the continuous narrative unified by chronology ("I hate the cyclic poem"). He wants no part of epic grandeur: "Let Zeus make thunder, not I." Hesiod, whom he calls "honey-sweet," is constantly preferred as the model. The reasons are not specifically stated, but the absence of any continuous narrative, the brevity relative to Homeric epic, and the factual subject matter would recommend the Boeotian poet as a model to the Alexandrian.

Alas, the poetry of Callimachus is poorly preserved and we are hard put to find in the fragments an adequate realization of Callimachus' aesthetic principles which, coming down to us in an exceedingly fragmentary state, are already ambiguous enough. But certain judgments seem possible on the basis of what we have.

His major piece was the *Aitia* ("Causes"), a poem of seven thousand lines on the subject of the origins or causes for things. Like Hesiod's *Works and Days* and *Theogony*, the poem reveals the antiquarian mind of the poet, the collector of lore and curiosities. The poem does not, so far as we can tell from the fragments, have any organizing principle, being episodic, a series of narrative vignettes in elegiacs, more a grand catalogue than anything else.

The ancients were highly enthusiastic about Callimachus' *Hecale*, which was an experiment in creating what we would call a mini-epic and which they called *epyllion*, a literary form which grew to be a favorite among the Romans. In about one thousand lines of hexameter narrative in a modified form of the diction of Homer, Callimachus tells the story of Theseus killing the bull of Marathon. But that in fact is not really his subject, merely the traditional mythological thread with which to weave quite a different pattern. His first purpose is to establish an *aition*, giving the reason for the naming of the Attic deme Hecale and the establishment of the sanctuary of Zeus Hecalus. Unlike (so far as we can tell) the several *aitia* of his aitiological poem, this *aition* has been expanded, given drama, local color, and emotion. More importantly, it is an epic account reduced, an experiment in making epic narrative without the vast perspective. We cannot determine if Callimachus was successful, since so little of the poem survives. The important fact is that Callimachus has achieved a remarkable emphasis in the poem. The story is that Theseus set out for Marathon to kill the bull, but stopped off at the cottage of an old woman named Hecale to seek shelter from a heavy rain. Next day, having enjoyed Hecale's hospitality, he continues to Marathon, kills the bull, and on the way home returns to Hecale's cottage only to find that she has died. In his grief he vows to repay her hospitality by establishing various institutions in her honor.

The traditional epic poet would have focussed his narrative on Theseus, building to his contest with the bull, making it the crucial moment, a variation on the conventional *aristeia* which we find so often in Homeric epic. Here instead Callimachus seems to have concentrated upon Hecale, not only giving the attention to a nonheroic figure, but taking the emphasis away from action, movement, and drama. A passage much cherished in antiquity was the description of the meal that Hecale set for her chance visitor. A brief portion which survives records the conversation of two crows. It is more like a magical episode from fairy tale than a device of the epic convention. Callimachus has radically changed perspectives, bringing what should be the background to the foreground, insisting upon the nonheroic in the very presence of a hero. T. B. L. Webster remarks on a similar tendency in art, describing a krater in the British Museum depicting a male and female centaur team: "A mixed centaur pair is a new idea; Hellenistic artists and poets were interested in the private life of monsters. When the *Argo* sails it is the Centaur Chiron's wife who holds up the little Achilles to wave good-bye to his father."[11] In both instances, the Callimachean and the Apollonian, the heroic detail has been domesticated.

Apart from a number of epigrams which reveal Callimachus' relentlessly impeccable taste and elegance,[12] six hymns from his hand survive to us. They adopt various tones and attitudes, but what is striking here, and most important for Apollonius, is the frequent presence of what we might call an amused tone. By this I mean something akin to the seventeenth-century use of the word *wit* when it refers to the elegant or stylish juxtaposition of the incongruous.

The *Hymn to Artemis* is the most obvious example of this manner. Callimachus has made his hymns more or less after the models provided in the corpus of so-called Homeric Hymns. The ancient Greek hymn to a deity had certain fixed elements: an invocation to the god complete with several of his epithets or titles; a description or narrative account of the god's birth; and a list of his powers or attributes. The *Hymn to Artemis* begins as a charming portrait of a little girl (Artemis) on her father's (Zeus') knee, first asking for as many epithets or titles as her brother Apollo has (6–7). She then asks for arrows, ritual title, clothing, maiden attendants, and a city. In this way the poet manages to introduce a variety of the conventional hymnal elements. And he has enough homely details to create a portrait of the little girl, a chatty thing (8), too small to reach her father's beard (26–28), sweet enough to palliate Zeus' problems with dreadful Hera (29–30), yet a tough little miss who once pulled out the hair on the chest of one of the Cyclops. Only the earlier Homeric *Hymn to Hermes* begins to approach the amused tone here, and it remains altogether serious, whereas the Callimachean hymn is constantly playful, emphasizing the ridiculous or the absurd. Callimachus is—partly, at least—laughing at his medium.

In the *Hymn to Demeter*, Callimachus goes still further. Erysichthon cuts down a tree sacred to Demeter and is punished, another variant of the story of the great female goddess and the young male who is destroyed. The story is told of Erysichthon's impious act and Demeter's punishment in causing him to suffer hunger without relief. The hymn begins with a reference to the sacred basket and to Demeter's search for her daughter, Persephone, and her refusal to eat and drink. Full belly, empty belly. Erysychthon begins to eat and eat and eat. What could be a horror story is made immensely funny. Callimachus describes the mother making excuses for her son's disappearance while he is in the back room gorging and the moment when the cooks and butcher must say no, since everything has been cooked, "even the cat before whom the mice used to tremble" (110). The worship of Demeter derives from the very real fear of famine in primitive society. Callimachus has given us a harsh, cruel, and exceedingly humorous portrait of a compulsive eater for an audience which is not much threatened by hunger.

Callimachus' ideal of poetry was fulfilled by Aratus[13] whose *Phainomena*, a poem of 1,154 lines of dactylic hexameters, was essentially a versification of the work of Eudoxes of Cnidus on meteorology. The poem survives complete. The first part is a description of the heavenly bodies, their names, and celestial positions; the latter part is a curious disquisition in verse of how animals, birds, and nature in general foretell storms. This succeeds in capturing the modern reader's interest because the information is charming, but the earlier part of the poem is, for us, a tedious and unending stream of proper names. Perhaps we must account this to be a poetical *tour de force*, setting so much factual information into verse, particularly managing the intractable proper names. The poem was immensely popular with the Greeks and later with the Romans. It was probably the Hesiod-like devotion to hard fact which won the approval of Callimachus, who says in one fragment, "I sing nothing false." [14]

Callimachus was Apollonius' teacher. The *Argonautica* is, on the surface of things, a continuous narrative centered more or less upon a hero, a narrative which bears marked affinities with the Homeric narratives. On the surface, therefore, Apollonius seems to have accomplished exactly what his teacher had so severely denounced. The poem is often held to be the product of a timid pupil's incapacity to proceed upon the course established by the master. Indeed the centuries have not been kind to Apollonius; he has been found wanting. [15] Yet anyone who even casually reads Virgil's *Aeneid* must be struck immediately by the extraordinary power of influence the Alexandrian has exercised over the verse of his Roman successor. Here is a more profound appreciation than one finds in the page of the traditional scholar.

Still more important, the readers of Apollonius must sense immediately the vitality of the narrator which the poet has created, beginning with the opening lines, a vitality particularly apparent in the glancing wit and irony—often the mock solemnity of a Hitchcock or Nabokov—with which the narrative progresses. The same strength reveals itself in the poet's brilliant control of the Homeric manner to which he hews closely so as to play off it in creating an absolutely new heroical epical narrative. The twentieth century's penchant for experimentation, for the absurd, for the process of deconstruction makes our era an ideal climate for the full enjoyment of Apollonius' poem. Now perhaps more than at any earlier time we can see the *Argonautica* as an innovative—perhaps rebellious—authoritative creative act. No timidity, certainly.

We say that Apollonius imitated Homer. To be precise, Apollonius knew how to re-create exactly the Homeric manner. The simile comparing Jason to Apollo in the first book (307–9) is an example of this. He knew also how to assemble Homeric elements into an entirely novel collage, a phenomenon which we may observe in, for instance, the description of the becloaked Jason on his way to Hypsipyle's palace. In effect, Apollonius managed to revitalize Homer's poems through the incongruities which he drew so often in his own poems between the Homeric view of things and that of the Alexandrian world. Here the *Iliad* and *Odyssey* have a life far more vivid than that guaranteed to them on the shelves of the Library. The first generation scholar-poets of Alexandria, notably Apollonius and Rhianus, used their poetry as a form of literary criticism, but often more importantly as a kind of scholarly exegesis of the Homeric texts. Apollonius goes beyond even this, self-consciously altering the traditional formulae and manner and thereby becoming a cracked-mirror image or perversion of his exemplar. Given the enormous pressures for conservatism in the tradition-oriented Greek culture and for conservation in the librarian's inherent role, Apollonius' peculiar Looking Glass performance of the creative act is an admirable feat of courage.

The first and most important element in the criticism of the *Argonautica*, then, must be a pervasive knowledge of the *Iliad* and the *Odyssey*. Apollonius is only barely telling a story; one does not much care what will happen next, except in a few moments of genuine suspense. The *Argonautica* is much more a statement about literature, about epic especially, about narrative, and secondarily about the psychology of man, about the nature of love and the relationship of men and women. Apollonius expects us to notice the manner in which he has assimilated and recast the Homeric narrative and the world view implied in it. For this is the means whereby he makes his statement.

It has been observed that a poet who uses the traditional epic language and conventions in the third century, some five hundred or more years after the style and the ideology which called that style into being had vanished, is invoking the naïve sensibility.[16] Whatever he may do with his narrative, there remains the ever-dominant reminiscence of the Homeric cast to the epic style, that is, the objectification of humanity through presentation of character types, the dehumanization of character, the abstraction of reality by the rendering of detail in formulae, the persuasive surface meaning achieved by the brilliance of the language. We may add to this the determination of the narrator who, after the manner of any raconteur, secures the floor *ad infinitum*. It may be summed up in what can be called the dread inevitability of the Homeric utterance, pretending to be as it does, and indeed is, the final truth of history in a world which knew no writing.

Homer calls out to the Muse to tell him the story, thereafter disappears from the narrative except to complain twice that he has not strength enough to tell the myriad details which in each instance his story demands. Essentially the story tells itself and demands absolute obedience. As Auerbach has observed, the *Iliad* and the *Odyssey* need no interpretation. The Muse who is the daughter of Memory has told everything there is to tell. Many object to Auerbach's seeming denial of subtlety in the Homeric poem. Of course, Homer does not tell us everything and we are free to make meaning. Homer, however, gives the *illusion* of telling us everything. He overpowers us with detail, alternative stories; the characters bombard us with their observations on everything that takes place. We are helpless before their onslaught. This is the poetry of oral presentation: the poet knows that we do not have the text and cannot reflect. He keeps at us, hectoring, seducing, amusing, but always demanding our submission to his narrative. In that sense he tells us everything. As Auerbach points out,[17] there is an enormous difference between the Homeric narrative and the biblical narrative. Consider the Abraham and Isaac story in *Genesis*. One can see how Kierkegaard can make so much meaning from the passage. The biblical narrative is so *sparse* that one is compelled to invest meaning into the bare lineaments of the story.

Homer never *invites* us to make meaning. That is important. It must remain unconscious. We are also not in league with the author ready to make sense of the narrative. He pretends to be its slave as well. Homer appears to be telling us ever so firmly nothing more than the facts of the case. He calls upon the Muse and seems to say, "Here is the story," as though it came to him whole, just as he will now recite it. That is the hallmark of the technique of oral poetry.

Since we know nothing secure about the poet known as Homer or about the composition of the *Iliad* and the *Odyssey*, everything said is opinion and probably will always remain so. My opinion is that there were probably two poets and that the *Iliad* and *Odyssey* are products of centuries of poetic experimentation, adaptation, and reworking of language, ideas, and narrative method—in sum, that they are traditional poems in a recognizable and widely used style, but at the same time that they represent considerable elaboration and rethinking by their authors. That is to say, that neither of them is the spontaneous outburst of a Greek bard in a smoky palace assembly room, as some extreme exponents of the oral theory of Homeric verse would have it. Nonetheless one cannot know to what extent the poet extemporized or dictated, memorized verbatim or employed writing (whether as an aid to memory or as a means to achieve posterity for his otherwise only too winged words). Those who wish to insist upon a literate poet must confront the extreme unlikelihood of an extensive reading public on the one hand and the great awkwardness of the papyrus roll on the other. Writing as a means to creation as we understand it seems highly unlikely; reading as an entrée to a verbal construct was well nigh impossible. Those who find the idea of an oral poet incompatible with conscious, sustained artistry will have to struggle with these facts or near-facts. It is better to imagine that the Homeric poet was indeed a self-conscious poet capable of all manner of subtleties, not a man compulsively delivering himself of patter, but yet a poet using the mannerisms we associate with oral poetry and the mentality that goes with it. That would explain how the *Iliad* poet manages quite authoritatively to arrange a series of episodes in logical narrative progression which at the same time hark back to distinctly antecedent moments. I mean the Catalogue of Ships, the *teichoskopeia* and the duel between Hector and Ajax followed by Paris' refusal. Each episode is well motivated in its present context, yet clearly reveals its original position in the Trojan saga. They are events from the war's earliest days. As the poem gets under way, this fact of structure allows for subliminal references to the war's beginning, while, at the same time on the surface of the narrative in the never-to-be-recaptured moment of communication between poet and auditor, these episodes are given absolute contemporaneity with the adjacent narrative. They resonate with times past; they seem to be, however, of the moment. All time converges, like the multifaceted alternative planes of a cubistic face and body painted by Picasso.

Similarly, Achilles' seeming ignorance of the gifts offered him in Book Nine when Patroclus begs him to return to the fight in Sixteen is the nonliterate response to narrative patterns. A sequence of pleading to a reluctant hero by authorities, family, friends, and wife is described by Phoenix in the Meleager story in the *Iliad*'s ninth book. This is the paradigm—or we might call it the author's program note—for a large narrative pattern where Odysseus (authorities), Phoenix (family), Ajax (friends) beseech the hero Achilles followed by Patroclus (stand-in for the wife). Several thousand lines have gone by and amends have long since been offered but the poet is still deep in the story pattern. For him and his auditor nothing has changed. Only a reader who could look back would note the discrepancy. Every reader does and complains, proof if ever it was needed that the poet, who was no dummy, never anticipated literacy as the fatal dust which would clog and slow the exquisite, finely tuned gears of his swift machine.

But things are altogether different with Apollonius. He is completely a literate poet. This is his poem, and he remains with it, like the sheep dog who barks and nudges his flock down the path. Apollonius insists that the reader acknowledge him as the narrator existing apart from the narrative. Sometimes he seems to establish himself as the artist and the narrative as his creation; at other times the relationship between author and work is more ambiguous, and the narrative seems to have an independent existence, or there appears what we might call the author's narrator.

When Apollonius chose to introduce the source of the narration into the narration itself, he was being strikingly original. He opens the poem with *Archomenos seo, Phoibe* ("Taking my start [or setting out] from you, O Phoebus [Apollo], I shall recall the famous deeds of men of old"). The initial phrase (which appears elsewhere in hymns and epic) sets up the conventional combination of poet and divine inspiration. After four lines of general introduction, the poet tells of the oracle which motivates Pelias to send Jason after the fleece. The oracle, which of course comes from Apollo's shrine at Delphi, suddenly offers additional meaning to *Archomenos seo, Phoibe*, that is, the poet shall begin the narrative with its original motivator, the prophetic god, Apollo. At the eighth line, the poet introduces Jason as the fulfillment of Apollo's oracle, "Not long afterward in accordance with your oracle, Jason crossed the stream." As the poet steps out of the narrative to address the god he places himself in some kind of other world before time and beyond human action where deity effects things. It is as though Apollonius were present at the creation, or as though he were with Apollo looking down onto the brightly lit stage of a marionette theater. (Callimachus does the same thing when he carries on a debate with Zeus throughout the *Hymn to Zeus*.)

The hymnlike quality of this opening line reappears at the very close of the poem (4.1773–76) when the poet abruptly stops the narrative with an apostrophe, this time however, to his heroes: "be propitious, O race of blessed chieftains. . . ." Hymns generally close with such a phrase in apostrophe, but to the deity who has been the subject of the hymn. The chieftains, albeit mostly offspring of deities, are human beings; the poem is not in fact a hymn. But Apollonius nonetheless emphasizes that this is the apostrophe of hymns by calling the chieftains "blessed" (*makar*), a commonplace epithet applied to deities in epic.

What does Apollonius achieve? It is a characteristic of hymns that the poet maintains his persona throughout the narrative as the devotee who has called the hymn into being. Apollonius at the last wishes to call the poem finished as a creation, like a painter who finally signs his canvas and hangs it on the wall. Then, just as the painter stands and gazes upon his creation, so Apollonius takes his stand with the reader, bidding his heroes and his poem farewell. The Hellenistic aesthetic depends on an understanding of the nature and meaning of form. By putting in bits and pieces of the hymn form, Apollonius invests his narrative with a special sensibility. This is bestowed by the associations emanating from an alien form which is introduced for its associations, not because the form itself belongs.

The poet has opened his poem with *archomenos* ("beginning" or "setting off"). The final word of the poem is *eisapebate* ("you stepped forth [from the boat onto land]"), conferring back upon *archomenos* the coloration of a sea voyage. Apollonius, in other words, begins his poem with the voyage and ends it with the return; but the voyage out evoked by *Archomenos seo, Phoibe* is the poet's own voyage, his journey through the narrative, and indeed, as we shall see, he often reminds us of his presence so that one comes to think of him to be almost a crew member, another Orpheus.

At the eighteenth line Apollonius proceeds to the subject of his first two books. Again he seems to compare himself to Apollo and in so doing seems to arrogate to himself a greater responsibility for his poem than does the traditional epic poet.

> To get to my subject: other poets previously
> have celebrated the ship, how Argo made it
> with Athena's instructions, but now I propose
> to relate the names and family line of the
> heroes, the journeying over the lengthy sea,

and what they did on their wanderings. May
the Muses be the interpreters of my song.

On the one hand Apollonius is acknowledging the poetic tradition from
which he springs, that is, the Argonaut story as an established *mythos*; at the
same time he allies himself with Apollo in the curious role which he assigns
to the Muses. *Hypophētōr* ("interpreter") is the priest who deciphers the
garbled, inspired message which the Pythia receives from Apollo. Here Apol-
lonius is Apollo; what he declares is the raw, divine truth; the Muses in effect
will make it into art, and hence intelligible.

Epic convention, particularly as we see it in the Homeric poems, assigns
the authority for inspiration or creation to the Muses. We would call it some-
thing like an artistically achieved tradition, since that is what the "daughters
of Memory" suggest. However much we can see the *Odyssey*-poet playing with
the phenomenon of authorship in Odysseus' first-person narrative, or his fic-
tive autobiographies, the Homeric poem stands essentially as a *donnée* inde-
pendent of its author. Apollonius' contemporary Theocritus takes a stand near
Homer and opposite Apollonius in his twenty-second Idyll. Since the subject
of this Idyll is the Polydeuces-Amycus boxing match (of which Apollonius
also tells), and since Theocritus uses the word *hypophētēs*, there may be some
special intent in the lines: "How did the son of Zeus overcome the gluttonous
man? Tell, Goddess; for you know. And I, as an interpreter to the others,
shall say what you wish and in whatever way is pleasing to you" (46–48).
Apollonius is rarely so obedient. Certainly, in his opening lines at least, Apol-
lonius, unlike Theocritus, makes the Muses subservient to himself, claiming
the poem his own.

Thereafter Apollonius stays resolutely with his narrative. Sometimes he is
its master, as we have seen. When he alludes to the numerous stories, reports,
or accounts, or the scholiast tells us of variant versions (presumably all of
them known to Apollonius' readers) we see him in the act of making a fiction;
in an era where myth and saga were no longer considered history, and there
was no one true account, choosing a variant is in effect creating a story line.
As another exhibition of his control, he has the habit of asking rhetorically
(sometimes it seems that he is really stopping to ask himself) why he has
developed a certain narrative line, as for instance at 1.648–49: "But why is
it necessary for me to tell the stories of Aethalides on and on this way?" He
uses the word *diēnekeōs* ("continuously") which we have noticed in the Calli-
machean fragment already quoted: "not one continuous song." A hallmark of
Homeric epic is that very relentless urgency, a never-ending, compulsive gar-
rulity—the bard *will* have your ear.

Apollonius by contrast insists upon his control. He wars against excessive verbiage in the narrative, generally with humorous intent. In the Hylas episode when Heracles has gone off to get a new oar and Hylas to get water, the poet begins to describe Hylas' background, then checks himself with "these details stray from my story" (1.1220) as though he were about to wander off as well. In "stray" he uses a verb which he repeats in describing Heracles' later departure from the narrative (1.1325). Just as Aeetes is about to embark upon a Nestor-like reminiscence he gains control: "but what pleasure is there in words?" (3.314). When Jason begins to describe his situation (3.386–95), Aeetes forestalls any lengthy self-advertisement in the manner of Odysseus with: "Stranger, why would you tell this out on and on?"—*diēnekeōs* again (3.401)!

At other times he seems to submit to the Muses. When describing the Argonauts carrying their ship for twelve days, a particularly fantastic feat, he says (4.1381–82): "This is the Muses' story; I sing obedient to the Pierian Muses." Pindar, in the second strophe of his *Fourth Pythian Ode*, alludes to this same event, which compels us to consider whether Apollonius means to say that since Pindar has made the event a literary tradition he will conform. We cannot know, of course, whether the twelve-day portage was a commonplace of mythology or Pindar's invention. In the same ironic way, Apollonius asks the Muses to be kind to him when he feels compelled to allude to the legend already found in Hesiod of Cronos' castrating his father ("it's not that I want to tell this story from olden times" [4.985]), conjuring up for us an amusing group of ladies of fastidious tastes, altogether unlike the hardy band of Muses who presided over Hesiod's poetic undertakings. Again he uses them as his moral yardstick when he apologizes for correcting a false tradition (2.844–45). They demand honesty, he must sing the truth. ("If I am compelled by the Muses to tell it out straight.") We are reminded of the Muses telling Hesiod that they can tell lies like truth or can tell the truth (*Theogony*, 26–28), his way of establishing the distinction between saga's fictions (Homer) and his own antiquarian, "true" poems, fact-filled poems of the sort fashionable in the Alexandrian period.

But again at other times the poet stands beside his narrative as though it breathed with a life of its own. "What other person then died?" he asks at 2.851, like Homer, secure in the conviction that the story will offer him the answer. And at 4.450–51 after the apostrophe to Eros which precedes the death of Apsyrtus he returns to his narrative with: "And now how did he do in Apsyrtus to his baleful doom? For that part of the song lies next on the way for us." Apollonius asks us to imagine that the ensuing narrative has already been worked out, like the footage of a film waiting to be run through the projector.

Again at 4.552–56, he has to call upon the Muses (*thea*) with questions which will lead the narrative forward. Here the questions have to do with the route. "How is it that beyond this sea . . . near the islands called Stoechades, the . . . tracks of the ship are mentioned?" Because there were alternative routes proposed by the geographers of the time, one could say that here the Muses are the representatives of learned inquiry.

At one point Apollonius tantalizes his reader and heightens the suspense of his narrative by showing a confusion over his story which casts him into the role of human narrator rather than omniscient author. This occurs in the invocation which opens the fourth book.

> Now you yourself, goddess (*thea*), the struggle
> and plans of the Colchian Maid sing, Muse (*ennepe Mousa*),
> daughter of Zeus. For in truth my mind goes
> round and round in me as I ponder, speechless,
> [presumably: I cannot verbalize to myself what I
> want to say, simply can't articulate my thoughts]
> Whether it was the pain of the catastrophe of
> cruel love or whether I should say (*enispo*)
> a panic flight was the motive which made her
> leave the Colchian folk.

What, we may ask, has happened to our narrator, so confident up to now, indeed revealing through monologue the innermost secrets of Medea's heart? It is as though he has let Medea slip from his grasp and has to call upon the Muse to sing the song, emphasizing his dependence by calling out to both Homeric Muses (*Iliad* 1.1, *mēnin aeide thea*; *Odyssey* 1.1, *andra moi ennepe mousa*). The ambiguity, the sense of doubt, is the fitting mood with which to enter the fourth book, where the Argonauts' *nostos* is portrayed as a kind of magical mystery tour. More importantly, Apollonius here as elsewhere establishes his characters' independence of the narrator. One of the sources of creative tension in the poem is the precarious balance between the narrator, the characters, and the epic tradition: no one element is consistently authoritative.

Throughout his poem Apollonius insists upon the peculiar nature of ancient stories based on traditional myth. A mythic story has a life of its own, an inevitability, a truth which no narrator can indeed alter. This can produce ironies which are tragic—for instance, Hector's saying to Andromache in the *Iliad* "I know in my heart that there will come a day when Ilium will perish" or absurdities as for instance Apollo's deus ex machina speech at the close of Euripides' *Orestes*, which forces the play's characters back into the inevitable but by now impossible, indeed outrageous patterns. Yet again when characters, particularly Euripidean characters, emerge from the traditional symbolic values assigned to their actions, we suddenly realize that they are psychological, intellectual, and spiritual beings existing independent of their stories, existing before and apart from their actions, such as the mean-spirited, murderous Electra and Orestes of the *Orestes*. Apollonius chooses to underscore the poet's role in the recasting of traditional mythic stories by creating a narrator who moves in and out and around his story. He is acting out what was by Alexandrian times the now-legendary response of the Muses to the shepherd-poet Hesiod, who said, "We know how to tell fictions as though they were true and at other times we can tell the truth." The Alexandrians working at their codification and purification asked: What is pure Homer? What is an epic poem? Apollonius is indeed asking the same questions but in a far more profound way. He wants to know and us to know what is the heart, substance, and spirit of this kind of poetic enterprise. His creation of the narrator is the decisive factor in his opening up of the epic genre.

Phineus, the ill-fated seer and prophet, is a counterpart to our narrator. While telling the Argonauts the details of the part of their voyage yet to come, he suddenly breaks off (2.390–91) to ask himself essentially the same thing Apollonius occasionally asks himself: "but why should I go against the command of god again and tell through mantic art everything, telling it out on and on [there is that *diēnekes* again]?" Phineus is the man who knows all, just like the poet who has the entire interlocking mythic tradition at his command. But Phineus has been told by deity to curtail his utterance. And what is deity but Art?

Like the seer whose vision is not hindered by the restraints of normal human frailty, Apollonius can address Apollo as we have seen him doing in his opening lines. In a curious way, the narrator calls out to gods from his narrative three other times in the poem, reinforcing both the idea that Apollonius is himself along on the voyage and the idea that simultaneously he, present at the creation, is privy to a supernatural world where all is manipulated (typically the author's world). This complementary and contradictory view of things is what the invocation in the fourth book is all about.

In one of the more curious passages of the poem (2.701–13), Apollonius so thoroughly identifies himself with Orpheus as to—so to speak—snatch the lyre from his hands and sing:

> Around the burning sacrifice they made a broad dancing place
> and sang out "Hail, god of healing, beautiful Apollo."
> Then with them Oeagrus' son [Orpheus] began a clear song
> set to his Bistonian lyre, how once upon a time
> beneath Parnassus' rocky ridge Apollo killed
> with his bow the monster of Delphi, still a young man then,
> a beardless youth, still glorying in his long hair.
> —Oh, Lord, may you be gracious, may your hair
> be uncut forever, always unsullied. That is as it should be.
> Only Leto born of Coeus touches it with her hands.—

Time and again the Corycian nymphs carried on the cheer
calling out "god of invocation" whence
arose this lovely hymn for Phoebus.

The change from the indirect discourse of Orpheus' reported song to the
poet's direct speech which is an apostrophe to the god is breathtaking. It is
another technique which Apollonius has taken from the Homeric Hymns.
Here because the narrator is so much less evident than a hymn poet, this
sudden breaking of the illusion is extraordinary. The narrator emerges from
the narrative into which he has completely immersed himself to call out to
the subject of Orpheus' song. It is like waking from a dream to discover that
one is in actuality shouting out what one has been dreaming.[18] The poet
departs from the narrative in the same radical way at the very close of the
poem, when at one moment he is addressing a farewell to a band of men
whom he has just been describing.

Similarly at 4.1198–1200 Apollonius calls out to Hera: "at other times
they sang alone, turning about in a circle for your sake, Hera, for you put it
into Arete's mind." And at 4.1706 to Apollo: "many times he [Jason] called
upon Apollo, . . . O son of Leto, you came down from heaven . . . swift to
hear."

In these two passages, Apollonius turns from the immediate story line and
moves out of the narrative to the side of deity in the greater universe where
humankind's progress through this world—that greater narrative—is cre-
ated. In the same way, he refuses to disclose the details of Medea's sacrifice to
Hecate (4.247–50). "What the maiden prepared . . . may no one come to
know, find out nor may my heart urge me to sing of it," implying, of course,
that he, the omniscient poet, knows it all.

The abrupt conclusion to the poem, where the artist asserts his authority
by demonstrating the absolute artifice of his narrative is equaled by the bold,
abrupt skeletal quality of the opening of the *Argonautica*. The principal sur-
prises for anyone familiar with the Homeric manner are, first, the very few
qualifying epithets and, second, the rapidity of the narrative, both of which
demand more effort from the reader. And, of course, it is to the point that
Apollonius was composing for a reader from whom he could expect consid-
erably more concentration than from the auditor, the listener present-day
scholars presume for the Homeric poet's recitation. The result is that his
narrative is everywhere more complex, more ambiguous, full of startling con-
trasts which only a reader would have time to assimilate. Apollonius is to
poetry what Thucydides is to prose, a writer who means to be read.

In the opening lines, the poet provides incomplete overviews of his poem
reminiscent of the proemia to both the *Iliad* and the *Odyssey*, mentioning the
journey out and the fleece but ignoring the love affair and the trip home.

After the manner of Homer, Apollonius recalls the entire Argonaut myth only intermittently, scattering allusions to it throughout the entire poem.[19] Here at the first he establishes the immediate motive for the voyage, that is, Pelias' desire to destroy Jason, but is peculiarly opaque about why Pelias will be visited by the doom which lies in store for him. The important facts of the myth are that Hera is determined to wreak vengeance on Pelias because he ignored her in his general sacrifice to the gods, at the same time wants to favor Jason who carried her over the river Anaurus at whose rushing streams she stood helpless, disguised as an aged crone; vengeance will come in the form of Medea who will persuade Pelias' daughters to cut up their father as part of a magical ritual to rejuvenate him, a ritual which not only fails in its intent but leaves the old king dead.

Apollonius begins this brief thirteen-line account of the antecedents to the voyage with the fact that Pelias had learned of a hateful doom which awaited him; then after introducing Jason as the author of this catastrophe, he observes that Jason came to the banquet which Pelias was offering "to his father Poseidon and to the other gods but he did not give a thought to a Pelasgian Hera." Anyone familiar with ancient myth will recognize that the exclusion, however inadvertent, of a deity from sacrifice can only wreak disaster for the human responsible for it. The Homeric poet would not leave the matter unexplained at this point, since the mention of the archetypal inadvertence would almost invariably trigger an allusion to the anger which it would engender in Hera. While Apollonius is silent here, in the third book when Hera is seeking Aphrodite's help in insuring Jason's success, she insists that she will get him back home at all costs, so as to destroy Pelias, "so that Pelias may not laugh at having escaped a wretched fate, he who in his arrogance left me without any tokens of honor at the sacrifice" (64–65).

After the manner of modern narrators, Apollonius presents the same event from two viewpoints. Pelias is intent simply upon Jason, who arrives with only one sandal, and thus fulfills the oracle's description of the man who will destroy him. Apollonius presents Pelias' omission at the sacrifice neutrally, because we see things only from Pelias' point of view here. Indeed, we can extrapolate from Apollonius' brief notice the scene in which Pelias, beset with fear at the sight of the barefooted Jason, quite absentmindedly omits to honor Hera, true to that Herodotean conception of things where a person carelessly acts out his doom although already warned of the dire consequences.

In the Hera-Aphrodite colloquy, Hera's love of Jason for his kindness to her and her hatred of Pelias for his omission—notice her assumption of his "arrogance"—cast the same event in another light. In the fourth book we get another sense of it. When Medea has joined Jason on the homeward voyage, the poet says in a striking sentence (here literally translated): "They—the wind blowing fast at the will of the goddess Hera so that swiftly Aeaean

Medea would arrive at the Pelasgian land as an evil for the house of Pelias—
on the third day tied up the ship's cables" (4.241–44).

Traditional epic dactylic hexameter would not have separated the pronoun
subject "they" from its verbal element which occurs here three lines later, but
Apollonius, since he is writing for readers, can compose extended sentences.
Often these will offend the sensibility attuned to the Homeric phraseology,
but they have their own immediate effect; here the poet has managed to insert
the sinister genitive absolute clause, so as to produce the sensation of an ugly
realization quite independently beginning to surface amidst the nautical ne-
cessities of the homeward voyage. And shortly hereafter indeed Jason will
begin to realize that he is hopelessly stuck with Medea, and perhaps subcon-
sciously to feel that she is dangerous trouble (and Apollonius' reader, who
recalls Euripides' *Medea*, knows exactly the trouble). Hera, in the third book,
makes no reference to Medea's role, far more important than Jason's, in Pelias'
doom. Again, Apollonius is presenting points of view and in the early part of
the third book Hera's sponsorship of Jason is essential. Medea is presented as
a victim there. The complexity of her person does not even begin to emerge
until she negotiates with Jason in their tryst at the temple, but more specifi-
cally not until they go to get the fleece, and the poet is true to this changing
view.

Historians of the culture of antiquity are fond of drawing parallels between
the aesthetics of the plastic and the verbal arts. Much has been written about
Homeric epic and geometric vase painting. One might venture to observe
here that Apollonius is attempting to show us an event in the round, so to
speak, giving us the view of things from Pelias' side, then Hera's, and then
what will soon become Jason's. This is true to the innovations in sculpture
made by Lysippus (c. 375–300) who introduced spiral torsion whereby dif-
ferent parts of the body faced in different directions and the viewer had to
look at sculpture all around instead of face on as one does with the sculpture
of the classical age.

Also, like Lysippus, who believed in the intellectual ordering of a work of
art, Apollonius demonstrates an intellectualist presentation of events which
ignores any true chronological progression and which argues against the need
to justify action in terms of outcome. Which is to say, little of that which
occurs in this poem matters to the story. For instance, the episode in which
Cyzicus is mistakenly killed (1.961–1077) tells us a lot about the failure of
outmoded heroism,[20] but it does not move us forward in the story. Its position
in the narrative does not stem from old-fashioned perspectives of cause and
effect. That is, nothing caused the Argonauts to come to Cyzicus' land, and
what transpires there does not motivate them to subsequent action. It is a
charm on a bracelet of vignettes which dangle and glitter all independent.
Only the land's geographical setting justifies its position in the narrative, but

the poet manages to extract from the events there psychological truths which make the Cyzicus episode a necessary transition from the Lemnos scene to the departure of Heracles. While the same may be said of the narrative of the *Iliad* particularly, the *Iliad* poet manages to introduce a sense of continuity which makes his audience wonder what will happen next. This is altogether lacking in Apollonius except for the sequence of events which leads us from Jason and Medea's initial meeting to the death of Apsyrtus when the narrative resumes its peculiarly flat pace, all passion spent.

Just as abruptly as Apollonius dealt with the motive for the voyage, he turns to the Catalogue of Heroes who accompany Jason. Nowhere is the naïve sensibility more extravagantly displayed than in this slightly more than 200-line-long passage (1.23–233) which in its technique was equally alien to the narrative style of Homer. The *Iliad* poet, however, overcomes the embarrassment of his lengthy Catalogue of Ships by means of an elaborate and dramatic motivation which fills most of the earlier part of the *Iliad's* second book and by a series of five powerful similes, one after another, which like circus trumpets prepare the entrance of the catalogue. Apollonius will have none of that; instead, riding over any attempts which the reader might have made at establishing contact with the story, he arbitrarily announces the catalogue and plunges ahead: "First, now let us recall Orpheus." We might well be at a lecture. The poet establishes a logical nondramatic structure to his catalogue similar to Homer's, following the geography of Greece and neatly bringing us back to Iolcus from which the expedition sails by ending with a notice of Acastus, one of the locals. Because his characters are sailors, Apollonius makes his catalogue a *periplous*, describing the districts of Greece by reference to coastal towns rather than inland cities. The lecture tone returns from time to time in the catalogue, as, for instance, in the reference to Heracles—like Orpheus, a major figure in the poem—"nor do we learn that Heracles . . . (1.122–23). The artificiality is reinforced by the fact that nineteen of the heroes mentioned in the catalogue are not dramatis personae in the poem.[21] This is true of the Homeric catalogue as well, which is in any case clearly a poetic set piece offered as catalogues seem to be in preliterate cultures as a special delight to the audience.

What is remarkable in Apollonius' description of this catalogue, however, is that he keeps the setting well in mind, so that he not only describes several of the figures in terms of movement which conjures up the moment of their convening at Iolcus but also introduces flashbacks which lodge the essentially static catalogue in the movement of time; and in addition, he alludes to events contemporaneous to the catalogue, such as Theseus' captivity in the underworld (1.101), so as to give the catalogue a realistic place in absolute chronology. When the catalogue concludes, the poet immediately places the heroes in a dramatic situation, "They went towards the ship through the city"

(1.237), completely at variance with the artificial and mechanical way in which he had introduced the catalogue. Yet with the character Acastus the poet manages to emphasize the two aspects of this assemblage, that it is at once a list and at the same time a moment of convening. Acastus was the last to be named in the catalogue, for the intellectualist reason that he is resident in Iolcus. This is true to the catalogue mentality. He becomes the last to arrive at the beach (1.321) as though the reason were that he had been the last to arrive in a group of men in the process of assembling. This is true to the narrator's instinct for describing action. It is as though someone were to thrust a playbill into our hands, and that playbill so arbitrarily pressed upon us were slowly to animate itself until at length it becomes the characters who begin the enactment upon the stage. But the catalogue does not really function as a playbill; many of its figures do not reappear. As Hurst remarks,[22] the catalogue is a list of men seen from the vantage of the tradition of the myth, not from the point of view of the poem. The catalogue, indeed, is Apollonius' most telling advertisement for the delicate balance he will maintain between form and content, artifice and realism, empathetic presentation and intellectual organization.

The Homeric manner of narration seems at first to be insistently artificial. Formulaic phraseology, stereotypic figures, and conventional narrative devices do not present the immediate moment. These devices achieve another kind of realism, however, because it seems clear that the poet always believes utterly in what he is saying, that beached and rotting ships are somehow always swift, that the hero in battle will always maneuver in a certain manner, that the sea will always be wine dark—in sum, that there is a universal and eternal truth which the poet has found. Then, too, he seems to be artless in his fondness for detail, those excessive and irrational details, seemingly unedited, offering up the full, extended, endless reality through which we move. But more than anything else, the Homeric habit of giving every figure the chance to explain himself in speech seems an extreme form of realism. There are no secrets in Homer; we are always in conversation with the characters.

Apollonius is never so generous. He uses few qualifying adjectives and few obviously formulaic phrases. The reader habituated to Homer feels bereft; there is no texture, everything seems accidental and particular. Apollonius presents things as peculiar, not universal. We see this in the very opening lines. Pelias has been warned against a man with one sandal. Jason crosses the Anaurus river and loses a sandal. "Straightaway he came to Pelias to share in the banquet . . . immediately the king saw him he began to ponder" (1.12–15). The reader is required to establish the connections here, that is, that Jason did not stop off to equip himself with a new sandal. The poet will not tell us all. Instead of comfortably rehearsing the obvious, the formulaic truths of human existence—for obviously anyone who loses his sandal will acquire another—he requires his reader to work out a particular, accidental, and peculiar circumstance.

Still more noticeable is the poet's indifference to the traditional epic speeches. Pelias who ponders does not tell us what he is thinking. When Argus and Acastus arrive late on the beach, upstaging Jason, all the narrator will say is, "But even so [tantalizingly vague: What is he conceding? The fact that they made such an entrance?], Jason refrained from asking them point by point each thing" (1.327–28). Was he angry? Surprised? Dubious? The effect is to make Jason enigmatic. Apollonius takes the narrative away from his reader, so we have a narrative which at times is inaccessible to the reader, at times as we saw in the invocation to the fourth book inaccessible even to the poet.

This silence from the characters is absolutely new in the history of Greek letters. In epic, tragedy, philosophy, and history, man and woman spoke out, advertising themselves,[23] justifying themselves, using themselves as vehicles to formulate certain absolute truths. Suddenly silence. The result is that the emphasis now turns upon the inner life of the characters, that which is left unsaid. Jason becomes deep, internal, and personal, as we know people to be. He is not public or emblematic. We have reached, in effect, the beginnings of the novel.

Apollonius achieves two of his greatest scenes through silence, letting the enormity of the ineffable emerge in the absence of speech, as Cézanne in his later career let the bare canvas reveal Mont St. Victoire. When Jason and Medea present themselves to Circe following the murder of Apsyrtus (4.693–99):

To the hearth they rushed in silence and speechless,
and sat there in the manner of miserable suppliants.
She held her face in both her hands, the sword he stuck
into the ground, that great hilted sword with which he killed Aeetes' son.
They could not raise their eyes to meet her gaze. But
Circe right away knew what it was, that they were
fugitives, and the crime was murder.

What deepens this awesome silence into the perspectives of tragic irony is the reader's memory that once before Apollonius has used the very same phrase "in silence and speechless" to describe the two. It is when they first meet. The poet details at length their physical carriage and emotional turmoil as they approach each other. Then where traditional epic would have opened with speeches, Apollonius writes: "There they stood facing each other, in silence and speechless, like oaks or tall pines, standing without motion, one next the other in the mountains, when no wind stirs" (3.967–71). The silence tells so much here that we remember it and its phrasing several thousand lines later.

Apollonius also uses indirect discourse. By this maneuver he succeeds in distancing the reader from the scene where Homer would have made everything completely immediate with direct speech. There is a vivid example of this in the third book. In this book places are very important, because the poet plots the narrative with much coming and going, as though it were comedy. At one point, he presents a major speech of Aeetes (579–608) in indirect discourse, thereby allowing the reader to follow along with Argus, who is simultaneously in the process of leaving for the city (572) as the speech begins and arriving there as it ends (609). Homer would have pulled us into the council chambers where Aeetes is speaking and then would have switched us back to Argus. By describing Aeetes' harangue through indirect speech, Apollonius only asks us to glance in the direction of Aeetes. What is more, after the fashion of a camera moving away from the scene, Apollonius stops the indirect speech, and begins to summarize or suggest toward the close of Aeetes' speech, "And he went on saying the most impossible things in his rage at the strangers" (606–7). With this technique, the poet prepares to withdraw even more from the scene.

The effect of distancing is to demand more of the reader. We wonder about the silences, the half-hidden acts, as we would not at the earlier, more open epic narrative. Similarly, Apollonius in describing Jason's cloak actively directs the reader to use his imagination[24] ("you could direct your eyes at the rising sun more easily than look at the rosy glow of the cloak" [1.725–26]; "if you saw this [the embroidered scene of Phrixus talking to the ram] you would stay silent to hear them talk" [1.765–77]). Elsewhere he encourages the reader to formulate a simile. As Jason's bronze weapons gleam out when he prepares for his contest, Apollonius remarks, "you would say lightning on a winter's day was shooting through the overcast sky" (3.1265). Elsewhere he is more insistent upon his reader's imaginative capacities: "you would not say it was a fleet, but a flock of birds" (4.238–40). In the same way, Apollonius is the first we know to employ the subjunctive mood in some of his similes (compare 1.1201, 4.933), making them hypothetical, analytical extensions of his narrative rather than true segments with authority equal to whatever else is written.

What is immediately apparent in the *Argonautica* is how much Apollonius needs his reader. He is by turns deliberately tentative, sometimes sketchy, overly self-conscious. His qualities are those of a flirt. He insists upon the presence of his reader, bringing him into the poem time after time. Very likely the Alexandrians were much intrigued by having a reading audience, still certainly a novelty. The third century was the first age of men of letters, of a reading public. Homeric epic and the subsequent literature of the classical period were all designed for public performance, oral presentation to a group. The exception is Thucydides whose prose is so complex as to reinforce by contrast the oral nature of all else, even when composed in writing. In the third century, literature for the first time becomes private, a transaction between two people. The reader has power that a listener would not know. Alexandria with its Library, where reading and working with a text were the major cultural industry, must have had a formidable impact upon its authors. The scholar-critics, themselves often poets, certainly were active participants in the reading of a poem. So it is only natural that a poet of subtlety like Apollonius might address this new sensibility by invoking the reader as a participant in the poem.

On the occasions when he makes similes into hypothetical statements, Apollonius demands that the reader readjust his thinking about the convention of the traditional epic extended comparison. Suddenly details matter much more. Indeed it may be said generally that Apollonius' similes require a greater attention to detail than do those of Homer. This is because as a rule Apollonius creates similes the details of which touch the narrative at many more points than Homeric similes are wont to do.[25] The scene of the simile suggests the narrative moment to which it is meant to be an analogy. An example is the simile at 3.291–95, describing the onset of flame enkindled from some twigs set to a burning coal, a flame which mirrors the rush of love's flame in the heart of Medea, deepened by the poet's description of the woman who starts the fire, a poor woman, who is a spinner (a tedious, painful occupation), lighting the fire while still dark, up very early (that is, she works long hard hours)—in sum, woman as victim, bound to the need to perform rote work long hours to survive. Medea, who has just been struck with the dart of love, is about to enter (hence consistent with a dawn scene) into the miserable state of woman's compulsive emotional dependence upon a male, which will render her a victim.

When Apollonius employs the subjunctive or locutions such as "you might say," he is directing the reader to enter the poem. He does this also with his learned descriptions. The present-tense description of the strong wave action in the Bosporus (2.169–71) is not an example of the historical present—which in fact is not used in epic—but is rather Apollonius' way of reminding his reader that he and the reader are contemporaries dealing with a contrived narrative which nonetheless relates to the real world, and they, the poet and the reader, must exercise their imaginations so as to make the bridge fast between reality and fiction. "The big wave," says Apollonius (2.173–74) at the close of his naturalist's description, "is made calm whenever it may happen to encounter a good ship's captain [the poet uses the subjunctive here—moving us into the hypothetical and thus toward our fictive narrative]. And so they sailed on, thanks to the skill of Tiphys." The same alternation between contemporary geographical or ethnographical truth and the narrative is reflected in the many *aitia*—over thirty historical explanations of present names and practices—which Apollonius introduces into his poem particularly in the second book. Homer's myriad allusions to other myths and stories imply an endless, variegated world. Apollonius suggests a similar universal complexity, but he places it in the contexts of time and reality.

Hence every detail counts in Apollonius because he demands so much of his reader. He can be very precise. When Jason is off to see Hypsipyle for the first time, he carries a spear (1.769) as any warrior would when anticipating arriving into the company of other men. For he does not know that he will meet only women. It is the instinctive gesture, just the detail to establish the conventional nature of Jason in this scene. It makes his subsequent downcast glance all the more amusing as he passes through the ranks of the Lemnian women. In the same way Apollonius establishes the essential suspicion and greed inherent in desire when he describes Eros counting his dice (3.155).

When Circe receives Jason and Medea at her house, the two women launch into the Colchian dialect (4.731). This subtle, realistic touch evokes in the reader Medea's homesickness, Circe's homesickness, their sense of family, and—especially important for the fourth book—Jason's occasional superfluity and impotence. There he is, the hero of this poem, twiddling his thumbs and staring out the window, while aunt and niece carry on in Colchian.

At the launching of the *Argo*, Apollonius considers the reality of men dressed for departure putting the ship into the sea: "they set their clothes, piled up one upon another upon a smooth stone, one which the sea would not strike with its waves, but which a winter's storm had long ago cleaned." Fastidious and practical gentlemen, they strip to their loincloths to keep their sailing togs dry, find a smooth stone—no rips or tears—a dry one and a clean one—no gull dung.

The launching scene itself (367–93) is a masterpiece of technical detail, an Apollonian version of the dactylic constructions of Aratus or of the poet Nicander who created a hexameter account of the nature of snake bites. Poetry and science meet. Even our hero is not immune to the new technology; his cloak, which he wears to meet Hypsipyle, was a gift from Athena when she first began the building of the *Argo* and "taught him how to measure timbers with the measuring rod" (724).

Precise detail, fit to the moment, does not create the universal, eternal scene, like the panoramic view achieved through Homer's myriad details. Instead, it portrays the accident, the special situation. And when the action itself is accidental, rather than inevitable, it has to be motivated and explained. Notice with what care Apollonius motivates the meeting of Phrixus' sons with Jason (1093–1121) by describing at length the storm which cast them onto the same island where Jason and his crew had stopped. Of course, it was also fate and Apollonius does not deny it. Phineus prophesies the meeting although in thoroughly ambiguous fashion ([2.388–89] "help will come to you which cannot be told"); Apollonius reminds us of this (2.1090–92) shortly before the meeting: "what then did Phineus have in mind that the divine band of heroes should land here? What kind of aid was about to come to them in their need?" Apollonius even introduces Zeus (1098) who moves the winds. All the epic machinery is in place. And yet the length and the detail of the splendid description of wind, storm, and shipwreck produce the impression that what has happened is more than anything else the accidental calamity of meteorology.

The same precision, the same exact detail, here psychological,[26] informs the three great monologues of Medea (3.464–70; 636–44; 772–801) establishing a kind of realistic interior process which almost goes beyond rhetoric into stream of consciousness, since it is too irrational to persuade. Homeric monologue is nothing more than a conventional speech delivered by a character to himself by virtue of that curious dichotomous sense of self which Homeric heroes display. It has been argued[27] that a major distinction between ancient and modern conceptions of character can be seen in prayer and soliloquy which in ancient poets is intended to have absolute validity for the audience. There is no awareness of the level of the psyche hidden by a person from himself, the subconscious. Thus a character may not lie to himself. But the monologues here reveal a Medea who, if not self-deceived exactly, is at least, to use a vague term, exceedingly muddled. Apollonius does the same thing in her highly agitated speech to Jason when she agrees to or argues for the killing of Apsyrtus. The logic falters so much that Fränkel argues that the lines are misplaced.

Medea has fallen passionately in love with Jason, but since it is the first time, she does not recognize the symptoms, and furthermore she is feeling guilty about an emotion which dilutes her affections for her family. Instead of the traditional "O me, wretched one" ("*o moi deileiē*") which establishes the other self to whom the monologue will speak, Medea starts out, "What is this ache which grips wretched me?" She talks and there is no object, truly an interior monologue.

> If he is going to die—whether the best of heroes
> or the worst—then to hell with him!
> [Literally: "let him go off (*erretō*)," but
> always in the sense of "away with him," something
> cruelly and angrily dismissive.]
> But, no, let's hope that he gets out of this unhurt.
> Yes, yes, oh Lady daughter of Perses, may that happen,
> may he get back home and escape his doom.

But if it is his fate to be vanquished by the bulls,
may he learn of this beforehand [and presumably go home],
so that I at least do not rejoice at his evil fate.

After dreaming that the stranger has actually come to woo her and that she herself has contested with oxen and won, provoking her parents to anger so that she must choose between her parents and the stranger, she awakens and says:

> I am a sad one; how these dreams have terrified me!
> I fear that this hero's voyage brings some kind of
> greater evil. My very senses flutter for the
> stranger [the Greek points up her confusion: *peri*
> *moi xeinō phrenes* . . . juxtaposing a *moi* with *xeinō*.
> In any case, is it flutter with fear or love? Of
> course, she could not know.] Let him go woo some
> Achaean girl far away from here among the Achaean
> people. [He has never mentioned wooing. She is
> bringing this from the dream.] Let me keep my
> virginity, and my parents' home. Nevertheless,
> [untranslatable particles, perhaps meaning some-
> thing like: if nothing else, well, damn it] I'll
> put on a dog's heart [that is, shameless], stop trying
> to stay out of this and approach my sister to see if
> she will want me to help in the contest, since she
> is so concerned for her son. And maybe this sore
> pain in my heart will ease up.

Again, as in the first monologue, Medea vehemently rejects the stranger ("Let him go woo") only to turn about face. And just as irrationally, she considers helping her sister, thoroughly confused as to her motives and the pain in her heart.

The third monologue follows a scene in which she wavers in her mind between whether to give the charms to Jason or not. Again she rejects him ("Let him die contesting, if it is his fate to die in the field" [778–79]), then again lurches to an alternative position. "How can I hide it from my parents if I prepare the charms? What lies can I tell them? What trick . . . ? And if I see him alone apart from his comrades, what shall I say to him?"

Like so many teenaged virgins writhing in embarrassment, she contem-plates suicide, but those questions quoted above tell another story; her mind is being made up. The brilliance of these monologues resides in the poet's display of Medea's irrationality and confusion, shot through with her consis-tently strong desire. The dynamics of indecision, the true emotional and men-tal movement in vacillation, make these interior speeches far more realistic than any of the classical period.

Control of detail gives Apollonius a special power in his descriptions. He achieves what we might call a painterly style, so well does he fix the spatial relationships of the objects or persons we are to visualize. What he describes become like tableaux vivants, scenes caught or frozen in his description, the narrative flow stopped. The rape of Hylas at the close of the first book (1.1207–72) is an especially good example of this. The episode is particularly revealing since it may be compared to a poem of Theocritus on the same subject. Theocritus' Idylls Thirteen and Twenty-two so closely parallel two passages in the *Argonautica* that we must assume one of the two authors wrote on the model of the other. The priority of either author can never be known; the arguments for either position are eventually idle, since nothing substantial can be proved or demonstrated.[28] In any case, since they do reveal characteristic distinctions in poetic technique, it is useful for any reader of the *Argonautica* to compare them. Idyll Thirteen is very brief, what we might call the suggestion of an epic, describing the rape of Hylas which Apollonius treats at greater length. Let us look at the Apollonian version.

Hylas approaches the spring to draw water for Heracles' evening meal. Apollonius begins with the background (1226–27): "All the nymphs who controlled the mountains or glens were far away in the woods." Then he narrows the focus. "But one nymph was just then emerging from the far-flowing spring." He moves still closer from her to Hylas. "She saw him rosy in his beauty and the sweet desire [he exuded]." The poet backs away to include them both in a larger picture. "For the full moon struck him with its rays and Cypris made her wits flutter; she was helpless, couldn't gather herself together." Two erotic agents from on high—the moon and Aphrodite—enlarge the scene. And the rays *strike* him; she is made to flutter, glancing as if the blow had knocked her askew.

Then Apollonius introduces the crucial sensual moment. "But at the very moment when leaning to one side he dipped the pitcher in the stream and the pouring water rang out against the resounding bronze, then she put her arm around his neck wanting to kiss his soft mouth; and with her right hand she pulled at his elbow and brought him down into the middle of the stream."

In the absolute stillness of the night energized by Hylas' moonlit physical beauty and the nymph's overwhelming desire, brought together in motion in "strike" and "flutter," the sound of the water against the bronze acts as a catalyst to erotic transaction. Apollonius has so carefully positioned the two figures that we cannot mistake any of the lineaments of that fatal rape; the scene in all of its detail is imprinted for our minds. By contrast the Theocritean version has none of the sensual erotic detail, no single nymph, and most important, none of the detailed positioning of the participants which mark the Apollonian version. It is far less precise and not at all pictorial. We may imagine what we choose.

The sailing out of the *Argo* (1.536–68) is another example of Apollonius' ability at staging a scene. He begins with a simile which describes the mood of the scene and the men: the crew cleaving the sea with their oars, to the rhythm of Orpheus' lyre, are compared to youths dancing in honor of Apollo to the sound of the lyre. Then Apollonius moves his reader farther away from the scene. He describes the armor glistening from the ship as it speeds along. We are taken still farther away with the comparison of the *Argo*'s wake to a path stretching over a green plain. This takes us to the horizon line where the poet pauses to recapitulate our now greatly enlarged view by describing the scene from the Olympian vantage point: all the gods, he says, looked down from heaven. Thereafter the poet begins to redirect our focus, moving us down and closing the view when he says that the nymphs gazed down from the top of Mount Pelion upon the heroes. Thereafter he continues the downward movement now to the lowest point and adds a scale figure to the foreground. "Down from the mountaintop came Chiron . . . and at the surf he waved, calling out bon voyage" (553–56). The final sentence of the description ("And his wife, carrying Peleus' son Achilles, displayed the child for his father") ties the foreground and the frame into the picture, adding a sentimental touch of human interest as well. The sense of perspective in this description suggests a painter, and critics have found the same painterly sensibility elsewhere.[29]

Perhaps Apollonius never more compellingly invites his reader to enter into the narrative than when the poet moves from the seriousness which we detect in so much of the *Argonautica* to an amused or ironic tone characteristic of the Callimachean hymns. One often laughs aloud at the Apollonian narrative. Consider the scene in which a leader is chosen for the voyage. When Jason calls for a vote, the reader's expectations (and no doubt Jason's) are upset when the crew unanimously chooses Heracles. Heracles' perhaps coy insistence that they choose Jason is of course the perfect ironic revelation of his own authority and Jason's lack of it. Likewise, the confrontation between Circe and Medea is described in terms which are reminiscent of a humorous comedy of bourgeois manners. As Circe says, in dismissing Medea, "get out of this house, you and that fellow with you, whoever he may be, this stranger you've picked up, against your father's wishes" (4.745–46). T. B. L. Webster, in commenting on this passage,[30] says: "The terrible but alluring magician of Homer has become the nervous aunt." More than anyone else, Jason is made to look ridiculous by the narrator's wit. For instance, when he is in the process of advancing his case with Aeetes and the reader expects an introductory speech common to such moments in epic poetry, Aeetes cuts Jason off with, "Stranger, why do you have to tell out each point on and on?" (3.401). Apollonius is obviously drawing attention to the unsuitability of detail and repetition in literary epic; he makes his hero, who would pretend to epic stature, stumble in this post-epic narrative. At the same time, he makes young Jason, who knows only the old ways, like any youth, appear foolish. His foolishness is more like vulnerability here. Elsewhere, the narrator is more malicious. When Idas rebukes Jason for relying on a woman instead of the traditional remedies of heroic men, there is murmuring but no response. Then the poet has Jason reply: "Let Argos go from the ship then, *since this is pleasing to all*" (3.567–68, my italics). We see a pompous, frightened boy.

The prevalence of this amused tone in the *Argonautica* and the Callimachean Hymns suggest that it was a commonplace in the Alexandrian literary scene. Euripides had begun to exploit this amused view of things in several of his plays. His *Electra*, particularly, and also the *Ion* are filled with ironic and unexpected juxtapositions which make these dramas brilliantly witty.[31] One thinks of Electra's describing her woe in terms of middle-class deprivation, or Ion's rejection of Xuthus' would-be fatherly advances, because he thinks he is a dirty old man. Theocritus' fifteenth Idyll, in which two vulgar women are described in dialogue as they set out to get some culture, has this tone. It is frequently to be found in the mimes of Herondas as well, where human existence is generally portrayed not as a predicament but as a folly.

Another favorite Alexandrian literary preoccupation which relates to this view of things is the collecting of paradoxes. An interest in the paradoxical seems to be translated in Apollonius' narrative into a perverse perspective which, like Nabokov's penchant for the perverse, can make the ordinary course of events appear highly mysterious. We can perceive this in two insights which Apollonius provides us into the characters of Jason and Medea.

Jason is shown to be a complicated person in two unusual similes. As he prepares to leave, his old mother throws her arms around her very young son, "just as a young girl crying out of control throws her arms about her gray-haired nurse, with no one else to protect her from a cruel stepmother" (1.269–75). True enough, traditional Greek society presents family patterns where the old are utterly dependent on the young, so that it is ironically true that in old age the parent once again becomes the child. But the poet has managed a brilliant stroke here. He is describing Jason at home, shortly before he steps forth from his house to become the public man, at which point he is compared to Apollo in a completely conventional simile. Here in the house things are more complicated. It is not that Jason must provide physical care for his parents; the description of the house retinue makes it clear that they shall not be wanting. Rather, it is the peculiar emotional nurturance which Jason as the aged Eurycleia figure seems to offer the little girl—mother figure, totally at variance with the way mother-son relationships in antiquity are presented. (But should we remember Telemachus? "Go back upstairs, Mother!" [*Odyssey* 1.356].) Something is clearly odd in Jason's house, which makes odder still the distinctly cold farewell he offers Alcimede

(1.295–305), ending ungraciously with a motif from an exchange between that querulous old couple, Hecuba and Priam (compare *Iliad* 24.218), in asking her not to accompany him to the ship: "Don't be a bird of ill omen to the ship." The gray-haired nanny has reached behind and untwined the clinging little girl's fingers from her neck. In a poem where so much emphasis is placed upon the youthful, boyish beauty of Jason, it is unsettling to see him compared to an aged crone. It shows that deep down he faces pressures and obligations which a lad does not usually have to take up.

When Jason at last acquires the fleece, his elation is expressed in an extreme image (4.167–73).

> And just as a young girl holds out her delicate gown
> to catch the full moon's beam as it rises above
> her high-roofed chamber; and her heart rejoices
> looking at the beautiful gleam; so at that moment
> Jason in joy held up the great fleece in his hands
> and from the flashing of the wool upon his gold
> cheeks and brow there settled a red just like flame.

A Homeric or fifth-century Athenian male who wins a prize or achieves a goal naturally would rejoice, particularly given the extraordinary competitiveness of their contest systems. But Apollonius uses this simile to establish an entirely other perspective. It is not the winning, not the success which animates Jason here, but rather the sensual pleasures of the fleece. This is the kind of sensibility which in Greek culture—as at any other time in Western culture—is generally reserved for the female sex. And Jason typically is compared to a woman. In terms of epic propriety, Apollonius has perverted a hero's natural instincts.

He makes Medea equally contradictory. Shortly before she makes her public appearance, while still alone in her apartments, she is compared to Artemis. She bathes and readies herself in the elegant and beautiful costume which one associates with maidens of high estate. And then Apollonius describes in great detail the charm which she will bring Jason. The circumstances of its creation are dread and loathsome (3.851–66); it is one of Apollonius' better descriptions. He follows it with: "And this she picked up and placed in her fragrant girdle which was fastened around under her ambrosial breasts." Likewise in the fourth book, when the young girl flees her parents' home in horror at what she has done and lovesick for Jason, the poet describes her escape sympathetically, comparing her to a helpless bond servant. This is followed by: "She had in mind to go to the temple. She knew the route well, since she had often gone that way in search of corpses."

Much has been written[32] on the curious reversals in Medea, as though we were dealing with Dr. Jekyll and Mr. Hyde. But Apollonius is far subtler than that. What he has done is to make her perverse. Both Jason and Medea, in fact, are made to be sometimes inscrutable, unpredictable. Nowhere is Apollonius more revolutionary than in this complication of character. Homeric figures, even the less than obvious Odysseus,[33] are monoliths. They are always predictable in their behavior,[34] so much so that sometimes the circumstances are in conflict, as when Odysseus lies, as lie he must, to his father. The complex character probably derives more from tragedy than anything else, since there we find figures who are caught between alternative courses of action and sometimes suffer anguish over it. For instance, Euripides' Medea must accept her destiny as a mother and thereby accept her husband's blithe disregard of her, a difficult act of self-abnegation, or she must be true to herself and force him to take her seriously by destroying his dynastic ambition, killing his children and his new bride. Clytemnestra in Euripides' *Electra* looks back with a mixture of regret, fatigue, and contentment; Agamemnon in *Iphigenia at Aulis* is tormented and confused. Nonetheless tragic action moves so inevitably that alternatives can only be suggested, never acted on, and in any case the ambivalence lies in the action; it does not spring from character.

The unpredictability, the deliberate strangeness, and amused ironic tone cancel the kind of coherence which is common to classical stylists. For many critics, this translates into the feeling that the *Argonautica* has no symmetry or unity. But of course it is there if we seek it. Northrop Frye, quoting Blake's "Every poem must be a perfect unity," says that this is a "statement of the hypothesis which every reader adopts in first trying to comprehend even the most chaotic poem ever written."[35] We must adopt it for the *Argonautica*. And Apollonius gives us confidence. His display of control time and again in the poem suggests that he knows what he is about from beginning to end. What does make a problem for the reader in search of unity is the fact that the narrative of the love affair between Jason and Medea seems so well-developed and so unified that the rest of the poem rather falls away; it is sometimes hard to see the connection between that tightly organized narrative and the episodic nature of most of the rest. The disparate nature of the narrative seems reflected in the division into books. The rationale for the division is not altogether clear, and the omission of an invocation at the beginning of Book Two is distinctly peculiar, even by Alexandrian standards.

We may begin to address this problem by noticing once again the firm, abrupt, and undramatic way Apollonius begins and ends the poem. Neither beginning nor ending is integrated into the narrative; they are arbitrary, as though a painter were to set down a frame over a portion of a painted canvas and say, "That is my picture." Homer does essentially the same thing at the beginning of the *Iliad* when he tells the Muse to begin at a certain point in what we can thus imagine to be the endless wheel of saga. Apollonius wants to make it more obvious that a story—a mythos—becomes just that by virtue of its having observable dimensions; hence the harsh beginning and end. He has, if nothing else, established a shape to his story.

The *Argonautica* is divided into four books. Book division in the continuous flood of Homeric dactyls was an arbitrary librarian's act which took place sometime during the third century. It is clear that divisions were made at what seemed a normal break in the narrative, the most obvious being the Homeric observation that his principals are going to sleep, for example, the end of the first book of the *Iliad*: then up to bed went Zeus and there lay down beside him Hera of the golden throne. Like the deaths in Elizabethan drama, sleep does bring down the curtain on action. At other times the divisions are less successful, as for instance the division between Books Five and Six in the *Iliad*, which seems arbitrarily to interrupt what is the *aristeia* of Diomedes. The *aristeia* is, our aesthetic instinct tells us, an episode, but the designation of the Greek letter *Z*, that is, Book Six, and the assignment of the number 1 to the first line following "having stopped manslaying Ares from the battle killings" in the Homeric text tells our intellect, if not our senses, that we are beginning again. As Mary Margolies points out, the physical act of turning from one papyrus roll to another would emphasize the division. Form, therefore, is a product of intellect or of instinct or indeed of physical sensation.

The Apollonian book divisions seem to be a conscious reflection of this observation. Consider that the first book closes with sunrise and that the second commences with no more than "here were the stables and farms of Amycus," or that the second book again closes with sunrise, and that the narrative thread between the third and fourth book hangs upon the pronoun "he" ("now he . . . was plotting" [4.6] referring back to "heavy sorrows came to Aeetes" [3.1404]), while the third book ends conventionally with nighttime and indeed cessation of action: "the sun sank and ended the contest thus for him."

Three books begin with an apostrophe to a presiding god or nymph of song: Apollo in One, Erato in Three, and Homer's traditional Muse in Four. To complicate matters, another invocation, this time to the Muses in general, appears at line 22 of the first book and the second book begins without any such introduction. To a mind accustomed to the relentless symmetry of classicism, this pattern is unsettling, but it is, again, part of Apollonius' experimentations with form.

The initial invocation to Apollo, as we have said, is followed by a partial statement of the story of the *Argonautica* after the fashion of the proemia which begin the *Iliad* and the *Odyssey*. It is not unreasonable to imagine, therefore, that it constitutes a proemium to the whole poem rather than to the first book. When the poet recommences, as it were, at lines 20–22—

"and now I hope to tell the name and lineage of the heroes, their journey over the sea and what they did as they wandered along"—he is in fact previewing the contents of the first two books, which constitute an introduction to the characters of all the major figures apart from Medea, and a description of the sailing from Iolcus to Colchis. Considered in this way, the narrative of Books One and Two constitutes a kind of unity for which a single proemium is enough. The passage between the initial proemium and the second (lines 5–16), which gives a skeletal account of a motive for the major action of the poem, that is, the voyage of the *Argo*, is really no different than the *Iliad*'s first book which dramatizes the motive for Achilles' wrath, itself the motive for the major part of the action of the *Iliad*, before the narrative proper gets under way with the Catalogue of Ships.

The invocation to Erato at the beginning of the third book—"Come, stand by me, Erato, and sing how Jason brought the fleece back to Iolcus through Medea's love for him"—is an ample statement of the contents of the third and fourth books, parallel to the passage at 1.18–22. And as we have noticed, the *entha* ("there") of the second book and the *ho men* ("he") of the fourth demand that the reader treat each passage as a continuation of the same episode with which the previous book ended.

But, of course, the fourth book actually commences (4.1–5) with an invocation which, by reminding us of both the *Iliad* and the *Odyssey* and by portraying the narrator as confused by his heroine's motives, effectively interrupts the action. But do we have a proemium similar to those we have discussed? Apollonius pauses to call on the Muses essentially to clarify Medea's motives in leaving home. These are her "travail and stratagem," not getting the fleece, not inspiring Jason to kill Apsyrtus, not any of the other things which fill the fourth book. The invocation is nothing more than an aside, it has no more force than the rhetorical questions posed at 2.1090–92; although it is more like the apostrophe to Eros at 4.445, it is slighter. What Apollonius has done is to insist that the narrative continues through "*ho men*," but on the other hand that our aesthetic instinct will tell us an episode has ended with 3.1407 "the sun sank." And still further, that our intellect will accept that a new pattern is being established at the apostrophe to the Muses. Apart from the intellectualist critical positions being developed at this juncture, the invocation which raises the question of Medea's motives has the effect of introducing her anew into the narrative, no longer the creature of Jason's will, but as an antagonist in the ensuing drama. With this invocation the poet signals that the *athlos* of Jason has ended; he must now share the narrative with Medea.

It is fair to say that the book divisions are relatively unimportant structural elements in the entire narrative. But a variety of balancing elements do create an architecture for the whole. Hurst argues, with elaborate charts to aid his exposition, that the narrative moves between *tour* and *retour*, even down to the rhythm of details. See, for instance, the anecdote describing Aethalides (1.640−49), who is described as dead and gone but never bereft of his memory; this is symbolic of that theme, in the particular form of presence-absence, in turn characteristic of the entire Lemnian episode.[36] Delage has argued[37] that the unity of the whole derives from the itinerary, that the geography is the rationale for the poem's organization, the one constant among episodes of considerable variety in terms of literary quality, narrative value, and tone, giving to the work whatever unity can be claimed for it.

There are several major structural elements. One is the central two-book element (Books Two and Three), which commences with the victory of good over evil, hero over monster, light over dark—Polydeuces vanquishing Amycus—and closes in the parallel victory of Jason over Aeetes. Another is the symmetrically placed mistaken killing of Cyzicus, 1.1030−52, and the foul murder of Apsyrtus, 4.467−81. Again the realistic sea voyage of the second book is reiterated in a through-the-looking-glass form in the mysterious travels of the fourth. The memory of Heracles runs through the entire poem as a leitmotiv, linking all the episodes in the narrative together.

Hurst's conception of the poem is that it is static, in the sense that it is recapitulative, more like a musical piece than an ongoing narrative. Does the poem go anywhere? Precise chronology is given in the first book; but it breaks down by the fourth.[38] The narrative of the first two books is so episodic that it seems held together solely by chronology. One could call it a kind of picaresque narrative, relying on wit and variety rather than empathy and suspense to maintain the interest of the audience. The same is true of much of the fourth book, except that the chronology, like so much else in the book, becomes vague. There is a lassitude which settles over the narrative of the fourth book which evokes the mood of the moral collapse of the characters at that point. It is as though the narrator empathized too much with his characters. Set within this episodic narrative, however, is a genuine story, or two stories, perhaps: Vanquishing the Monster and Winning the Fleece (Girl). They are thoroughly integrated yet separate stories, but together constitute a suspenseful ongoing narrative where details materially affect the outcome. It is not clear that Apollonius has handled these disparate materials successfully. In the first two books of the poem, he accustoms the reader to a very different tempo than what is found in the tension-filled love story and fleece story. Once energized by this tension, the reader has trouble settling back again at the end of the poem into the slower pace.

While the book divisions do not seem to clarify the narrative nor to reflect the narrative, they do perhaps mark off portions of the narrative which demonstrate various devices of story telling. This will be argued later, but briefly here we may identify the first book as a narrative meant to establish and delineate character and the interaction of personality; the second book as on the one hand a demonstration of the narration of events from more than one point of view—clearly the most timid, least successful narrative gambit—and on the other, the evocation of mood, partially through landscape, the third a narrative of what is essentially a comic drama, and the fourth again a description of psychological states through correlative description, principally of landscapes.

It is a commonplace that the subject of Alexandrian poetry is poetry. Apollonius offers his poem as a commentary on Homeric epic, Homeric scholarship, and the nature of narrative. But we must remember that the poem is much more than that. The poet manages to unveil for our inspection a gallery of special persons, some of them memorable, particularly Medea. But all of them—Heracles, Jason, Aeetes, Idas—display the Hellenistic preoccupation with characteristic personality which so distinguishes the sculpture of that era from the serene, detached classical exemplar. They, as much as the peculiar narrative style, give the distinctive stamp to Apollonius' poem.

2

The Tradition

When Alexander founded his city on the Mediterranean shores of Egypt in 331 B.C., he commanded a Greek presence to appear in alien land. In the decade before his death Alexandria, the city, grew quickly, already well on its way to becoming the major cultural center of the Greek-speaking people in the third century. But as we have earlier remarked, the city was a colonial enterprise, planted self-consciously, encouraged to send forth blossoms in imitation and in rivalry of those which made the flowering of Athens two centuries earlier so irresistibly brilliant forever after. To be Greek was to be like Athens; even the emergent *koinē* ("common") dialect of the Hellenistic period was forged from the Attic dialect of Athens. Parodies or crude imitations of things Athenian were not wanted, however, just the deep wholesale knowledge of everything that had gone before in the rich Hellenic tradition centered there. Never before as at that time in Alexandria had a poet been able to play to so much tradition, nor an audience asked to know so much.

The twentieth-century reader comes at the surviving Alexandrian literature with only the merest fragments of this tradition which the chance of history has preserved. But it is fair to say that there is enough remaining for us to form a general understanding of the myth which furnishes the story of the *Argonautica* and of the major variations which writers before Apollonius made in their telling of it. And we can read here and there in epic and drama and history to see the way mankind and the human condition were presented over the centuries before the Alexandrian Age. It is important to do so because Apollonius, who is so self-consciously modern, exhibits his newness by casting before us the long and variegated past which formed the baggage brought by the émigré Greeks to Egypt's shores, and then playing with this past in new and unexpected ways.

The myth itself was very old. Athamas, son of Aeolus, fathered two children on Nephele (Cloud), named Phrixus and Helle. Ino, Athamas' second wife, true to stepmothers in fairy tales, plotted against the children. Through a series of stratagems she obtained a false oracle which declared that Phrixus or (by another tradition) both children should be sacrificed. Nephele intervened, bringing them a golden-fleeced, flying ram which bore them off across the sea toward Colchis. Helle fell off in the area we call the Dardanelles, to the Greeks Hellespont, in honor of Helle. Phrixus, upon arriving safely in Colchis, married Chalciope, daughter of the Colchian king, Aeetes, and sacrificed the ram to Zeus, hanging up its fleece as a trophy in a grove where a huge snake guarded it. Phrixus had four sons, then at last died and was buried in Colchis.

The father of Phrixus and Helle, Athamas, had a brother Cretheus who was king of Iolcus in Thessaly. When this Cretheus died, he left a natural son, Aeson, and a stepson, Pelias, who was the child of his wife Tyro by Poseidon. Although Aeson was the legal heir, Pelias took the throne (in one way or another—the stories differ). Aeson's son, Jason, was sent to the Centaur Chiron where he grew up in safety, enjoying the culture and education Chiron had a habit of bestowing upon the better princes of Greece's mythological houses (Achilles was sent there when Thetis left home and Peleus embarked with Jason to find the fleece [compare 1.557–58]).

After he has grown up, Jason one day carries an old crone across a flooding spring stream. The old lady turns out to be the great goddess Hera in disguise. Throughout his life thereafter, Hera favors Jason as much as she hates Pelias, who neglected to offer sacrifice to her. (H. J. Rose has conjectured, plausibly enough, that originally—in lost versions—Pelias refused to help the old crone across the river.) While bringing the disguised Hera across—or on some similar occasion while fording a stream—Jason loses a sandal in the mud and proceeds to Iolcus with one bare foot. Pelias, warned by an oracle to beware a one-sandaled man, is of course frightened by his nephew's appearance. By one argument or another, he induces Jason to sail off to Colchis to recover the golden fleece, which Phrixus' ghost has been demanding. His thought is, of course, that Jason will perish en route.

Jason calls together the best and brightest of the Greeks and sets sail. After a number of adventures getting there—the principal one being the negotiation of the ship between the Clashing Rocks—the Argonauts arrive in Colchis and discover, hardly to anyone's surprise, that Aeetes has no intention of simply handing over the precious fleece. Instead he proposes a horrendous contest in which, Aeetes thinks, Jason will almost certainly be killed. Aeetes has figured wrong. The king's younger daughter, Medea, falls in love with the handsome stranger and gives him magic that can save him.

When Jason wins, Aeetes is furious. Medea flees to her beloved under cover of night—or alternatively the crew takes her away. Medea subdues the serpent, and Jason snatches the fleece; thereafter, they are in flight from her pursuing brother until they kill him. (An alternative version has it that her father pursues them until Medea dismembers her young brother whom she has brought aboard and flings the pieces over the side, causing her father to lose their trail when he stops to reassemble his son. This grim story contrasts with the prettier story of Atalanta's race; on the advice of Aphrodite, three apples of Hesperides are thrown upon the racetrack and Atalanta, stopping to gather the apples, loses the race to her competing suitor.)

After another set of adventures, Jason and Medea arrive in Iolcus. Hera has claimed that these two will prove a torment for Pelias, and indeed they do. The princess persuades the daughters of King Pelias that she has the means to rejuvenate their old father if they will cut him into sections and boil these in a stew of magical herbs. She demonstrates with the sections of an animal which, by real magic or fake, skips merrily forth after the treatment. Pelias, needless to say, does not. Hera has her revenge, and Jason and Medea must flee the country.

The story of the voyage of the *Argo* is generally thought to have provided the poet of the *Odyssey* with a number of the fabulous adventures which Odysseus recounts to the Phaeacians; so Apollonius was retelling a story which had been current for possibly six or seven centuries. Because he lived in an age of antiquarianism which collected old traditions and curiosities, an age which likewise delighted in interpretation and had developed at least a rudimentary form of the science of anthropology, the folkloristic origins of the story may well have been important to him. (At any rate, in the poem he at times seems to parody the scholarship of his day.)

Various Alexandrian literary-anthropological interpretations from antiquity survive to us. Diodorus Siculus interprets the voyage as a warlike enterprise, demystifying the fire-breathing bulls as being no more than a poetic way of saying that the inhabitants of those eastern lands had the habit of killing strangers (4.40). Strabo analyzes the golden fleece as being the gold of Colchis which was washed down the Phasis river and collected by the Colchians on fleeces (11.499). Suidas (under the heading *deras*) claims that the golden fleece was a book written on parchment on the subject of how to obtain gold by alchemy.

These interpretations are typical of the method of rationalizing myths which began as early as Hecataeus of Miletus in the sixth century and gained great favor as it was practiced by the fourth-century scholar Euhemerus. The method survives to this day, of course; one modern-day interpretation[1] of the *Argo* voyage connects it to the opening up of the Black Sea to trade. Indeed, the Cyzicus episode is said to be possibly a genuine relic of a Black Sea raiding expedition. More probably the episodic nature of the voyage, structured as it is upon place names and geographical detail, reflects the tradition of the *periplous*, the early sailor's versified (for easy memorization) account of the stations on a typical journey along the coast of one or another part of the Mediterranean.

The folk motif represented by the Medea-Aeetes-Jason story is a commonplace around the world.[2] A young prince comes to the home of a hostile being who puts him to severe trials in which he is helped by the daughter of his host. After succeeding at the imposed task, he elopes with the girl and is pursued. They elude their pursuer by throwing things in his wake which must be collected. The immediate analogue is the Ariadne-Minos-Theseus story in which Minos sets for Theseus the task of entering the labyrinth and killing the Minotaur, and Minos' daughter, Ariadne, out of love for Theseus, gives him a magical ball of string which will lead him in and out of the maze. Apollonius recognizes the similarity, for he uses the Theseus tale ironically in his own narrative more than once (3.998–1004, 1074–76). And there is a secondary correspondence, in that Ariadne is helping Theseus kill her half-brother just as Medea assists at or causes the death of Apsyrtus. The same emotional nexus appears in the Hippodamia story, the legend of the princess who falls in love with Pelops, who is competing—as all suitors must—against her father in a chariot race; she contrives to wreck the father's chariot so that her beloved will win; her father becomes the victim of this love just as Medea's brother is the victim of his sister's love for Jason. Again a minor detail links the two: Hippodamia's father, Oenomaus, has set up at the palace gate the heads of her previous suitors who failed in the race; in Apollonius' version, the way to Aeetes' palace lies past corpses (although not of her suitors) strung from the trees. Apollonius briefly mentions Hippodameia (1.754) in the Hypsipyle episode, and shortly thereafter he mentions Atalanta (1.769), another powerful princess much sought after, who somewhat resembles Medea in that she, the only woman in the Caledonian boar hunt with Meleager, was the one to strike the initial and finally fatal blow. She is powerful like Medea, who alone amongst a band of men is the one who subdues the snake.

If we remove the maiden from our Argonaut story, we confront a common fairy-tale type: the prince who is sent after a precious prize who must perform impossible feats to secure it and who is aided by a number of companions possessed of magical talents. Grimm's tale number 134, "The Six Servants" ("Sechs kunstreichen Diener"), is often cited[3] as the obvious parallel. The addition of Medea to the story twists the folk motif toward irony: her talent in magic makes the special talents of Jason's crew appear negligible. Orpheus, for instance, if he can charm the Sirens (4.905–9), ought to have been able to put the snake to sleep. Not that these special talents of the crew have no value in the poem. If nothing else, the talents of the crewmen enable Apollonius to create powerfully individualized characters—in contrast to the mostly faceless, forlorn, weak, and cowardly men who tag along after Odysseus.

From the beginning of the tradition, some of the helpers seem to have been, like Orpheus, men with supernatural abilities, for instance the speedy sons of Boreas who pursue the Harpies. Others have been analyzed as having been animals in origin: Echion (*echis*, or "serpent"), "skilled in tricks" (1.52) as a serpent is thought to be; Lynceus (or, *lynx*: our word lynx) "with very sharp eyes" has the supposed super-vision of a lynx.[4] Others are not men, not animals, but demonic figures, supernatural forces, not unlike fairies or gnomes in our *Märchen*. Their magical traits are not of much importance in late Greek tradition; we may assign this to the Greek anthropocentric way of viewing things, which tends to elevate all things human and deny the non-human.[5]

A story which tells of a trip to the east to procure a shining golden object which is then brought to the west may rouse the suspicion that we are dealing with some kind of solar story. There are fairy tales which describe magical ships which must cross the sea toward the rising sun in search of the sun's house. Mimnermus (fragment 11.5) describes Aeetes' realm as the place where "the rays of the swift sun rest in a golden storeroom." Apollonius makes heavenly light, solar or lunar, an important imagistic element attached to Jason and the other heroes much as Homer uses fire as the emblem of heroism.

Aeetes' realm is in any case at the edge of the known world. Such a voyage is inherently mysterious. Jack Lindsay explains the voyage in the following way. In the original story, the *Argo* is sailing out of the known world into the stream of the ocean which surrounds the world. It is sailing beyond the physical world, bounded by time, into the spirit world, and the Clashing Rocks are the point of entry. Pindar says (*Pythian* 4.210–11) that the voyage of the

Argonauts brought *teleutē* ("death") to the rocks; they never moved again. That *teleutē* is, it is argued, some kind of initiation, a *rite de passage*. The voyage through the rocks is a *teleutē* for the Argonauts as well, an ordeal, and thereafter they move on to a new sphere.[6]

Whatever may be the source for the bare events of the heroes' voyage, the aura of magic and strangeness persists. It is apparent when one considers Odysseus' account of his travels, so much of which is borrowed from the *Argo* story. For here, in plain contrast to the rest of the *Odyssey*, Odysseus, the unconventional but genuine Achaean hero, enters Fairyland.

Meuli, who was the first to pose the separate existence of the *Argo* story and its priority to the·story of Odysseus, believes that the journey into the underworld (the so-called Nekyia) is the invention of the *Odyssey* poet. But the theme is far older; many critics would argue that Gilgamesh's journey from the time he leaves Siduri until he meets Utnapishtim is a third-millenium precursor of the Odyssean underworld visit to Tiresias, and the twelfth tablet of the *Gilgamesh*, from the Akkadian version, is explicitly a journey to the underworld. In addition, there are those who would argue that, in early tradition, the *Argo*'s voyage to Colchis is some kind of underworld voyage, much diluted as we have it in Apollonius' poem.

At least Colchis suggests a Never-Never Land. The *Argo* sails off to the end of the earth to a place called "Land" (*Aea*); its dread king is "Landman" (Aeetes), son of Persis, who is Hecate, a relative of Circe and Medea. As keeper of the grove and snake sacred to Ares, Aeetes is a kind of infernal ruler. The *Argonautica* belongs to a story type where a band of heroes "sails over the sea to the land of the dead, where they meet a demonic being, overcome obstacles, . . . finally defeat the forces of death."[7]

Coincidence or no, the Lemnian women, in one version of this story,[8] are like Circe in the *Odyssey*; they hold the crew back forcibly, as though they too partake of the demonic, infernal mentality. Then Phineus who prophesies to the Argonauts is like Circe when she describes to Odysseus the underworld journey. In fact Jane Harrison has remarked[9] that the geographical instructions of Phineus are like the aids printed on Orphic tablets found in southern Italy which enable the owner to find his way safely through the underworld. Phineus has been likened[10] to a demon of the house who befouls the food of his visitor until a stronger hero appears to force him to desist, whereupon he is forced to tell the hero the future path of his adventures. That again reminds one of Circe, the men transformed into swine, the *moly* carried by Odysseus to overcome her, and her submission. Phineus has also been compared to Nereus who is forced by Heracles to show him the way to get the apples, or the Graiae whose shared eye was stolen by Perseus so that they would tell him where to find the Gorgons—although here Phineus responds to kindness rather than to threats.

Like Circe, who instructs Odysseus in the proper means of approaching the dead, Phineus gives Jason elaborate instructions for his future travels. There are other suggestions of the underworld:[11] Tiphys is perhaps a doublet for Charon, the infernal boatman, as is Erginus who wants to become steersman after Tiphys' death. When Ancaeus takes the helm, he sails down the Acheron river and into the sea. Tiphys the pilot and Idmon the seer have just died, Idmon gored by a boar, an animal which has a chthonic association. Elpenor's death in the *Odyssey* is an essential prelude to the infernal voyage of Odysseus. Perhaps the same can be said of the deaths of Tiphys and Idmon.[12]

If there is a hint of the infernal voyage in the poem, then we may also say that Jason's return with Medea at his side follows the paradigm of the so-called rape of Korē, the snatching—whether attempted or successful—of Pluto's bride Persephone from the underworld. Orpheus, who is a constant presence in the poem, is associated with a similar feat, the abortive attempt to bring back his wife, Eurydice, from the underworld. The poet alludes to the Persephone story in the Catalogue when he excuses Theseus' absence by remarking that he is at that very moment with Peirithous in the underworld (1.101–4), where, as we know, they have gone to snatch away Persephone to be Peirithous' bride. There may be special emphasis here. Apollonius seems to be in error in his chronology, or has purposely altered it, since the accepted order of mythological events calls for Medea to have met Theseus in Athens after her disastrous mariage to Jason, long before this adventure or for that matter before his trip to Crete, a trip to which Jason alludes as to a *fait accompli*. Possibly Apollonius, whom we may imagine to be careful about such things, since he is writing for readers rather than composing for listeners, as we assume Homer to have done, is deliberately drawing our attention to Theseus' underworld trip so as to underscore the nature of the voyage in the second book.

But more than anything else the voyage of the *Argo* is, as we have said, mysterious, deriving more from the ambience of *Märchen* than of saga. This is not surprising, given the Alexandrian penchant for the perverse and the paradoxical. The essence of the literature of the preclassical and classical period is its emphatic conventionality. The Alexandrians only bent to convention to achieve what was odd. Thus one can see how the poem failed to meet with the approval of nineteenth-century classical scholars and why it is much more sympathetically studied today.

The extensive scholia which accompany the ancient text of the *Argonautica* demonstrate a well established literary (as opposed to folk) tradition for the *Argo* story. The obvious learning of the period gives us a clue to the extent to which Apollonius wrote for an audience of cognoscenti who would be able to detect new emphases, subtle reworkings, and allusions. Simply by bringing their knowledge of the literary past to a reading of the text, they incorporated that knowledge into the poem. In an age of learning, highly conscious of history, the reader is *auteur*.

Odysseus, when he mentions the ship *Argo*, calls it something with which everyone has dealt (*Argo pasi melousa* [*Odyssey* 12.69]). The story was already, as we have observed, a mythological commonplace, and the very oblique reference implies another fully developed narrative line with which his listener would be familiar. But in fact the surviving early references are few: Odysseus sees Jason's grandmother in the underworld (*Odyssey* 2.254–59); Jason's son by Hypsipyle brings wine to the Achaean troops at Troy (*Iliad* 7.467–69); Circe is referred to as "sister of the dangerous Aeetes" (*Odyssey* 10.137). The *Odyssey* poet's near contemporary Hesiod recounts the basic story in his *Theogony* (992–99) without a fleece, without the murder; it seems to be no more than the story of a prince performing prodigious feats to win a princess. Our evidence is, of course, so scanty that we cannot confidently make any claims about the elements in the story known in Homeric times. But there are other clues. When, a century later, we find a reference to the fleece in Mimnermus (flourished about 630 B.C.), the very brevity of the reference again implies a well-known element of the story. Various scholia to the *Argonautica* suggest that there was already in Hesiod's time a tradition of a voyage (Schol. Ap. Rhod. 4.284; compare also Strabo, *Geography*, 1.12), of Phineus and the Harpies (Schol. Ap. Rhod. 2.181), and of Heracles' departure from the expedition (Schol. Ap. Rhod. 1.1289).

The *Argo* story was used in the eighth century to promote Corinth. Eumelus connected the genealogy of Aeetes with Corinth and then introduced the story of Medea's arrival in Corinth when the royal line fails of male issue so that Jason can rule. A scholium says Apollonius borrowed verses from Eumelus in which were described the men springing up from dragon teeth. One cannot tell which verses are meant, but G. L. Huxley plausibly points to 3.1854–58 which have a kind of early epic style. [13]

One fragment of a version of the *Argo* story composed at and for the city of Naupactus—hence a fragment misleadingly known as the *Naupactica*, dating possibly from the mid-eighth century—describes Idmon urging Jason to undertake the task which Aeetes commands. This shows that, unlike what we have in the Apollonian version, the seer has in this version lived to arrive at Colchis. What then does it signify that Apollonius has him gored to death by the boar (which Idas kills, we must remember) as a duplicate death to that of Tiphys? The one would seem sufficient. Another fragment describes all the crew members as willing to take on the bulls, whereas this is not the case in the Apollonian version (*Argonautica* 3.521), where the majority shrink back and the poet takes pains to create a mood of uncertainty and incipient despair (3.492–504). The *Naupactica* also tells us that Aeetes was going to kill the Argonauts after the feast, but that Aphrodite roused his desire so that he went to bed with his wife—love entering the action in a more direct and heavy-handed way than in Apollonius' poem. Idmon, foreseeing danger, tells the men to leave, and Medea, hearing their footsteps, follows with the fleece. The crew's seeming indifference to Medea is strange. If she had not pursued them, would they have left the fleece—and her—behind? Aeetes, besotted with love and unmindful of his obligation to be the baleful king, may remind us of some fairy-tale giant temporarily diverted from his oppressive cruelties—the drunken Cyclops, for instance.

According to Diogenes Laertes (1.111), the mid-seventh century Epimenides composed an *Argo* story in dactyls in which the building of the boat was the significant feature. Is it to this that Apollonius is referring when he says (1.18–19), "Others before me have sung of the boat, how Argus built it to the instructions of Athena"? Probably so; perhaps the lines are meant to be, among other things, the Alexandrian version of a scholarly reference in dactyls.

The earliest extended story of the *Argo* appears in Pindar's Fourth Pythian Ode. It is his longest ode by far. One might be tempted to call it a very small epic, except that the aesthetic—the manner of narration—is so different. (Perhaps if we knew more about the hymns of Stesichorus which are said[14] to have contained much narrative, we would find it comparable to them.) In praise of Arcesilaus, king of Cyrene, Pindar's ode consists of thirteen triads of which eight comprise the *Argo* story. There is a suggestion of a catalogue which reminds one of the manner in which Theocritus in Idyll Thirteen achieves the sense of epic panorama in a few large sentences in the opening twenty lines before narrowing to the seduction of Hylas. The *Argo* episode comes into Pindar's poem with the thoroughly epic device of two rhetorical questions ("What was the start of the voyage . . . ?" [70]).

The poem is notable for its geographical confusion. The *Argo* sails from Ocean to the Red Sea to Lemnos. Equally perplexing is the notice that with Medea in tow the crew stops at Lemnos, and there, says Pindar, makes love to the women. Scholars who worry about Medea's virtue when she travels alone with the crew in Apollonius' fourth book narrative must find this assault on her sensibilities impossibly trying. But, of course, we are not to worry. What Pindar says makes little difference; he has achieved the absolute separation of form from content. What *is* important is that Pindar makes the motive for the voyage to be the urgent desire of Phrixus' ghost that the fleece come back to Iolcus so that his soul can be at rest. Pindar is the only poet to establish this motive, says the scholiast (in a remark on *Pythian* 4.281). Apollonius does not repeat this motive; in fact, the peculiar absence of motive is remarkable in the Apollonian version.[15]

Incidentally, Pindar's account of the voyage contains one of the better expressed descriptions of the basic underlying impetus to heroic adventure. He writes (184–89): "Hera put sweet desire (*glykon pothon*) in the demigods for the ship *Argo* so none would remain at home, out of danger at his mother's side, wasting his life, but rather in valor together with his peers he would find the nicest remedy (*kalliston pharmakon*) for death." In the heroic world, a man's love affair is always with adventure; adventure provides the fame which is a male's guarantee of immortality. The use of the erotic phrase *glykon pothon* implies the parallel: a woman's love affair is with a man; the male provides her with a child which is, of course, the superior claim on immortality.

Jason, in Pindar's Fourth Pythian Ode, is the archaic hero par excellence. One imagines the traditional *kouros* statue in "he arrived . . . marvelous . . . a garment held him . . . fitted to [that is, clinging to] his [wonderful to look at] attractive limbs . . . and the glorious locks of his hair fell uncut; they blazed out all along his back" (78–83). "Could it be Apollo? Or Ares . . . ?" someone in the awestruck crowd of onlookers (88–90) asks. There comes to mind the way Apollonius plays on his reader's memory of this passage when Jason first steps forth from his house to go to the harbor, a passage in which he is compared to Apollo (1.307–9) as he goes through the crowd of onlookers.

To the conventional questions put by Pelias—What's your homeland? Who are you?—Jason answers "boldly but gently" (*tharsesais aganoisi logois*). The answer in which he delays naming himself ("they call me Jason" [119]) might superficially recall Odysseus' opening remarks in the ninth book of the *Odyssey*, but in fact the difference is instructive, for the man of many turns is clearly manipulating his audience, whereas the young gentleman here is all modesty if also defiance. It might as well be the young Gary Cooper. No wonder his father rejoiced through his tears seeing "his exceptional and most beautiful of offspring" (123–24).

The distinctive feature of this Jason, which sets him apart from the Homeric heroes (except perhaps for the deferential Diomedes of the *Iliad* (4.411–18; 5.436–44; 6.212–33) is his *politesse*, his gentleness. Pindar stresses it. At a banquet Jason received his kinsmen "with gentle, soothing words" (*meilikhioisi logois*—one of Apollonius' constant expressions). Again in speaking to Pelias he uses a "mild voice" (*malthakai phonai* [138]), an adjective, we may note, which is just as capable of the pejorative connotation "feeble," "cowardly," as of a favorable one.

For all his mild manner and courtly turns, Pindar's Jason is a man of action. Once home, he holds a dinner party; once the decision for the voyage is made, he sends out heralds, and after the brief catalogue Pindar notes: "Jason had collected them together and he approved" (189). Once at Colchis, they seem to engage immediately in battle with Aeetes' men (212–14), "then they came to the Phasis where they mingled strength with the black-footed Colchians right by Aeetes himself." Aphrodite gives him tangible power over Medea.

She "taught the wise Jason prayers and spells whereby he might remove from Medea respect for her parents, replace it with love for Hellas . . . " (216–19). He successfully fights the bulls, kills the dragon and, as Pindar puts it, "stole Medea, not against her will" (250).

The description of Medea is negligible in this ode. Pindar ties the *Argo* story into his praise of Arcesilaus at the beginning by describing Medea prophesying the founding of Cyrene to the Argonauts while they are in Libya: "the word which the mighty daughter of Aeetes breathed out from her immortal mouth, the lady mistress of the Colchians." Prophetess—powerful, but no magician—she is less impressive here than in the *Iliad* poet's allusion to her who says (11.739), "She knew the healing powers of all the plants that grew upon the earth." Her name, Medea, means the cunning one, the planning one. In the Aeetes-Jason complex she is the ogre's daughter.[16] Strabo, looking back on all the major literature of Greece, says (1.38[45]) that Circe is a doublet for an older version of Medea. But a modern who has reviewed the extant literature says, "When the literary tradition is viewed dispassionately it is remarkable how often Medea appears not as a murderer but as a saviour," and adds, "In childish language, Circe is the bad, Medea the good fairy."[17] In Pindar's story because she is so slightly treated we are, I think, to imagine her to be essentially a conventional young virgin, a princess, who falls in love and under that spell tells her prince how to succeed in her father's contest and consents to elopement. She is pretty much Jason's victim, or at least his creature. Of course Pindar does mention the killing of Pelias (*Pythian* 4.250). The killing of her brother goes unmentioned by Pindar, although perhaps it was an established story by this time. Medea's fundamental ambiguity—or better, perhaps, ambivalence—is probably already a fact by Pindar's time.

Where Medea has earned her bad press in the Western tradition is from the Euripidean tragedy and Seneca's adaptation of it. It seems that Euripides came up with the idea of having her murder her own children, a crime which used generally to excite the wildest condemnation of Medea. The murder, however, is the very pivot which changes the action from a high-class soap opera into genuine tragedy, making the heroine sympathetic, if frightful (pity and fear again). In fifth-century Athens, a respectable woman's only function was to serve the dynastic interests of the house into which she had married, a polite way of saying that she was little more than a brood mare. And it is clear that at times she commands little more respect than that animal. In any case, an Athenian woman's sole reason for existence was her children. Take these from her and she is nothing; this is why the Aeschylean Clytemnestra must kill Agamemnon who has killed their daughter, Iphigenia. She cannot tolerate his utter denial of her. (It is Aeschylus' genius, of course, to transform the murder in the very moment of its enactment into an adulterous wife's revenge on a two-timing husband.) The Euripidean Medea, who is being rejected by her husband, and hence denied, must insist that he acknowledge her. She has little choice then but to act in terms of the one faculty which he, like any other male, notices in a woman, childbearing. The tragedy of the play, certainly, is that while she murders her children to gain her husband's attention, she is at the same time denying the only force of her own existence, her only identity.

The twentieth century's increasing articulation of the woman's point of view has in some quarters considerably altered the traditional reading of this play. It has now come to seem, at least to some, to be a stinging rebuke to male chauvinists, a scathing attack on male supremacist notions of marriage, which makes Jason to be the villain of the play. This is, of course, a little inaccurate. The play was written by a male, chosen for a festival by a male, mounted and performed by males at the expense of a state in which only males voted and administered, to an audience made up—we assume—principally of males educated in a culture which insisted upon the absolute superiority of the male sex. Only someone with an advanced capacity for self-flagellation could imagine that a feminist interpretation of the *Medea* would go down well with that audience. A Christian audience, perhaps; pagan, no.

Jason is beset as males traditionally were in that culture with the problem of providing security for his family, and while emotional security is wonderful, the bottom line is food, shelter, and clothing. What can an unemployed prince—a hero—do? He must have land, of course, and material goods and power. Where do men get these things if they are traveling men? Through marriage, just as Oedipus did, just as the suitors of Penelope hoped to, just as Odysseus could have done if he had accepted Alcinous' offer of Nausicaa's hand in marriage. So Jason is being prudent in contracting this marriage with the Corinthian princess. At the same time he is poisoning his relationship with Medea. He may be breaking dubiously legal but possibly sacred vows to a barbarian, although this is not stressed in the Euripidean version. He is walking out onto the quicksand. Agamemnon had to make a similar choice in the *Agamemnon*. We do not see the action from his point of view, but he is damned if he does, damned if he doesn't. Euripides explores Agamemnon's position in *Iphigenia in Aulis*, where he appears as a man caught in the grip of his ambition, moving along in the train which it has activated, weakly submitting, but just as we all might, or males might in any case, who always have to think about making a living before they can think about those for whom the living is being made. In a traditional society there is a rather thorough separation of roles.

What makes Medea the fearful witch in this play, from a familiar male point of view, is the demands—emotional and sexual—which women place

on men beyond the obvious obligation of material support. Clearly in late
fifth-century Athens the women were coming out of their *thalamoi* to demand
a piece of the action. There is a remarkable speech by Medea on the predica-
ment of being a woman (230–50) which commences with almost the same
language as a memorable speech by Odysseus on what one once would have
called the human dilemma but now perhaps only the male predicament (*Od-
yssey* 18.131–50). This new awareness and need can be tragic for all concerned
if in a given case the conflict is unresolvable, as Euripides shows it to be in
this play. It can also be exhilarating, as it clearly is to the chorus of women
who sing about rewriting history from a woman's point of view (410–30).
And it can be frightening, as it clearly is to Jason who has, he thought,
managed to find a safe berth for himself, an annuity for Medea and the chil-
dren, only to confront what from his view is a raving malcontent who wants
proprietary sex more than anything else (Jason: "Because of sex and love you
have killed them [*eunēs hekati kai lechous*]?" 1338; Jason: "You decided that
because of sex it merited killing them [*lechous*]?" Medea: "Do you think that
is a small sorrow to a woman [that is, the absence of sex]?" 1367–68). Males,
who see sex as orgasm—which in their case happens also to be the mechanism
of reproduction—something neutral to be performed whenever and wherever,
finally cannot understand the emotional intensity with which women endow
the sex act. Even Freud asked, "What is it women want?"

Medea is a foreigner in Greece, permanently exiled from her home. The
situation is used to reinforce the notion of dependency. The circumstances are
such that Medea has absolutely no one else. As her wise old nurse says, "A
woman's maximum security remains with her so long as she doesn't go in
opposition to her man" (14–95). I want to die, Medea declares, because "he
was everything to me" (228). Everybody—Creon (284), Jason (529)—agrees
however that she is intelligent, a quality which she declares makes her hated
and envied (293–305). Every master must view an intelligent slave with
suspicion; the Greek husband and father was probably no different, especially
regarding a woman who considers Hecate to be her special protecting deity
(395–98). "You were born smart (*sophē*)," Creon asserts, "and skillful at every
kind of evil" (285). A little later Medea says sarcastically, "We women were
born absolutely helpless when it comes to doing good, but the cleverest (*so-
photatas*) dealers by far of every evil thing" (407–9). The irony of it all is that
she chooses to become a monster of evil before the play is out.

Love has thwarted her intelligence, perhaps. The ancient Greeks more
often than not called love a dread disease, a destructive force above all else.
Love is castigated by all in this play (330; 526), particularly in a choral ode
(627–41). And of course the bitterness which comes from an unshared bed
has driven her mad. Jason (567–73):

You wouldn't think my plan so bad, if your
empty bed weren't grating on you.
You women—if everything is OK in bed, you think
the whole world's rosy,
But let a little trouble come in bed,
And you grow hostile to the best and finest things.

It is a wonder she did not try to kill him too, after remarks like that. Poor Jason, poor Medea! Euripides' play shows us once and for all that the relationship of a man and a woman, whatever its benefits, is problematical.

The problem in the play is Medea's dependency upon Jason. Euripides is able to use her foreignness, her essential alienation, as a sign of this. A bride is a Stranger. The family house will always be alien and she will thus be utterly dependent upon her husband until her children grow old enough to be her allies (poor Clytemnestra, a bride into the house of Atreus, always its victim, never was able to get the children to see her point of view). Jason, normally enough, sees Medea's dependency as material. But she wants "something more." She wants an emotional life, something more than making out with her female companions up in the *thalamos*. She wants sex with her man for recreation and self-fulfillment. This is an utterly new and preposterous idea. He's done his bit, settled them in Corinth, got a small place across town for Medea and the kids. Does she think he's going to *enjoy* sleeping with the Royal Princess? No, that's just part of *his* job, like Odysseus' seven years with Calypso. He'll go on getting his physical and psychic pleasure from his courtesans and boys and his male friends as well down at the coffee house. This conflict of roles, interests, needs is what is problematical.

Jason thinks of himself as amiable: "Even if you do hate me I would not be able to think hostilely toward you ever" (463–64), to which Medea cries out, "You filthy coward!"[18] The characterization exactly foreshadows the curious ambivalence, even self-delusion, in his *politesse* and courtly way in the *Argonautica*. Their *agon* of debate in the Euripidean version is only one step away from *Who's Afraid of Virginia Woolf?* "I will begin at the beginning," she says. "I saved you . . . I killed the snake and held up to you the light of salvation (in effect, I gave *you* security [*sōtērion*, compare 14 *sōtēria*]). Betraying my father and home, I came with you . . . Now, where am I to go?" (475–505). Jason replies, "Aphrodite was the salvation (*sōteiran*) of the voyage, no one else. You do have a subtle mind, but it would be nasty of me to point out that Eros fixed you with his arrows to save my skin . . . in any case you got a lot more in recompense. Instead of some barbarous country, you got to live in Greece, where they use law instead of force [an idea repeated at 1330], you have all the Hellenes acknowledging you as wise and famous. If you had stayed in the boondocks there would be no word of you" (526–75). A curious speech, this one of Jason's, but it rings with sincerity. Sincerity, not profound honesty. His villainy stems from the deepest level, that is, he believes what he says.

A century and a half after this play, Apollonius' readers could remind themselves that this impassioned verbal duel lay ahead of the couple even as they meet at Colchis, could indeed forecast it when first Jason mentions Ariadne, would be sure of it once the tensions mounted, as the Colchians pursued them. When Apollonius' Medea says, "In Hellas I suppose good things happen, like honoring agreements, but Aeetes is not that kind of man in his relation with other men . . . " (3.1105–7). Euripides' Jason will someday say, "You got to live in Greece," in defense of his own dishonoring of his marriage vow. Most of all, Euripides established love between man and woman as serious and dignified enough to be the subject of tragic action, thereby preparing the way for its entry into epic.

When Euripides' Jason tells Medea that he brought her out of obscurity into the limelight (540–41), a twentieth-century translator might be tempted to write, "Medea, I made you a star!" Apollonius portrays the young woman long before she hits the big time; Jason, too, Apollonius never tires of telling us, is just an ingenue. The star in the *Argonautica* is Heracles who upstages everyone throughout the first book. Even when he has left the narrative, he proceeds to leave his impression by being remembered with nostalgia or enthusiasm at numerous critical junctures. There was an early tradition of his participation in the voyage of the *Argo*; no gathering of heroes would be complete without him. Just as early, there is the tradition of his leaving the ship; no gathering of heroes could function with him.

There is a story of his own expedition against Troy which he sacked because its king, Laomedon, reneged on an agreement. This event took place in the generation before the time when Agamemnon led out the Achaean armada to make war on Laomedon's son Priam. The *Iliad* contains only the briefest references to Heracles' Trojan war, but it is there as another and older *mythos*. In the *Odyssey*, speaking of Heracles, Odysseus says that he cannot compete with men of earlier generations (8.223–25). Apollonius has exploited the sense of these references to capture in Heracles a past irretrievable. Again he relies on his readers' knowledge of the main events in the mythological life of Heracles as they are captured in the major literary interpretations of them. And we again have only the fragmentary view; it is particularly vexing not to have the lengthy epic on Heracles by Apollonius' contemporary, Rhianus, or the fifth-century Heracles epic by Herodotus' uncle, Panyassis, the last of the old-style epic poets.

Both a man and a god—very unusual in Greek mythology—Heracles is too much for any assemblage. The impression we have of him is self-sufficient and alone. When Odysseus visits the underworld he sees Heracles standing apart in majesty (*Odyssey* 11.601–15). Unlike Odysseus, another loner, whom

Athena watches over and accompanies (almost like Cinderella's fairy god-mother), Heracles is even naked before the gods, constantly harried and per-secuted by Hera whose name ironically he bears in his own (Glory of Hera). Of all the heroes of Greek mythology the most important, the one truly Panhellenic hero, Heracles is the hardest to come to see whole. He seems to be so many things at once: a heroic master of prodigious feats, a tragic figure, a buffoon, even a philosopher and civilization builder.[19]

Karl Galinsky quotes the excellent epigram of Wilamowitz "Mensch gew-esen, Gott geworden; Mühen erduldet, Himmel erworben" ("Born man, be-came god; labors endured, heaven earned").[20] A hero and then a god by virtue of the twelve tasks which he performed for Eurystheus to atone for the murder of his wife and children, Heracles is the Greek hero par excellence who achieves immortality through performance. If we consider children, as most do, a form of immortality, it is pertinent to note Karen Horney's remark that a woman can bear a child simply by being, but a man must perform. The labors of Heracles, as they are usually called, would be better translated as challenges or contests, from the Greek word *athlos* which is invariably used to signify them. More than simply getting a job done, Heracles is out to prove himself. Some of the labors show in disguised form an attainment of immor-tality, carrying off the apples of Hesperides for instance, or the Hound of Hades.

Heracles was endowed with monstrous strength. Even in his crib the infant bested the serpent which Hera sent to destroy him, just the first in a series of monsters and giants he spent a lifetime fighting. There was a cult of Heracles called the Guardian Against Evil (*Alexikakos*); in a parallel conception he later came to be considered a bulwark against barbarism, victor that he was in all those contests with giants. His strength was fit to the extraordinary tasks Eurystheus demanded from him, such as killing and skinning an invincible lion, harnessing a team of man-eating horses, and other similar fairy-tale feats. Why Eurystheus had power over him has no real explanation, except that it provides the kind of constraint and bondage against which certain kinds of excessive figures need to struggle. Otherwise their lives would have no shape.

Excessive strength gave Heracles a gargantuan temperament, too strong to be humble, always prone to violence, a symptom of his infantile megalo-mania. For instance, in a fit of pique he killed Iphitus when he was a guest in his home, a violent act against all the rules of hospitality. The *Odyssey* poet disapproves while narrating the story (*Odyssey* 21.27–30). Heracles had wanted Iphitus' sister, a young maiden named Iole. Her family declined to give her to him, and when Iphitus was visiting at Tiryns, Heracles threw him from the walls. He then journeyed to Pylos to seek purification from King Neleus, who refused. Returning to Tiryns, Heracles mounted an expedition, returned to Pylos, killed old Neleus and all his sons save Nestor. Then he went to Delphi for absolution where he quarreled with the god Apollo himself over possession of his holy tripod. Finally he went back, sacked Iole's town, and stole her away for his sexual satisfaction.

The same monstrous selfishness animates the portrait of Heracles in the Sophoclean play *The Trachinian Women*. At the end of the play he has violated Deïanira's feelings—she kills herself as a result—and then without remorse learns of her suicide. Sometime before he has raped Iole, and now he forces his son Hyllus, altogether unwilling, to take the shopworn Iole as his bride. *The Trachinian Women* is a play about lust, violence, victimization, and repressed rage in which gentle, sweet, and long-suffering Deïanira inadvertently kills Heracles with an unguent which she thought would restore his love for her, an unguent made from the sperm and blood of a monster named Nessus whom Heracles killed as Nessus tried to rape her. Heracles appears (in this play) as a man who does not respect or even like women; certainly he cannot love them, he can only use them after the manner of a powerful wanton with his victim. Sophocles does not make this emphatic because the male-female inequality in fifth-century Athens precluded undue notice of Heracles' behavior toward Iole and Deïanira, but his actions are certainly there in the play. Deïanira's death-dealing ointment, then, has the inherent sense of being somehow her, all women's, revenge, revenge for loving him and receiving no fair return. Wittingly or no, she *does* kill him.

One can see, then, why Heracles is never portrayed in a group; his egoism even in a society of such heroic prima donnas as Agamemnon or Achilles is extreme, accompanied as it is by legendary brute strength. His violence and selfishness fall just short of madness, and indeed one of the more important stories about him describes a fit of madness which Hera sends to him, during which he kills his wife Megara and their children. It is usually for this that he is described as required to perform the labors—although Euripides composed a play in which his madness and the family murders occur after he has succeeded at the labors, at the very peak of his success. It is a strange play, made up of two phases of action which do not easily cohere in the viewer's imagination: Heracles, flush with success, returns to avert some doom threatening his family. No sooner is he successful in that than he goes mad and destroys them. There is much talk of the force of Necessity, and of enduring. Apart from strength, endurance is Heracles' most obvious quality during the twelve years of labors; for a man of Heracles' psychological makeup, endurance appears as a cleansing passion.

It is not hard to see why all of Greece took Heracles as its favorite culture hero. In a society so confining, where family, group, tribe, and city exerted so overwhelming an influence that the individual was always submerged, Heracles appears as the appealingly antisocial criminal personality. The quarrels, the killings, the rapes—fueled by the superhuman strength—are the gestures of a man always straining, yearning for more, necessarily aggressive before the malevolent Hera who will batter him down, cheat him in every way she can.

His lust was proverbial. No maidservant or stableboy was safe from it, nor respectable woman for that matter. Lecherous Heracles was the stuff of comedy, as well as Heracles the glutton and Heracles the drunkard. The prodigious strengths and endurance appear in belly, brain, and genitals in the comic theater. Indeed, no other Greek hero was so easily translated from the tragic to the comic mode. We have a portrait of him in Euripides' *Alcestis* (a problematic play supposed to have been performed as a satyr play) in which he appears drunk. This is the persona of the comic Heracles immediately recognizable to fifth-century Athenians who were rather rigid about genre distinctions. But Heracles is comic in the greater sense of the word in this work. The play has to do with death and with hypocrisy, itself a kind of death of the spirit. Heracles shines forth in comparison with mean, spiritless Alcestis and her husband Admetus. He loves life, he is generous. He fights Death and wins Alcestis back. His strength is his vigor, his saying yes to life, his vigor of spirit.

Something of his symbolic significance is suggested by the fact that Heracles was as important to the philosophers of the fourth century as he had been to the playwrights of the fifth. The most famous instance is a parable by a late-fifth-century philosopher, Prodicus, who conceived of Heracles being met by two allegorical figures, Virtue and Vice, and being asked to choose to follow in the path of either the one or the other. The endurance which the Heracles of the labors exhibits, which Euripides spiritualized in his play *Heracles*, becomes here the will to choose. Heracles becomes a moral person. Thereafter—the fourth century—Isocrates (5.109) emphasizes Heracles' mind rather than his strength of body, and concentrates upon the implications of a hero figure with a cult title of "Guardian Against Evil," demonstrating his philanthropy, his sense of justice, his capacity for honor. The fourth-century Diogenes the Cynic purified what we have called Heracles' criminal mind and regarded Heracles as a kind of child of nature—asserting individual freedom against the artificial constraints of convention and tradition, that is, the social existence. [21]

This was the complex tradition to which Apollonius and his readers were heir. Apollonius' Heracles seems immediately more archaic, as does the Heracles of Theocritus. The two Alexandrians were being true to the deepest memories the dactylic hexameter evokes. The absence of any suggestion of the fourth-century concept of Heracles makes Apollonius' archaism all the more deliberate for his reader, throwing Heracles into sharper relief in contrast to the more obviously Alexandrian Jason.

Most early cultures seem to have produced epic poems composed orally. These generally relate the adventures of some man or men of the ruling class, all enough alike that we have come to speak of the "heroic age" of a culture. Nowhere has the main figure been better delineated than the two central figures in the two poems surviving from early Greece, Achilles of the *Iliad* and Odysseus of the *Odyssey*. "Hero" is a Greek word, used from early times to describe the men of saga whose existence was not blessed or immortal, like a god's, but not so commonplace as that of everyday man.

The hero is the major legacy of epic in Greek literature. Forever after narrative of whatever sort needed some human figure for focus. The fifth-century historian Herodotus, wanting to develop a theory of causality, structured it around the fortunes of King Croesus of Lydia, then when describing the Persian invasion and defeat in Greece, conceived of it in terms of the personal ambitions of the Persian king Xerxes. It is significant that the books of his history dealing with descriptions of peoples—an ethnographic survey more or less—are far less organized, lack a controlling point of view. Surely this is because there is no human figure upon whom he might hang the narrative. His successor, Thucydides, writing a history of the Peloponnesian War, manages to endow the two major antagonists, Sparta and Athens, with enough personality to make the conflict one between two persons. Again the legacy of epic.

But the most obvious re-creation of the epic hero is in the tragedies. Whatever the difference of genre, whatever the differing cultural and social imperatives which brought epic and tragedy into being, many of tragedy's antagonists recall the epic, having been themselves part of the saga world: Agamemnon, for instance, or Ajax, Menelaus, Odysseus, Philoctetes. Aeschylus called his plays "slices from the banquet of Homer." His manner is sometimes deliberately epiclike, as for instance in the list of warriors—a small epic catalogue no less—who await outside the gates of the city in the *Seven Against Thebes*.

What the tragedians brought over from Homeric epic was a sense of the larger-than-life field of action, the greater-than-average forms of behavior—in general, the hugeness of things. Homeric epic is vast in any number of ways. By alluding to a variety of sagas, by similes which move us instantly to another context of equal and independent validity, by introducing the view from Olympus—*sub specie aeternitatis*, one might say—by depicting characters who sufficiently replicate one another so as to suggest action and attitude stretching to infinity, likewise insisting that the known world is stereotypic and hence endlessly repeated, the Homeric poet creates an immense vista.

The modern Western world has no equivalent of the saga of ancient Greece. It was a period of time lodged in "once upon a time" and therefore without a chronological bridge to the contemporaneous. Hence it was not subject to revision but existed immutable and absolute, peopled with all the familiars of the Greeks' collective cultural memory, lodged in their palaces in the great Mycenaean citadels throughout the Greek land, citadels which as often as not survived into the classical period as mute ruins, testifying with terrible insistence to the grandeur of that time gone by. Anyone today who leaves the banality of the Argos-Nauplion highway to walk among the enormous stones of the ruins of Tiryns may still sense this.

Tragedy and history are the outcomes of epic. The latter is an investigation into the record of events in order to separate the true from the false, to establish some kind of chronology and with it a sense of cause. History deals in particulars. Tragedy strips epic action of its accidents of place and person so as to see it skeletal, as the irreducible framework of reality, analogous to Pythagoras' discoveries in mathematics. But tragic action is also problematical; the genre demands this. The hero must choose or pretend to choose between impossible alternatives. The result is a concentration upon behavior, a defense of action which brings us far closer to the workings of the human psyche than epic narration chose to go. Homeric characters accept their actions as an inevitable part of the continuum. It has always been this way; so the poets have sung it, the auditor knows it this way and is complicit with the characters in anticipating results. Nowhere is this more dramatically displayed than in the ninth book of the *Iliad* when Achilles refuses the pleas of three Achaeans who have come to him. As in fairy-tale narration these are the fatal and irrevocable three noes. But in fact each one of his speeches of denial ends with a slight tilt toward accommodation, since no matter how much Achilles may refuse to return to battle, the narrator knows, the audience knows, surely Achilles, Odysseus, Phoenix and Ajax know, that he will return. In tragedy nothing is so easily laid to rest. Consider Electra and Clytemnestra rehearsing again and again from play to play their positions toward Iphigenia's sacrifice and Agamemnon's murder, or Antigone arguing with Ismene and then Creon her duties toward brother, uncle, king, state, beloved. However much Anouilh may insist that tragic action is comfortable since no one is responsible, there is a good deal of urgent verbal prelude to these inevitable acts. And so we know the tragic Clytemnestra, Electra, and Antigone far better than we do the epic Odysseus and Achilles.

Heracles, the hero par excellence, is characterized by his violent rages, expressive of his unbridled power and lusts. Epic and tragic hero-figures alike demonstrate power more than anything else. All epic heroes are confident in themselves. Apart from the help of protecting deities—help they feel so much to be their due as to be simply a natural extension of themselves—epic heroes are autonomous. What is more, they are from time to time privy to the divine. They talk with gods, act in concert with them. Sometimes, as in the case of Diomedes in the fifth book of the *Iliad*, a god favors a hero with a view of things as a god sees them. Even when their cause is lost, they are supremely confident in the rightness of things. See Hector's speech to Andromache when she begs him to stay in the city and he refuses, acknowledging at the same time that he and Troy alike are doomed. There are no regrets, no hesitations. Everything, however sad, is as it should be. The narrative breathes the confidence of its narrator and his audience in the eventual outcome.

A similar strength emanates from the figures of tragedy. One thinks of the mad Ajax rushing the cattle of the Achaeans and his subsequent suicide, or the suicidal Antigone's refusal to give Creon the satisfaction of her starving to death in the cavern, or Oedipus willing to torture his aged witness so as to learn for sure the hideous truth which he now fully suspects, or the mad Hecuba wreaking her vengeance on Polymestor. See the power, confidence, exultation, and pride of self which fills Clytemnestra's apologia in the *Agamemnon*.

Finally, epic and tragic hero figures are the center of the narrative because they themselves are so preoccupied with self. It is the extreme of ego; nothing else matters. As Helen says to Hector in the *Iliad*, "Maybe all these things have happened to us so that we may become the subjects of song for the coming generations" (6.357–58). This view of the individual ego as the center and cause of things is an expression of the ancient Greek capacity for viewing things anthropocentrically.

Whereas the Hebrew people believed that a god had created man in his image, the Greeks believed men and gods to be coeval in origin and to look alike. Twins, as it were, but with a difference; gods are immortal and, when pressured, omnipotent. Nonetheless the arrogance of these thoroughly anthropomorphized deities, the boldness, sureness, the certitude of their every action is a projection of the confidence of their human counterparts. When the Olympian deities became obsolescent, at the close of the fifth century, human action came to be seen as far more problematical, more tentative.

During the fourth century there arose two philosophical systems, Stoicism and Epicureanism, which served as answers to the collapse of the traditional religion and the culture of the city-state which had supported it. Both philosophical systems offered justifications for action and behavior which remained popular for centuries; in fact our knowledge of them comes more from Roman documents than from the original Greek sources.

Mainly Stoicism taught that there is a divine being, call it what you will—Zeus, Fate. It is like an eternal fire, which is encased in the physical body of every human being. Whatever accidents affect the body—poverty, illness, death, success—are of no consequence, for they do not touch the immortal part of man's being. Ultimately they can have no ill effect, since whatever happens is the action of the divine order of things which is beneficent. Several ideas are clear by this view: all men are equal, for each share equally in the eternal flame; the seeming differences produced by happenstance are inconsequential, for no man is truly king, no man is truly sick; and the universe has meaning, for everything works out for the best.

Epicureanism has a less interesting ideology. The principal idea relating to human conduct is contained in the Greek word *ataraxia* which means "not being shaken," or better, "quietude." The universe as Epicurus conceived it is a constant rain of atoms upon which man can have no effect and gods choose not to. In this mechanistic view of things, man's best course is to lie low, avoid grief. The common view was that devotees of Epicurus pursued pleasure. It is more accurate to say, they sought to avoid pain. The self-centered, alienated, apolitical, antisocial person is the Epicurean ideal.

Alexandria was the repository of every idea which had been born during the previous centuries in Athens. Stoicism particularly, but also Epicureanism. It is fair to say that some mix of the two formed the educated Alexandrian view of man. For this reason it will be useful to read the *Argonautica* in the context of these two philosophical systems. While the pastoral heroes of Theocritus' tranquil fields and rustic paths are more obviously direct expressions of the Epicurean *ataraxia*, it is possible to read into Jason's melancholia the traces of dread at destiny's inevitabilities and nature's indifference. Of course, Apollonius is never topical, and of course never so simple.

The *Argonautica* is of the period but not altogether of the time: a poet who chooses to create an epic poem long after the epic age instantly makes an archaic statement about the human condition, because that genre is inescapably locked to the bygone notion of the triumphant human will and the importance of the human being. An epic poem is about a hero. Let us look at a few of the implications of this.

One of the important ideas in early Greek epic is heroic *aretē*. The concept is difficult to elucidate. Werner Jaeger devoted a fine chapter to it ("Nobility and Arete"), probably the most enduring piece in his three-volume history of Greek culture, *Paideia*. Recently Robert Pirsig has treated the same idea, calling it "Quality" in his *Zen and the Art of Motorcycle Maintenance*, a so-called novel, but really a treatise thinly washed in the bath of some kind of fictional narrative. *Aretē* is that factor in a person or thing which is the realization or definition of it. For instance, the *aretē* of a knife is not its handle or its shape, but the cutting surface. Similarly the hero of the *Iliad* will realize himself most fully on the field of battle where he uses his brains and body to the utmost. That is the moment his heroic quality emerges. Ultimately, the Homeric hero is most perfectly realized in that moment of greatest exertion which immediately precedes his death. The sixteenth book of the *Iliad* depicts Achilles' friend Patroclus cutting through the ranks of the Trojans in a glorious assault. Three times he swings out and in the fourth he is downed, but he has clearly fulfilled himself as a warrior in the high-flying, manic, overextended thrust of his initial "three times." That is what heroism is all about, and the *Iliad* contains a number of solo performances on the battlefield like that of Patroclus. Called *aristeiai*, in the *Iliad* these performances generally end in the hero's victory; otherwise, the Achaean forces would be decimated by the poem's conclusion.

The hero is inextricably linked to death, to competition, man pitched against man in a win or lose contest system, to war and violence. That is an early epic tradition found almost everywhere: the proving of the male through killing. Whereas moderns have castigated the nexus between fulfillment and killing—notably Simone Weil—the Homeric narrator accepts it as the inevitable fact of life. The *Odyssey* poet makes, perhaps, a commentary upon this warlike way of life in the twenty-fourth (and sometimes disputed) book, when he describes the last war encounter in the poem. Odysseus and the relatives of the suitors are fighting, he once again to secure himself in the home, they to seek revenge, just as the suitors had fought Odysseus to survive and he had attacked them for revenge. The weary wheel of violence seems to be turning on endlessly when Athena tells the relatives of the suitors to stop fighting (24.531); they run toward the city "anxious to stay alive" (24.536). Odysseus starts after them when Athena tells him to stop fighting or Zeus will be angry, and Odysseus, the poet says, rejoiced in peace (545). Some preparation for this is to be found in Circe's remonstrance when Odysseus wants to fight Scylla and Charybdis (12.116–17). "Oh, you compulsive man (*skhetliē*), are you still concerned with deeds of war and its labor?" Odysseus remembers this a hundred lines further on (12.226–27) when he says "I forgot Circe's painful command when she told me not to arm myself." Will fighting no longer work?[22] W. B. Stanford is his commentary to the *Odyssey* (24.537–38) says of Odysseus as he starts after the suitors in the twenty-fourth book, it is "the exit of the Iliadic hero."

The hero of the *Odyssey* is better known for his wandering than for his fighting, more remembered for his desire to return home, for the women he meets, than for anything else. The travels of Odysseus constitute a theme already present in the centuries earlier Near Eastern epic poem on the adventures of Gilgamesh. We can also find in that poem the three conceptions of womankind which appear in the Homeric epics, as well as the theme of companionship as though the *Epic of Gilgamesh* were a kind of matrix, an ur-epic from which the others take their shape.

Very briefly, the *Gilgamesh* poem describes a great king obsessed with how death will nullify him and anxious to live on in the community's memory. He goes out to find adventure and, through it, fame. He has a companion, Enkidu, whom the narrator describes as a child of nature, subsequently civilized and alienated from nature, who becomes Gilgamesh's bosom companion after a wrestling match in which he is vanquished by Gilgamesh. It is a relationship of the male and his alter ego as enduring as anything in the Western tradition—in America, for instance, in Ishmael and Queequeg, Huck and Nigger Jim, the Lone Ranger and Tonto. After an adventure in which they kill a giant, Enkidu dies and Gilgamesh, unable to assimilate the loss, travels the earth and through the underworld, eventually to find an old man, Utnap-ishtim, who he hopes will grant him immortality. His wish is denied, and Gilgamesh returns home to die.

In the *Iliad* the Achilles-Patroclus relationship has clear affinities with that of Gilgamesh and Enkidu. The wanderings of Odysseus, including his best-ing of the giant Cyclops and his descent to Hades to speak with Tiresias, is in some ways like Gilgamesh's adventure and travels. Odysseus, however, re-turns home to success; Gilgamesh goes home in despair. Gilgamesh is helped by his mother Ninsun, propositioned sexually by the goddess Ishtar, and encouraged to stay his wanderings and settle down to sensual and domestic pleasures by the vineyard woman Siduri. In the sixth book of the *Iliad*, Hector is offered wine by his mother, invited by Helen to sit by her, and encouraged by his wife Andromache to stay inside the walls. In the *Odyssey* Odysseus is protected by Athena, propositioned sexually by Circe (in a more discrete way by Calypso), encouraged (in veiled hints) to settle down by Nausicaa.

Whether directly related or not, then, epic narratives of Greece and the Near East share patterns and typologies. These are the archetypal aspects of epic, and we may safely assume that Apollonius plays to them in one way or another. To what extent, for instance, does the Medea-Jason relationship re-flect the Achilles-Patroclus relationship? Or could one say that the allusions to Heracles constitute a new way of dealing with the idea of alter ego or shadow figure which we see particularly in the Enkidu-Gilgamesh relation-ship? The journey into the cedar forest, in which the challenger Humbaba is killed, is the cause of Gilgamesh's glory, but also the source of Enkidu's down-fall and therefore Gilgamesh's final despair. The desolation evolves from the exhilaration, just as Gilgamesh predicted before killing Humbaba. If we kill Humbaba, he asks Enkidu, then where will be the glamor and the glory? Does the deepening woe after Jason's triumph over Aeetes somehow reflect this manic-depressive swing?

Critics often distinguish between the so-called comic sensibility of the *Od-yssey* and the tragic sensibility of the *Iliad*.[23] Odysseus is a hero whose main imperative is the return home and the subsequent integration into his envi-ronment, reuniting himself with his son, his servants, his wife, even his old dog. Achilles on the other hand has everything stripped from him, first the community symbols of his worth, and then his alter ego. His withdrawal from the society of his peers is an outward expression of the fundamental isolation in which he finds himself. The *Iliad* looks toward death, the *Odyssey* toward life. This distinction is the inheritance Apollonius received, and a measure of his originality is to be seen in the way in which he alters and mixes the tragic mode with the comic. The same curious blending may be observed if we consider that, in Northrop Frye's category of modes,[24] Medea is a heroine of romance whereas Jason is a hero of the high mimetic mode. As Medea's nurse suggests in the Euripidean play, although for quite other reasons, they should never have met.

By the time Apollonius began to write the *Argonautica*, five centuries or more had passed since the *Iliad* and the *Odyssey* were composed. Whatever one may decide to call the *Argonautica*, formally it is an epic poem in the style of the Homeric epics. It was the genius of the Greeks to adopt as their principal aesthetic the imitation and adaptation of existing literature. True to their conservative instincts, re-creation was more important than innovation. The tragedian Agathon and his fictive plots, the epic poet Antimachus of Colophon and his outré vocabulary, Lycophron and his obfuscating pedantry are representations of an impulse to break away from that other current. The great writers of the Alexandrian age, however, came back to the tradition exercising the greatest decorum in the way in which they impressed themselves upon it.

Apollonius wrote an epic poem which necessarily invites its reader to case back in his memory across those centuries to the Homeric exemplars. But in passing through the centuries neither reader nor poet can ignore the modifications and accretions which the tradition has undergone. A variety of literary forms sprang up after Homeric times to confront the *mythos* once more. Medea and Jason have lived other lives, the *Argo* has sailed before. Apollonius and his reader recall all this as they take on the poem. This is the freight with which Apollonius' *Argonautica* must inevitably set sail.

Only a book devoted to close textual analysis could satisfactorily demonstrate the manner in which Apollonius is constantly using and reworking the texts of the *Iliad* and the *Odyssey*. There are, of course, other less subtle allusions to or imitations of the Homeric manner, for instance, the catalogue or the battle between the *Argo*'s crew and the Doliones (1.1025–52) or the description of Jason's cloak (1.721–67) which recalls the description of Achilles' new shield in the eighteenth book of the *Iliad*. There are important verbal echoes as well, immediately recognizable, such as Aphrodite's initial greeting to Hera and Athena which almost exactly reproduces that of Charis to Thetis in the *Iliad* (18.385–86) when Achilles' mother has come to ask Hephaestus to make her son a new shield. "O, Thetis, . . . why have you come to our home? Previously you didn't use to visit at all." To Athena and Hera, like Thetis, on a mission of petition, Aphrodite says: "Dear friends, what plan and need brought you here? Why have you come, you who previously did not frequent this place often?" To which Apollonius has Hera reply in her traditionally bitchy way, but in repartee which is true to the Alexandrian world: "You're making fun of us / trying to pick a fight / being nasty (*kertomeeis*)."

It is important to Apollonius that he establish a tone to these borrowings which Homer had offered without commentary. The same might be said for the initial meeting between Jason and Medea (3.956–74) which recalls that of Nausicaa and Odysseus. In the scene from the *Odyssey*, the hero advances gently and tentatively although the simile recalls a warrior. Principally one has the sense of a battle scene from the language used to describe Nausicaa: "She awaited him," "The goddess put strength in her." As such it is a charming scene. Apollonius makes the meeting between Jason and Medea a little harsher by employing a simile—Jason as Sirius, the baleful star—suggested by something similar applied to Diomedes (*Iliad* 5.5–6) just as he begins his career of mayhem and violence which fills the subsequent thousand lines. Medea, like Nausicaa (9.64), holds her ground but not through courage, but because she is too afraid to move. The Sirius simile suggests that she has more reason to be afraid than Nausicaa did. Apollonius has taken the Homeric idea, that is, man meets woman on some kind of battlefield, and charged it with a special aggression and urgency. It says something about male-female relationships as well as Jason's character, especially when we remember that Apollonius uses a reminiscence of Achilles' final fatal charge against Hector (*Iliad* 22.26) to depict Jason's arrival at Hypsipyle's palace (1.774).

Homer narrates his story by apposition and analogy. The opening lines of the *Iliad* are instructive of the former technique. The poet begins: "The wrath sing, O Goddess, of Achilles, son of Peleus," he defines wrath, "destructive," then defines that by "which caused countless woes for the Achaeans," and "woes" is in turn defined by "many . . . souls . . . it sent to Hades . . . " and "made their bodies as food . . . " and the entire development is defined in "the will of Zeus was accomplished."

Even in casual, less programmatic, moments, he does the same, as for instance in Priam's saying: "And now my two sons, Lycaon and Polydorus, I cannot see, among the Trojans crowding into the city, whom Laothoe bore me, preeminent among women," where the latter half of the first line is a restatement of "sons" and the third line is a definition of the first, and the latter half of the third line redefines Laothoe. The thrust of the narrative comes in the first half of the first two lines, "I cannot see my two sons," and everything else is some kind of modification, amplification, redefinition. The effect in line after line of the Homeric epics is thrust-rest, thrust-rest. Of all the elements in the verbal construct which is the *Iliad* or the *Odyssey*, that rhythmic phenomenon is the most elemental and pervasive.

A similar feeling for apposition in the *Iliad* poet begets the curious reiteration of the initial structural element of the narrative. After leading his auditor *in medias res* (in the first book), the poet commences the poem formally with the Catalogue of Ships, then proceeds to a scene which is an alternative survey of the Achaean forces (the *Teikhoskopeia* of the third book) begun in this version of the poem but not fully realized, then on to a review of the Achaean forces in the field (the *Epipolesis* of the fourth book) so as to be able finally to begin his story with the *aristeia* of Diomedes (in the fifth book). We have had a review of the Achaean forces from the poet's point of view, from the Trojans' point of view, and from Agamemnon's point of view. Likewise through that curious telescoping of time similar to Picasso's simultaneous presentation of all planes of the body, we have had first the Achaean forces at Aulis and then their line-up at the start of the war before Troy's walls (where the theme of princess contested for by suitors—the duel of Paris and Menelaus—is appropriately played out), and finally at their stations, or preparing to hold them on the field of battle at the present moment.

The two poems proceed by rehearsal and recapitulation. The Telemachia in so many of its facets rehearses the wanderings of Odysseus. The Meleager story, in the ninth book of the *Iliad*, told by Achilles' surrogate father Phoenix before petitioners, prepares for the petition of Patroclus (playing Cleopatra to Achilles' Meleager) in the sixteenth book of the *Iliad*. The story of Nausicaa and Odysseus, the princess and suitor, has any number of resemblances to the final reunion of Odysseus and Penelope. It is clearly important to the *Odyssey* poet, because one of the very few repeated similes in either poem describes Odysseus after washing off the salt brine at Scheria and the suitors' blood at Ithaca (6.232–35; 23.159–62).

Similarly, the language of the two poems seems to be created out of analogy. Milman Parry noticed near similarities as opposed to repeated elements. Michael Nagler's *Spontaneity and Tradition* took the data further and demonstrated the manner in which words and phrases will come where they do because they are phonemic or grammatical or ideological analogues of each other. The phenomenon functions after the fashion of word association as psychologists understand the term.

The use of analogy and apposition parallels the normal manner of speaking. What we are describing is a product of the oral creation of poetic narrative as opposed to a written version. Such a style is really not available to a thoroughly literate poet unless he chooses to imitate rather exactly, as Quintus of Smyrna does in his *Posthomerica*. But not to do so poses a problem, it seems. The style of narration in the great exemplars, the *Iliad* and the *Odyssey* (and no doubt in the other poems deriving from the oral or immediately post-oral poetic milieu), is the epic poet's view of things. It is characteristic. Together with the hero, this style represents the heroic world. Apollonius' problem becomes how to arrange action and description as an epic poet and as a literate poet, so as to give them coherence as well as a kind of epic sensibility. Some-

times he succeeds; sometimes he seems to be less successful. Immediately, his
style is much tighter. There are scarcely any repetitions.[25] There are no typical
scenes. Note how the initial launching and sailing out are described in con-
siderable detail (1.363–558), and thereafter the poet never again describes
the men's daily harboring or meal taking or launching.[26] The reader may
never relax with Apollonius at the helm, and this marks an enormous change
in the epic style.

To make the stylistic differences and similarities clearer, let us consider two
passages. The Homeric passage comes from the close of the eighth book
(554–65) as the Trojans, after their very successful fighting, are bivouaced on
the plain of Troy, close to the Achaian ships.

> . . . they sat all night; many fires burned for them
> as when in the heavens stars around the shining moon
> shine forth conspicuous when there is no wind in the air
> and all the mountain peaks and promontories shine forth
> and the glens; down below the heavens the infinite air is cleft;
> all the stars are to be seen, and the shepherd rejoices in his heart.
> That's how many fires of the Trojans burning them shone forth
> between the ships and the streams of Xanthus before Troy.
> A thousand fires burned on the plain; and by each flame
> of a burning fire sat fifty men.
> Horses feeding on barley and white oats
> standing by their chariots awaited the well-throned Dawn.

The *Iliad* poet redefines the fires with the star simile and then proceeds to
establish their brightness with a panoramic view ("all the mountain peaks
. . . ") which also has the effect of lighting the plain at Troy in the real
narrative. He then restates his proposition ("down below . . . ") recapitulat-
ing and adds the human scale figure, but only to give a human response to
the scene. We do not know where the shepherd is as we do, for instance,
know where Chiron is in Apollonius' scene of the departure (1.553–55). The
shepherd's pleasure is probably no more than the conventional response (that
is, it's a clear night; he will not have to sleep in rain), just as the poet intro-
duces again and again in his poem the conventional or inevitable response or
observation, as in "and the will of Zeus was accomplished" (*Iliad* 1.5) or "an
ornament for the horse and a thing of glory to its rider," which is the conven-
tional addition to the simile of staining ivory (*Iliad* 4.141–47).

A starlit night is a shepherd's pleasure, human action is the accomplish-
ment of the will of Zeus, the staining of ivory is the creation of a thing of
beauty and value. These are generic truths. One would like to extend the idea
of the shepherd's pleasure so that it could be the Trojan viewer's pleasure at so
many of his army's campfires on the plain. Or one would like to see irony here

because the very next episode will tell of the tearful reaction of the shepherd
of the Achaean army, Agamemnon, to the fact of the Trojans camping so close
to his own forces. But it is unlikely that the *Iliad* poet intended either asso-
ciation. The *Iliad* poet closes the passage with a conventional description of
the horses feeding, that is, he simply amplifies the sense of the men sitting at
campfire. The description of the horses feeding amplifies "sat all night" (the
adjective *pannukhioi* is immediately more closely parallel to the numeral than
the adverb in the translation is). The phrase "sat fifty men" is also a restate-
ment of the initial idea, typical of the so-called ring composition device used
by Homer.

The Apollonian passage describes the late night during which Medea tosses
and turns in her indecision as to whether she should help Jason or not (3.744–
50).

> Then night brought the dark over the earth. Sailors
> on the sea looked out from their ships to Orion
> and the Bear. Both the traveler out there on the road
> and the gatekeeper by this time were longing for sleep.
> And a heavy slumber enclosed all around that woman
> whose children had died, nor was there any more dog barking
> through the town, nor the echoing voices of men.
> Silence held the black darkness.

Apollonius recalls the Homeric manner in his ring composition, in reverting
at the close of the description to the darkness with which he had begun,
although differing significantly from his exemplar by not repeating any of the
words and by having brought "silence" into the statement, whereas Homer
would have repeated the word "night." Like Homer, he presents the conven-
tional night figures with one exception: the bereft mother deep in slumber.
The image is unusual enough to be startling, hence to mar the conventional,
obvious development of the passage. What is more, the bereft mother is the
pivotal element in the passage for many reasons.

The description passes from earlier to later night, to traveler still on the
road to no sound of men's voices. So it goes from wakefulness, the sailors'
purposeful wakefulness sliding into the unwilling wakefulness of traveler and
porter, to sleep, that is, no sound from the dogs, no men's voices. Sleep is the
relaxation of all care, the giving up of this world. So Apollonius takes us from
the porter who must stay up to await the traveler at the gate to the woman
with the dead children, now in deep sleep, because there are no more de-
mands to be made upon her as a mother in the night. Her cares are over and
she can sleep as the porter cannot. But her sleep is perverse; we can imagine
it as the heavy sleep of the depressed and recently bereaved mother, the sleep
of escape. Her sleep is indeed the sleep of the world between three and four

in the morning, a world sunk in sleep. It is the only time in a village when one will not hear men's voices and the respondent bark of the random dog. "*Adinon*," he calls the woman's *koma*. It means close-packed, often used of sound to signify loud, intense. Does it have the sense here of insistent, oppressive, that is, the sleep which is no sleep which presses upon sorrowing people to blot out their woe? It is the heaviest sleep and fittingly complements no barking of dogs, and so forth. At the same time by describing the suffering nurturent woman, Apollonius prepares us for Medea ("sweet sleep did not hold Medea" [751]), who suffers in the night, in her concern for another, pondering the protection she might give him, which act, as we know, will eventually destroy her family for her in one way or another, and her family will be dead to her through alienation or, as in the case of Apsyrtus, truly dead. Apollonius has made a subtle passage which has movement in time, movement in space (the sea and the sky to the traveler on the road or the gate where the porter waits to the woman in her bedroom and then out to the village street in general so as to get to Medea in Aeetes' palace), in which each element mentioned adds considerably to the richness of the entire description, in which the central element, the woman, is baffling and upsetting, hence problematical. What is so conspicuously absent in this passage is the Homeric sense of the *déja entendu*.

The epic poems orally conceived and transmitted constituted the only source of history and cultural self-consciousness in a preliterate society. As such, they had the same value as archives, and were held to be absolutely true. Contemporary investigators find that today's oral poets imagine what they sing to be true and to be sung exactly the same each time as though they were able to maintain an exceptional orthodoxy. Shortly thereafter the distinction between truth and fiction came to be made. The *Odyssey* poet is already clearly intrigued by it;[27] Hesiod makes it a feature of his initial poetic inspiration. When the Muses first visit him and give to the simple shepherd the gift of song, they point out to him that they can sing falsehoods as though they were truths, just as well as singing the truth (*Theogony* 26–28). Hesiod's two surviving poems have as their principal subject matter cosmology and agricultural lore, both suggesting an author who is a researcher and organizer and antiquarian first rather than a storyteller. It is significant that in the early third century it is Hesiod rather than Homer who is set up as the exemplar by Callimachus. Hesiod is the high priest of fact as Homer is of story, and Alexandrians cultivated the science of their age in every aspect of their tradition.

As we have remarked earlier, Callimachus' *Aitia* is *the* Alexandrian poem, being a poetic exposition of fact in the Hesiodic manner, where unity comes from the idea of the list or catalogue. So, while it is clear that there were epic poems made throughout the Hellenistic period, it is nonetheless true to say that Apollonius' determination to tell a *story*, moving as he did in the higher circles of the avant-garde, is interesting. For Apollonius is deliberately adopting a naïve narrative style, recalling an understanding of the real world utterly at variance with that of his contemporaries. Because there seems little justification for the tradition of open and strident hostility between Apollonius and the rest of his circle, we must try to understand how he saw himself as the heir to Homer—and to Hesiod, as well, since Apollonius, the narrator, never ceases to remind us of the distinction between fact and fiction.

A traditional story, legend, or saga is different from an outright self-consciously conceived fiction. Extant Greek literature shows little real fiction. Its strength lies in the *mythoi*. Even after the distinction had been established, the *mythos* was thought to have a veracity which was not accorded fiction. The earliest historical research dealt in *mythoi*. As Hecataeus of Miletus said: "I am writing what follows as it seems true to me. For the stories (*mythoi*) of the Greeks are both inconsistent [literally *polloi* "many," but thus in the sense of conflicting] and laughable, or so it seems to me." Hecataeus did not disown the *mythoi*; he wanted to rid them of their manifest absurdities so as to enhance their veracity. Gradually, however, there grew up the distinction between *mythos*, a story, and *logos*, a researched account. In the fourth century a distinction is drawn between recent events and the events of the Persian War and earlier.[28] These last belong to the heroic past whereas recent events are for prose history because they have never been treated in *mythos* form (*oupo memutholētai*). Historians of epic remark on the late-fifth-century Charitus of Samos, who composed an epic on the Persian War because he is using a "true" subject, but it is not clear that the Persian War constituted a "true" subject to the writers of that period. More likely it was altogether a *mythos* and not a *logos*.

It was less than a decade after Xerxes' disastrous defeat at Salamis in 480 that Aeschylus treated certain details of the Persian War in his *Persians* in 472. Already the event is amenable to a treatment which makes it legendary, larger than life, almost fabulous. The great historian of the Persian War, Herodotus, follows Hecataeus in gathering together all the *mythoi* which in any way relate to the event. Although writing in prose, his manner is definitely Homeric in the magisterial command of myriad details; as in Homer's narrative, Herodotus shows a disinclination to subordinate human experience. He is the last surviving practitioner of the paratactic mode in Greek culture. Unlike Homer, he devotes himself to writing on two planes, the heroic and the historical; there is constant tension between the endless procession of his facts and the lovingly told careers of his extravagant hero-figures. The result is history with glamor, exactly that which his younger contemporary, Thucydides, banished from his own history of the Peloponnesian War. "Perhaps I shall bore some because there is no *mythos* style narration in my work," he acknowledges in his introductory chapters (1.22). What he will not do is yield truth to art or to his audience's need to be entertained (1.20).

Thucydides is more representative of the fifth-century mind. His historical writing is thoroughly impressed with the dominant intellectual and artistic experiment of that period, namely, tragedy. That aspect of tragedy which is important for Apollonius is the centrality of a dialectical view of things. The Greek mind had always emphasized dichotomies and alternatives; it is the basis of their compulsive symmetries. The tragic form is shaped from conflict. The oppositions between static singing (ode) and dramatic action (episode), between group (chorus) and individual are constant in tragic drama. What in the earlier part of the century is a dramatic confrontation between two persons—Agamemnon and Clytemnestra before the palace door, for instance, when the queen urges her returned husband to step upon the carpet and he resists—becomes a real debate, an *agon* between two antagonists, Jason and Medea, for instance, in Euripides' play. Antitheses are everywhere in Thucydides; the opposition of word and deed, the effable and the tangible (*logos* and *ergon*) is one example, the contrast between Sparta and Athens is another. The dialectical way of arranging things gradually increases the importance of a second person in narrative. The heroic figure has his Patroclus or Enkidu; Croesus has his admirer in Solon, as Xerxes has Mardonius and Artabanus. But in tragedy, equals confront equals. The emergence of Medea in Apollonius' poem from the passive virginal princess to the commanding woman of the fourth book narrative is not so much the result of Apollonius' devotion to Euripides' play as it is a new understanding of the importance of developed relationships to narrative construction. The dialectic is traditionally and probably inherently eristic, which stamps the narrative with a pattern which heroic narrative does not have. There is no central conflict in the epic narrative. The quarrel between Agamemnon and Achilles does not have the same importance as the love between Patroclus and Achilles. At bottom, the paranoid Odysseus' quarrel is with his total environment; the suitors are no more than an obstacle on the way to his queen.

We have a far larger range of examples of Euripides' work than of Aeschylus or Sophocles. One of the directions in which Euripides was moving was that which led to the fourth-century so-called New Comedy. Very few of these survive from the Greeks; we have what we believe to be reasonably accurate imitations in Plautus and perhaps Terence (whose invention and use of the subplot beclouds our estimation of his models). If we can judge our scanty remains, New Comedy is principally a comedy of manners. The beginnings are to be found in Euripides' *Ion* and *Alcestis*, both of which end happily and which treat human relationships with an amused tone. Two other of his plays, *Iphigenia in Tauris* and *Helen*, have plots somewhat like Apollonius' Jason and Medea story. A wicked king holds a princess in his power until she is delivered by a clever stratagem in which a male takes an active part. The play, *Iphigenia in Tauris*, which is more like the Apollonian story, tells of the priestess of Artemis, Iphigenia, subject to uncouth King Thoas (31), saddened because she does not live among Greeks and is forced to do barbarian things (217; 389). Apollo tells Orestes to go to the mythical land where she is (somewhere beyond the clashing rocks [124; 242; 392–406]) and steal Artemis' statue from the temple there; then he will be freed of the madness which has gripped him since he killed Clytemnestra. Orestes hesitates, unsure of himself (80–90), until his friend, Pylades, encourages him (103), and moments later Orestes rallies with the thought that everything is possible to the young (121). One of the major themes of the play is the strong brotherly love between Pylades and Orestes (601; 674–723), who appear together almost always in this myth on the model of Gilgamesh-Enkidu, Achilles-Patroclus, and so forth. Here we have the cruel and barbaric Never-Neverland, the cruel king, the theft of one of his prize possessions, the sometimes timid prince, his encouraging companion, accent on youth, enthusiastic connivance of the indentured maiden, and friendship between males. The story is far removed from the conventional tragedy. It is more like a dramatized romance.

More than one critic has suggested that the *Argonautica* is a prototypical romance.[29] Nothing is more difficult than a generally accepted definition of the romance when we are only tracing elements. Some will argue that the epic and the romance are essentially the same, that they are both narratives of adventures of individuals told for entertainment and the sake of the story, but what makes a distinction between epic and romance valid is the differences in the societies from which they derive. Epic is a product of a closed society, conservative, conventional, with established beliefs, whereas an open society which is centrifugal and questing, without fixed beliefs or set answers—a problematical society—produces romance.[30] Alexandria is an example of the open society by this definition. Romantic love and the theme of the quest, both common in romances, seem the response to this open society.

But it is possible to distinguish epic by its social role. It is a narrative that belongs to society "which poets as a class are entrusted with," as Northrop Frye says.[31] Put another way, "his [the poet's] primary allegiance is not to fact, not to truth, not to entertainment, but to the *mythos* itself—the story as perceived in the tradition which the epic storyteller is recreating."[32] But Apollonius, as we can clearly sense, is a private person writing a special poem. In Frye's terms he is not writing epic. Nonetheless in terms of presentation[33] Apollonius insists often that he is *telling* a story so that the reader will forget that he is reading. In this way Apollonius allies himself with the poem as performance, the hallmark of the older epic.

While the word *romance* refers to a genre, it also describes a mode of apprehending reality. Scholes and Kellog trace a line which emerges from epic and subdivides into empirical and fictional. The fictional branch replaces its allegiance to the mythos of epic with allegiance to the ideal. It further subdivides into romantic and didactic. "The world of romance is the ideal world, in which poetic justice prevails and all the arts and adornments of language are used to embellish the narrative."[34] This is the opposite of mimetic narrative. Perhaps one could add Frye's notion that "the romancer does not attempt to create 'real people' so much as stylized figures which expand into psychological archetypes."[35] Certainly one would agree that Apollonius makes epic "more literary and fictional."[36] While it is true to say that Aeetes and Medea represent archetypes, as do the minor figures surrounding Jason, it is equally important to notice that Apollonius is trying to develop a complex character in Jason, ambiguous and tentative, which is much more a product of *mimesis* than anything else.

Students of the Greek romances like to identify elements of the novella preexistent in the *Odyssey*, such as the theme of the return of the husband, the Aphrodite-Ares story, the story of the mantle which Odysseus tells to Eumaeus in the fourteenth book, the shroud motif as well as Eumaeus' autobiography.[37] Odysseus' experiences on the island of Scheria have the ring of a marvelous little fiction set right into the larger stream of traditional story motifs. There is a well-plotted beginning and end in Odysseus' meeting with Nausicaa and his journey outward bound on the Phaeacian ship (a story given real finality when the ship is turned to stone). The lovingly developed conversations within the story are the finest example of the *Odyssey* poet's abilities at creating a comedy of manners. In many ways Apollonius has created a through-the-looking-glass version of this narrative, with Medea playing Nausicaa, Jason Odysseus, Aeetes Alcinous, and Chalciope Arete—as though he recognized that the real story or fiction in the *Odyssey* was that passage for which he would more than anywhere else in his own poem create an analogue. In any case the story of Jason and Medea is a love story, as is the story of Odysseus and Nausicaa.

For many critics the presence of love defines a work as a romance, a novella, a fiction. Some of the themes of the Athenian novella[38] are sentimental love, love faithful through adversity, and the sufferings of love. These are set within a series of disasters into which the principals fall; they are separated, set upon by pirates and other evil folk, then in the end reunited, finally recognizing one another. Through it all the heroine's chastity is preserved. This again is the story of the *Odyssey*: Penelope and Odysseus are separated and after a series of fabulous adventures, trials, and sufferings, are reunited, her fidelity unalloyed. Love's sufferings, so important to the romance, mark the *Argonautica* as belonging to this type.[39]

In the fourth century, love stories begin to appear among the anecdotes in historical pieces. Xenophon's life of his great hero Cyrus, *The Education of*

Cyrus, is designed as a didactic piece, to instruct by the example of Cyrus' manifold virtues. Along the way he narrates an anecdote that has all the qualities of romance. Xenophon reports Cyrus' remarks on the power of love (5.1.12–18) which is then illustrated in the story of his lieutenant Araspes who falls in love with the captive woman Panthea who forms part of Cyrus' personal baggage, whom Araspes is supposed to be guarding. Xenophon wants us to read this story as an example of Cyrus' tolerance; lieutenants are not supposed to lust after their chief's chattel and Cyrus laughingly forgives him, after the young man had taken the position in debate with Cyrus that falling in love is voluntary and can be avoided. But the story is strong enough to take over. What we have is the sad tale of the love of Panthea and her husband, Abradatas. When Araspes falls in love with the captive woman she resists and finally tells Cyrus of his lieutenant's advances (5.1.18; 6.1.31). Then Panthea tells Cyrus to send for her husband who will be a true ally (6.1.45). Abradatas arrives, embraces his wife, and pledges loyalty to Cyrus (6.1.47). He then goes off to battle in splendid armor which Panthea has made (6.4.2); his departure occasions a loving farewell between the couple and Panthea's notice that it is Cyrus who has preserved her chastity (6.4.4–11). Abradatas fights bravely and is cut down (7.1.29–32). At his funeral Panthea commits suicide (7.3.2 to the end). Here indeed is a story of love's power and pain, an illustration of everything in Cyrus' remarks on love, reported by Xenophon so many pages earlier.

Among the many other ways of characterizing the post-classical age, one may cite the growing interest in heterosexual love, romance, conjugal love, and tender sentiments, the absence of which clearly marks Greek culture prior to this time. One can only speculate upon the reasons. Certainly the growing freedom of women is important; for it meant that a woman could become an object of esteem in a man's eyes. The widespread upper class habit of homosexuality in preceding centuries may in part have derived from a tendency among soldiers and men of affairs to find housebound, uneducated, naïve girl-brides a trifle boring. Respectable women began now to be something more than household possessions. But that of course does not explain the emphasis upon love, only the possibility of it. Perhaps in the increasing breakdown of an established culture, together with the enormous growth of the Greek world through the conquests of Philip and Alexander, the Greek, now deprived of his minuscule and psychologically secure city-state society, turned to love as the one way to realize himself. In a time when persons are alienated from their society because its political, social and cultural benefits seem inaccessible to them, individuals can turn only to individuals for affirmation. This they find in an erotic life. The Theocritean herdsman, for instance, believe that they are in control; no external power, no god, is to be blamed if love goes wrong.[40] In love they themselves make their destinies. Women become significant love partners in literature because the society has granted dignity to women, perhaps also because the increased social importance of women makes them part of the poet's audience and then exerts pressure for more feminine subject matter.

Thus love becomes paramount as a form of validation. Whatever the reasons, romantic interest begins to appear everywhere. In the third century, Theocritean pastorals play on the pleasure of love (narcissistic suffering is one of its chief pleasures) in a way unthinkable in earlier centuries. It is an entire way of life, as much a "love culture" as now we speak of the drug culture. The erotic element enters even Rhianus' historical epic of the Messenian War. Neda, the woman responsible for the Messenian betrayal, is sleeping with a Spartan herdsman who overhears her husband's military information (Pausanias 4.20.5–10).[41] Aristomenes' escape from his captors is made with the help of a Messenian girl. In art in the Alexandrian period, the most prominent deity is Aphrodite.

New Comedy is filled with the stratagems of love, some of which remind one of the third and fourth books of the *Argonautica*. A common plot describes the travails of a young man in love with a girl who is held captive of either a pimp, if she is a prostitute, or her father, if she is respectable; the action of the comedy turns on his maneuvers for helping her escape. Fathers are often tyrannical; they are the butt of the deception. One thinks of Aeetes claiming that he has not the slightest suspicion of his daughters (3.602–603). Aeetes may be compared, too, to the stock miser figure, another creature hostile to love. In comedy, the lovers are always youthful. Often the boy lover seduces the girl and then wishes to make amends. Sometimes the girl is seduced and abandoned. Comic love is pernicious. Lysiteles in Plautus' *Trinummus*, based on a Greek play of Philemon, recites a long monologue on the danger of love which describes something like the love affair of Jason and Medea. Another common comic figure is the swaggering braggart soldier (who invariably loses the girl), a figure comparable to the exaggeratedly old-fashioned "heroic" Heracles who disdains the Lemnian woman only to lose his catamite Hylas to a nymph's embrace. Yet another staple of the New Comedy of thwarted love is the go-between: the comic action is pushed along by bribed maidservants, male guardians, messengers running to and fro. Even a wife takes a hand in arranging the intrigue in Plautus' *Casina*, based on a Greek play by Diphilus. In the *Argonautica*, Chalciope, Eros, and Arete take the roles of go-betweens.

The comedy of Menander clearly shows the new mood. Love, we have said, validates the individual. Menander's comedy depends directly upon the "new assertion of the value of the individual, not as in the early fifth century as a citizen of an imperial state, but as a private individual in a larger whole."[42] As a complement to the Hellenistic popularity of portraiture in art, Menander stressed character drawing. He preferred to pair opposites, the slave with the master, or the hetaira with the wife. The same tendency toward the balancing of caricatures appears throughout Apollonius: Idas and Jason, Heracles and Jason, Polydeuces and Amycus, Aeetes and Jason, Arete and Alcinous and, of course, Jason and Medea. Clearly, Apollonius has managed to create caricature personalities for several of the crew. Jason, however, has been so well realized that he becomes not a caricature but a character-in-the-round, a person independent of the myth from which he is derived.

There remains to describe one further work with which Apollonius was undoubtedly familiar, Xenophon's *Anabasis*. It bears a resemblance in many ways to the journey of the *Argo* and her crew. We are unfortunately so ignorant of what books were read in antiquity—and of how many people read them— that it is hazardous to say that Apollonius could count on his reading public to measure Jason's problems of leadership—and the entire crew's problems in wandering through unknown territory—with Xenophon's account of a similar experience.

A principal feature of the *Anabasis* is Xenophon's descriptions of the Persian Cyrus, which amount almost to hagiography. The man was a brilliant figure whose untimely death reduces his band of mercenaries to all the miseries reality can present. More recent Greek history, it might be mentioned, offered a parallel to Cyrus' tragedy. Only a scant half century before Apollonius composed his poem, Alexander had led an army through strange lands in the same general direction Jason was taking. Alexander, who had a strong sense of theater, self-consciously presented himself as a hero in the antique mode, and his tragic because untimely death gave immediate impetus to the emergence of a body of legend attached to his memory. A modern historical figure thus moved rapidly and easily into becoming an heroic figure of the sort Herodotus or Xenophon described. In both instances—the life and legend of Alexander, on one hand, Xenophon's *Anabasis* on the other—the heroic stance has been discovered in contemporary historical action. In the *Anabasis* we see it mingled with the petty, tiresome facts of daily existence. Apollonius, by constantly reminding his reader through the *aitia* (the sonorous allusions to how places got their names) calls attention to the fact that his epic narrative is lodged in a "real" world, and he achieves by this means, far more fully than does Xenophon by his trivia, the curious and ironic blend of heroic and mundane. Apollonius' characters undergo the grand actions and adventures of the *Argo* myth, but Jason especially brings to the mythic story a realistic psychology, in effect blowing up the mythic arena.

Xenophon's *Anabasis* was composed in the second and third decades of the fourth century. It records a march made by a band of Greek soldiers-mercenaries from Sardis into Babylonia and back by another route to Pergamon. Initially they were led out by the Persian prince Cyrus, who wanted to dethrone his brother Artaxerxes. Cyrus was killed at Cunaxa (at the confluence of the Tigris and Euphrates rivers) and it fell to Xenophon, who had come along for the adventure and for sight-seeing, to assume leadership and get the demoralized Greeks out of strange territory and beyond pursuit. Schoolboys, inching their fingers across the page, used to yawn over the interminable marches Xenophon records; but read rapidly, the *Anabasis* holds one's interest easily enough. Politics, lively anecdotes, descriptions of the landscape, and ethnographic observations keep the story of the constant march flowing.

At one point Apollonius and Xenophon coincide, describing the peculiar habit of the Mossynoeci of copulating in public (*Anabasis* 5.4; *Argonautica* 2.1019–25). But a larger parallel is more important. Xenophon's story concerns a great and heroic man (compare 1.9) who is taken away from his followers, after which they must settle for second best. Xenophon's power is forever being challenged, like Jason's in the *Argonautica*; like Jason, he is unwilling to assume absolute control (3.1; 5.6; 6.1; 7.6). We find many other parallels. Stratagems of leadership are described: (feigning faint heart 1.3; shaming the common soldier by besting him at his tasks 3.4). The Great King, Cyrus' brother, is a pursuing villain (2.1; 3.1) whose agents are treacherous (2.5); Xenophon relies heavily, almost fatuously, on divine assistance through oracles and omens (3.1; 3.2; 4.3; 5.7; and so forth). Throughout the trip he records ethnic observations (1.4; 4.7; 5.4; 6.1), geography (for example, 1.5), and little anecdotes of human interest (for example, 1.5 a marvelous description of the Persians in fancy dress down in the mud; 7.4 a charming story of a beautiful boy and a pederastic army officer).

Xenophon, in short, provides us with an ingenuous historical account of a band of men who must somehow make do when their natural leader dies. Bereft of their superior, the surviving equals must stifle the impulse to anarchy which threatens their alliance. Their problems are compounded by their unfamiliarity with the terrain and by the relentless pursuit—both personal and through agents—of the Great King. As we have said, one cannot be sure how much ought to be made of the seeming relationship of the *Anabasis* and Apollonius' poem. But much of what Apollonius describes—the tensions between the prima donnas in the crew, the desolation in wandering, the group's loss of its natural leader (after Heracles drops out)—reflects historical facts previously set down by Xenophon. One suspects that Apollonius is asking us to consider heroic feats and prowess, the material of epic vision, through the lens of a grubby reality.

3

The Heroes

〓〓〓〓〓〓〓

TTTTTTTTTTTTTTTTTT

Apollonius proposes to sing the deeds of famous men of old. After the briefest notice of the circumstances motivating the expedition, he grows more specific, announcing that he will tell the name and genealogy of each of the heroes who sailed, and launches into somewhat over two hundred lines of catalogue. Unlike the *Iliad*'s "wrath of Achilles" or the *Odyssey*'s "man of many turns" the narrative of the *Argonautica*, it seems, will be about the voyage of a *group* of men.

And yet, of course, it is not. Jason is far more center stage in this story than are his friends and enemies. It is Pelias' fear of Jason that gathers the men and launches the ship in the first place; and however faltering or inept Jason may appear, it is usually he who gives directions, he to whom the sons of Phrixus address themselves, he with whom Aeetes parleys; in short, it is

Jason whom the poet consistently presents as leader of the group. Jason's beauty captivates Medea and thus wins the day on Aeetes' magical field; and it is Jason who snatches the Golden Fleece from the tree. Generations of critics have faulted the poem for not having a strong central character upon whom the unity of the narrative could be built. Jason, say they, is too weak, too often absent at decisive moments, to be a real hero; he is made to share so much of the important action with the other Argonauts that the narrative focus becomes uncertain. At one time, they say, we are supposed to be entertained by the doings of a group of men, at the next moment we are supposed to follow the career of Jason in Aeetes' palace. It won't work.

One has heard the same arguments in other places: Achilles' absence from books two through eight of the *Iliad* is said to damage the poem's structure; call those books an interpolation and take them out. The *Odyssey's* Telemachia (Books One through Four), in which Odysseus does not appear, must be another poem tacked on. The hero cannot make his first appearance in the second act, as it were. Thus we need not be surprised to encounter arguments that the Argonaut story is inherently unsuitable as plot material because it has no unity, with the result that Apollonius' poetic undertaking is doomed from the start. Scholars who specialize in classical antiquity have a habit of establishing certain a priori standards (usually, in the case of epic, standards derived from nineteenth-century novels), and then chastizing ancient authors who do not meet them or excusing those authors by hypothesizing textual corruption.

The fact of the matter is that, from the myriad stories available to him, Apollonius *chose* the Argonaut story, and critical good will requires that we try to understand why he chose as he did. He must have liked its essentially dichotomous structure (fleece and voyage or love and adventure, or Jason and the crew, or Jason, Medea, and the crew). And in the same way we need to assume, tentatively at least, that he chose to make the narrative perform without a dominant central figure. After all, Pindar had sketched a strong Jason, so the thing was possible. And it is clearly true that Apollonius' Jason is not a poorly drawn Achilles or Odysseus, but an entirely different kind of man.

It has been argued that Apollonius meant the crew collectively to be the hero. [1] Having chosen a narrative which traditionally emphasizes the qualities of individual crewmen, whether they be magical or animal or typically heroic, Apollonius had no room for—did not want room for—a traditional central character. According to this argument, Jason is no more than one among many, a specialist whose particular heroic qualification is his gift for dressing up and getting naïve young virgins to fall in love with him. Finally, in this view, the importance of Medea defeats the initial premise of the story line: her magical powers render the crew impotent to use theirs and the crew sinks into unimportance, as in effect Jason does too. Hence, Apollonius seems to be saying that there are no heroes anymore.

Another theory[2] which concentrates upon the qualities with which the crew is endowed has established four almost allegorical categories: man of brawn (Heracles); men of skill (Tiphys, Polydeuces, Ancaeus); men of valor (Telamon, Peleus, Idas); and men of piety (Idmon, Phineus, Mopsus, Orpheus). These groups represent various ways of coping with life, none of them finally successful. Acting as foils to Jason, they demonstrate the failure of grandeur, skill, intellect, martial impetuosity and piety, whereas "success attends the initially weak, always unadventurous, the circumventive, compromising, treacherous and finally impious Jason, a man of resounding success whom no reader has ever found himself able to admire."[3] The *Argonautica*, by this reading, is a poem of the antihero. Such an interpretation has much to be said for it, but the usual presentation may rouse our suspicion; it has the characteristic emotion and accusatory tone of someone who feels betrayed: led to expect heroic matter, the reader is cruelly mocked, cynically tricked.

The critical problem does reside in our expectations. Apollonius has contrived to write what is *formally* an epic, yet in a sense *not* an epic. Homeric epic is, like all public and social literatures, essentially conformist; that is, it implicitly judges persons and actions as they promote or inhibit the common good. One is reaffirmed in the community's values upon hearing the *Iliad* and the *Odyssey*; indeed, such is the quality of Homer's exploration and exhibition of the deepest instinctive responses of the human community that these two epics transcend the parochial limitations of their original milieux to win favorable responses from centuries of audiences throughout the world. But Apollonius is not writing as a spokesman for the community. To the contrary, this is a private narrative about private people. In that sense, the *Argonautica* is like the romance or the novel. Apollonius does not ask us to admire Jason or to consider him a specimen of the community's values.[4] He asks us to believe in Jason, and in that Apollonius is successful. Critical reaction would not be so vituperative if the credible, lifelike Jason did not betray our idealistic expectations.

Apollonius brings us to Jason through the group, that is, he amply describes the crew before he turns our attention to Jason. Unlike the men of Odysseus' crew, who remain faceless throughout the voyage, many of the men who will sail on the *Argo* are given immediate definition. Apollonius does not dehumanize them with conventional epithets, but instead points up their special attributes: the keen vision of Lynceus; the speed of Euphemus; the lameness of Palaemonius (inherited from his father Hephaestus); the marvelous wings of Zetes and Calais; Idmon's skill at augury; the magic of Orpheus; the aged body and youthful spirit of Polyphemus; Periclymenus' ability to change shape.

Homer's Catalogue, by contrast, which is political, does not attempt to describe characters; it lists territorial leaders and the contingents they lead. In fact, Homer's Catalogue presents almost no distinctions between these leaders; in the narrative of the *Iliad* they are for the most part replicas of one another, created on analogies, as we expect in conventional poetry. The distinctions Apollonius establishes are surface, but they present the image of an assemblage of men in which effective interaction, deriving from special gifts, peculiarities, or idiosyncracies, becomes possible. And the crew is not only a group of specialists, like a bomb squad or a football team; since the poet often describes the different motives which led each man to join the crew[5] and will guide his actions later, each man has at least some measure of individual personality. They are not simply presented in the story as data; as the catalogue unfolds, they effectively and willfully enter the story, each for his own reasons. Clearly the poet thinks of this enumeration as more than a list. He has created an exactly efficient body of men, that is, enough to man a fifty-oared boat, with sufficient backup men to handle death and desertion.[6] Whereas the *Odyssey* poet has so broadly and simply sketched in the band who followed upon Odysseus that they are remembered as no more than "the crew," the men of the *Argo* stay in the mind's eye as a group of individuals, united only at this moment for one special task, specifically chosen and especially competent for its completion.

Although nineteen names from Apollonius' catalogue never recur in his narrative, many of the catalogue figures are part of saga. Among them are members of that older generation whose sons will fight at Troy—Achilles, Patroclus, Ajax Major, Ajax Minor, Podarces, Eumelus, Leonteus, Schedeus, Epistrophes, and Nestor's older brother. There is even someone old enough to have fought the Centaurs (Polyphemus 1.40–43). We have been placed at a point prior to the heroic age, when baby Achilles can wave to his father (1.558), when the resident bard (Orpheus) sings a cosmology rather than a heroic lay, and Circe's creatures are not men transformed into swine but half-shaped creatures just starting on the Empedoclean road of evolution, a time when magic succeeds at what human effort cannot do. Pindar chose to make Jason and crew "heroes" who are true to the traditional Homeric ideal; Apollonius seems to have established his story at an earlier moment in mythological time.

Whatever hoary ur-time we may wish to assign the story to, we are not to forget the youth of the crew throughout the poem,[7] a point Apollonius stresses. In the catalogue, Meleager, for instance, is *eti kourizōn*, young enough to have his half brother with him as chaperon (1.194), and when the group is dismayed at Aeetes' demands, young Meleager—one of those who springs up to fight—is described (3.519) as still waiting for down on his cheek. Jason himself is obliquely described as a very young man. When he meets Cyzicus, the new groom is characterized as late adolescent (1.972): "like Jason, the hair on the side of his face was just sprouting out." Homer does not really assign any age to his heroes, but by their temperament, as well as (in most cases) the age and size of the families left behind, we may imagine them to be, in general, in their late twenties to early thirties. The emphasis upon youth in the *Argonautica* gives the epic story a special character: The themes of men baffled when confronting mystery or depressed by their loss of innocence may be ascribed to the story's oldest traditions; in Apollonius' poem, those themes reflect the natural psychology of young men.

Homer, in keeping with the competitive ethos of the early heroic world, precedes his catalogue with a notice of Agamemnon, who stands out preeminent among the converging men (2.483–84, *ekprepe theke*). In an epilogue, he singles out Telamonian Ajax as the greatest hero at Troy after Achilles, who has at this point withdrawn from the battlefield. True to the group ethos, as opposed to the competitive, Apollonius focuses on his entire band after the catalogue: "they stood out" (1.239, *meteprepon*). We are almost two hundred and fifty lines into the poem, and no notice of Jason except for the preliminary reference to the single sandal, Pelias' fear, and the proposed voyage. Apollonius presents Jason initially without reaction to Pelias' demand, with no motive for going. Contrast this to Pindar's *kouros*, all plans and negotiations, or to members of the Apollonian crew who are described as enthusiastic for the voyage. Jason, who has been curiously absent, is now about to appear. Apollonius has marvelous sense of theater; he moves us from the assemblage (who play the clouds to the crew's stars in the simile), through the crowd of murmuring male onlookers to the women onlookers, grouped as they would be in that kind of society to themselves. While the men have been exclaiming over the crew's powerful appearance, the women are lamenting the tribulations of Jason's mother and father. We move from the *agora* mentality of the men to the *thalamos* mentality of the women and thus Apollonius brings us into the palace and finally to Jason.

In contrast to all the other heroes, Jason is presented in the bosom of his family. His leave-taking is marked by a melancholia[8] which distinguishes him from his exuberant fellow crewmen. Theirs is the public arena of the Homeric hero; his is the private, domestic scene of Euripides, Callimachus, or Theocritus. The serving women are in grief, the father groans, and the mother, who is, as we would say, "all shook up" (*bebolēmenē*), has a conventional speech of parental lamentation ("would that I had died first . . .") which stresses— in a newly sentimental context—Homer's theme of the physical dependency of the old upon the young. Apollonius emphasizes the parents' age quite naturally. But just before, with the brilliant simile equating the old mother to a young girl hanging on the neck of her old nurse (who is Jason), the poet underlines Alcimede's *emotional* dependency upon her son, turning the conventional order of things around. It foreshadows Medea's dependency, with which Jason is equally—though less understandably—uncomfortable. Apollonius first presents the young man as he tries to improve the mood in the room (*katapreunen tharsynōn* [265–66]). He has much to contend with, his mother hanging upon him, the female servants surrounding him and crying continually. His first speech has no effect; he tries again, still polite (*meilikhioisi epeessi* [294], one of Apollonius' favorite expressions), but certainly a bit exasperated. For he can be blunt. "Mother, do not pour out your bitter grief too much, since you can't stop evil with tears; in fact, you just add to the misery. Stay here. Do not come to the ship like a bird of ill omen" (295–305). Jason is flexing his wings. Odd as it is—chilling, too—the scene of the impatient boy is also charming.

Then Jason emerges to the public gaze, and, as it were, straightens his shoulders. For Apollonius describes him in the most conventional of similes, comparing him to Apollo. The flatness of the simile, the absence of concrete detail, is completely Homeric; Apollonius reinforces the resemblance by employing traditional wording which falls into the conventional metrical position. This, the narrator is saying, is a hero. But no sooner does Jason emerge triumphant in the Apollo simile than the poet begins to complicate his character by deliberately undercutting his heroic progress. Immediately after the Apollo simile, Jason is met by an aging priestess of Artemis (Apollo's sister), "who kissed his right hand, but was not able to speak to him, though wanting to, as the crowd rushed on, but she was left by the side, as the old are by the young, and he disappeared from her, going off far away." Here the dependent old woman repeats the drag upon Jason which his mother had produced, and the melancholia deflates Jason's triumph.

Apollonius repeats the sensation when Jason arrives at the beach. This will be his first encounter with the assemblage of heroes. Early epic practice would demand that Jason's distinction be established at this moment, and Apollonius prepares us for it. "He arrived at the beach of Pegasae where his companions received him as they waited by the ship. He stood at the entrance, and they were gathered together to meet him (*antioi*)." With *antioi*, literally "in opposition," the poet stresses the special nature of Jason, set apart as he is from the group. The reader anticipates the conventional epic poetical observation upon Jason's glitter or strength or some other heroic quality. But Apollonius continues: "Just then they noticed Acastus and Argus hurrying from the city, and they marveled, seeing them" (321–22).

The amused tone of the interior palace scene becomes stronger, more ironic in this bit of upstaging; subsequently the poet turns to flat-out comedy. Jason speaks, and Apollonius gives him a conventional Homeric line of authority ("Aeson's son spoke amongst them with goodwill [*euphroneōn meteeipen*]" 331). Everything is ready, he says, now let us choose as our leader the best (*ton ariston*). In Homeric narrative, made inevitable by formulae and stereotype, true choice at this juncture is inconceivable. This is Jason's moment; he has called them together; they stand upon his family's demesne; he, as we all know, will get the fleece. And he will be leader. Apollonius says: "Thus he spoke. The young men looked around at bold Heracles sitting in their midst, and with one voice called upon him to lead." Poor Jason! Witty as the poet is in this scene, he is also cruel in his betrayal of the poem's hero. And Apollonius piles on humorous details. Heracles remains seated, contrary to usage, and hence immensely condescending and arrogant, declines: "Let no one offer this honor to me, I will not agree. And I forbid anyone else to stand for the post. Let him who gathered us together lead the group." In full authority, the true leader, he orders the crew to choose Jason, and not because of Jason's worth, but because in the tradition of the *mythos* Jason is, formally, the leader. Jason, who at the first was curiously innocent of any motive for making the voyage, is now denied any qualities of leadership in directing it. The dread and loathing which this bondage to a destiny unsought and unwanted provokes was taken over by Virgil, whose Aeneas is a far more volubly unwilling instrument of fate.

Yet some foreshadowing lurks in Jason's suggestion that they vote for "someone who will care for each detail, who will deal with our quarrels and our compacts with strangers" (339–40). For if nothing else, Jason has politesse and patience, which will win the day in the coming quarrel with Aeetes and the compact with Medea. Nonetheless, on the surface of things, Jason has definitely been established as second-best. No wonder he is often downcast or in tears. Like Orestes in Euripides' *Orestes*, or Electra in his *Electra*, who act out with reluctance and distaste their inevitable destinies, wearily, always, wearily,[9] Jason is the prisoner and victim of his myth. One could probably say the Alexandrians were enslaved to their tradition in the same way. As a metaphor for the Alexandrian literary scene, Jason functions as the young and therefore tentative new direction in poetry which must contend with the moral authority imposed by the centuries of superlative creativity in the past. The inescapable fact was the Library, the stone Heracles of Greece's literary past, the repository of a literature which was powerful, authoritative, and heroic. Just as Jason escapes from Heracles into love and the perversion of heroic values which love demands, so the poetry of Alexandria found its own voice in eroticism and narcissism.

Having briefly shown us what the rest of the crew really think of Jason, Apollonius again paints the conventional scene. "Then warlike Jason sprang up rejoicing and spoke to them in their eagerness" (349–50). Since the poet uses few epithets, particularly traditional Homeric ones, "warlike" assaults our ears as almost too insistently ironic. Jason's speech resumes as though the interruption had meant nothing. "Since you bestow upon me this honor to cherish, let nothing delay our going, as I was saying to you earlier (*hōs kai prin*)." He proceeds to call, as a good leader should, for sacrifice, for prayer to Apollo. He has ordered his servants to bring sacrificial animals. As Fränkel notes in discussing this passage, this is the one instance in the *Argonautica* where we find the epic habit of narrating the command for action and following it with a description of the action. Together with the Apollo simile earlier, this very traditional speech reinforces the conception of Jason as a leader altogether in the convention of epic poetry. With a call to the crew to launch the *Argo*, Jason "was the first to turn to the work, and they stood up obedient to his command" (363). Yet again Apollonius undercuts Jason by having him conclude his speech in a manner that can only recall Heracles: "by sacrifice [to Apollo] I shall begin my labors for the king."

This remarkable assemblage of scenes and descriptions establishes Jason as the single most important figure of the narrative, the traditional leader of the crew of the *Argo*, but—and it is this that is unusual in ancient literature—the poet has shown Jason's role and personality to be not all they might be. Jason is a captive to his mother's emotions; melancholia and a hint of things failed attend him; he has not the *auctoritas* to command center stage; the group, which is the narcissistic Homeric hero's mirror, clearly does not prefer him; and they are themselves highly individualistic and powerful figures.

While the story of the *Argonautica* can be called an allegory of the obsolescence of the hero in the Alexandrian age as well as a symbolic statement about the end of conventional epic poetry, it is also the personal story of a very young man caught up in an undertaking in which he is supremely insecure. The voyage out and Jason's performance in it has been likened[10] to the Telemachia; in his voyage and discovery, according to this view, Jason learns about love and war, the failure of heroic action and the power of intellect. This is an attractive idea, though it may perhaps underemphasize the poem's irony. It is true that Jason, at this point, is very like the ineffectual, irresolute Telemachus who loses his composure before the suitors (*Odyssey* 2.81). One remembers, in fact, the old nurse Eurycleia's lamentation at Telemachus' departure (2.361–70). The simile of Jason as the old nurse recalls, if in a perverse way, that moment; one thinks particularly of the freedom of Odysseus' son, who can say to Eurycleia (3.372), "Say nothing to mother about this," and hence get away without the emotional encumbrance which threatens to smother Jason.

The *Argonautica* is not simply about the decline of the Homeric ideal; this seems evident from the fact that the poet fashions for Jason enough personality to make him an individual, an accident of creation rather than the characteristic type. The key to Jason's personality is there in his first appearance as he tries to soften the grief, calm the prevailing mood, and speak soothing words. His tact and diplomacy are the characteristic manner of an accommodating person: he achieves his goals through the kind of manipulation we associate with the courtier. Throughout the work, the emphasis is upon his seductive verbal skill ("win her over with clever words" [3.946]) as well as his seductive physical charms. The poet even uses the word "fawning"[11] to describe Jason's immediate response to Aeetes' hysterical and barbaric tirade (3.396) and, later, his first words to Medea as they stand alone together (3.974). No wonder he had no reaction to Pelias' initial request. His instinct was to obey and to keep still.

In the same way, Jason is defenseless and silent before Idas' outburst the last night before sailing. The scene is, in fact, a dramatic expression of the conflicting values which maintain the poem's tension. Idas' challenge to Jason's authority reminds the reader of Achilles' rebuke to Agamemnon in the opening scenes of the *Iliad*; though his crudity makes him more like a second Thersites.[12] But the scene is fundamentally different from anything in Homer. Instead of an assemblage called to discuss strategy and politics, this is a drinking party, the kind young men are wont to have, says Apollonius (458), when *hubris* is far away (459). Genteel camaraderie is one of the typical social values of this poem. Even when the crew has just finished battling with the Bebrycians, they turn the evening, after tending to the wounded, into a pleasant get-together of song and good cheer (2.155–63).

Jason, as he so often is, is sunk in melancholy, lost in his own thoughts, going over every detail, as the poet says (460–61), obsessed with and borne down by the problems of leadership. Idas is besotted with drink. Neither belongs at this drinking party. Idas speaks competitively and aggressively (*neikēse* 462): "Son of Aeson, what plan are you turning over in your mind? Tell us all your thoughts. Or has fear got you . . . ? Let my impetuous spear witness . . . that no test fails when I am there." "Impetuous" is *thouros* from *thrōskō* "to leap," "spring," or "rush." It is the direct, unanalytical response of a simplistic person for whom physical strength has always battered down all the barriers. Heracles is a similar sort, called *thrasys* at 341.[13] When one of the men regrets Heracles' absence from the boxing match with King Amycus, it is in these terms. If Heracles were present, he declares, there would have been no contest after the king's announcement of his mad regulations; one swing of Heracles' club would have made Amycus forget the whole business (2.145–53).

Although he is sarcastic and cruel, Idas means well. That is why Idmon can say, "There are other words at hand with which a man might encourage his comrade" (1.479–80). And surely Idas does mean to encourage when he speaks of his prowess and his spear. It is only that he is tactless, crude, and self-aggrandizing after the manner of traditional heroes. There is nothing *meilikhios* ("gentle, cozening") about Idas' manner. It so offends the courtly Jason that he cannot find a response.

The Homeric Thersites is physically deformed; in a society of perfect bodies, we know what that means. The warmest sympathy he can command when Odysseus strikes him is embarrassed snickers. Apollonius is describing a world where—instead of physical perfection—politesse, verbal communication, manners are all-important. At this pleasant drinking party Idas is drunk, and we know what that means. After his challenge to Jason, he tosses down a full goblet of unmixed wine, splashing it over his face. After Idmon's polite if haughty response, Idas menances the seer, but first the poet says, "He laughed long and hard and, winking at him, he started in with words that cut to the heart." It sounds like old Karamazov. Idas' strength and power, which allow him to challenge the gods (467–68) and thus earn Idmon's rebuke, give him the freedom to be idiosyncratic. He is a boor and a buffoon, but like all authentic persons, completely at ease with himself.

Jason, who depends upon seduction, cannot answer a word. It is Idmon who handles the man, or tries to, by invoking the traditional means for controlling impetuous upstarts. He rehearses the conventional pieties about the dangers of provoking divine jealousy (Idmon does not seem to know that in this poem the gods will not matter); but Idas couldn't care less about divine jealousy.[14] Idmon's words only provoke him to murderous wrath. Elsewhere, pious Idmon is equally ineffectual, and when he dies, gored by a boar, Apollonius reminds us of this by noting that it is Idas, still flourishing, who kills the boar with his trusty spear (2.830–31). The reader will not be surprised to learn that when it comes time for the crew to put their trust in a woman and magic, Idas will indignantly grumble and complain (3.558–63). He is finally shown to be ineffectual in his attempts to damage Jason's magical shield (3.1252–53), and thereafter never reappears in the story.

In the present scene, as Idas and Idmon come to quarrel, only Orpheus can calm them through the magic, literal and figurative, of his singing. The expression *thelktron aoidēs* ("the narcotic charm of his song") is indicative of what has power in Apollonius' world. It is that which mesmerizes, hypnotizes, enchants, and seduces. Therein lies the greater *aretē*. Apollonius begins his catalogue with a reference to Orpheus, so as to assign first place to music, magic, and supernaturalism. As Rose has remarked: "it is noteworthy that there is rather an overplus of prophets in this story, Phineus, Mopsus, Idmon, and Orpheus all taking part in one way or another."[15] Orpheus is the most important, being central to eight incidents in the poem: here, three times in the second book, and four times in the fourth.

The quarrel at the beach party is a curious scene, then. Idas is the most interesting figure, because he is so much better described than are the others. But the description renders him, if not repulsive, then outrageous, set in the polite atmosphere of the party. Idas' strength seems Jason's weakness; yet Jason's silence is provoked by the very quality of personality which will render

him effective later when Idas is useless. In turn, Idmon's conventional pieties
are offered in a poem where challenges to deity and later murder itself go all
but unnoticed.

Once more in the first book, Jason is publicly attacked to his face. This
time is is Telamon, another of the old-time heroic figures, who rebukes Jason
for setting sail without Heracles when the latter has disappeared in his fren-
zied search for Hylas. Initially the quarrel and anger are generalized (1.1284–
85) between, one may presume, those who feel that group enterprise cannot
wait on a prima donna and those of a more conventional mind who still
support the star system. In any case, Telamon turns it all on Jason and pro-
jects upon him a motive so utterly unlikely for this unadventurous mild
young man that we recognize it as surely deriving from Telamon's own anach-
ronistic sensibilities. To Jason, whom Apollonius describes as completely at
a loss in his sense of failure and inadequacy (*amēkhaniēsin atukhtheis* [1286])
and who has stayed out of the crew's argument, Telamon says: "you sit here
so smug (*eukēlos*). It was your idea to leave him behind so that his *kudos* will
not eclipse your own throughout Hellas . . . But what is the point of talking?
I'll go [to find him] alone, with none of these who have helped you plan this
deceit (*dolon*)" (1290–95).

In the *dolon*, in the *eukēlos*, in the thought of fame, Telamon completely
misunderstands Jason. Later he apologizes with the same energies with which
he attacked, hugging Jason, and lamenting his "haughty and unendurable
language" (1334). Jason's highly ironical reply speaks to the same cast of
mind which initially sparked Telamon's anger. "I shall give up my wrath
(*mēnis*)," he says, reminding us of the obdurate and petulant Achilles, and
then he paraphrases Homer: "It was not for flocks of sheep, nor possessions
that you raged with anger, but because of a companion," reminding us of
Achilles' last fatal pursuit of Hector around the walls of Troy (*Iliad* 22.159):
"No holy victim . . . were they contending for, . . . but the life of horse-
taming Hector." In this speech, Jason disavows the kind of egomaniacal com-
petitiveness and self-aggrandizement which marks Achilles and, in this
poem, Telamon, Idas, and of course—first of all—Heracles. We may notice
that Idas and Telamon attack Jason on occasions when, as Apollonius remarks,
he is particularly weak and vulnerable. Like all competitive heroic males,
their instinct is to go for the kill in human relationships.

Apollonius has truly dramatized a group. Idmon's prim little speech, Tel-
amon's bear hug, Idas' slurping the wine, Heracles' sitting while command-
ing are master strokes of portraiture. Apollonius keeps these figures in char-
acter. Telamon, for instance, after Aeetes' outrageous demands, is about to
open up in rage when Jason, ever the courtier, stops him (3.385–86).

Elsewhere Apollonius uses domestic detail to give insight into an estab-
lished character. In the narrative Peleus has the cooperative group-oriented

spirit Jason needs, rallying the men when they are desperate (2.1217–25), offering himself as a substitute for Jason (3.504–14), good at strategy (4.494–502), and at interpretations (4.1368–79), willing to enter the thick of the fight (2.828–30), in at the vote (2.878–84)—all of which contrasts him with his petulant, self-centered son, Achilles. The poet also introduces his quondam wife Thetis. "Go help him," Hera says to Thetis, "Why does your anger remain so firm?" (4.816). Thetis agrees, flies to her husband's side as he is playing ball with the rest of the crew, only touches the tips of his fingers, delivers her message, and flies away. Sharp pain hits Peleus (4.866) for, as the poet explains, it was the first time he had seen her since she had left when he bungled Achilles' immortality (*mega nēpios* [4.875]). Like so many commonplace men of good cheer, Peleus carries a private domestic tragedy in his bosom. The glimpse we are given of this breaks the surface in a way entirely foreign to the traditional epic poet.

The poet concludes the overture to his poem in the description of the departure, one of the happiest, most triumphant scenes of the poem. The poet assembles all the gods so that they may witness the sailing out (547–52), and he concludes the account with a joyful simile: Orpheus, playing as fish gambol alongside the *Argo*, is like a shepherd piping to his flocks. But even here, Jason's presence sounds a discordant note. Early in the description of the embarkation, a simile compares the crew's activities to those on a festival day for the god Apollo (1.536–39)—a jubilant, seemingly ingenuous and old-style heroic simile. Because the immediately previous simile (1.307–9) compared *Jason* to Apollo, Apollonius makes the irony hard to miss. Just before this, the poet has described the far more godlike Heracles stepping into the boat, his great body so heavy that the boat sinks deeper into the water (1.533); and directly thereafter, the poet tells us that "Jason, crying, turned his eyes away from his fatherland." Scarcely ten meters off shore and Jason is homesick! The poet will never let us forget that Jason does not want to be on this voyage. Jason calls the voyage "a painful labor" (1.841) and wishes the gods would free him from it (1.903); he tells Phineus that he would only be happy if he were on the way home (2.442); and when he has the chance to ask the prophet about the fleece, he only inquires about getting home again (2.414–15).

At the close of the fifth day and 600 lines into the poem, the *Argo* harbors at the island of Lemnos and here, finally, Jason acts importantly in the narrative, meeting and acquiring carnal knowledge of the princess Hypsipyle. The old phrase perfectly suits the event; one has the sense that this is Jason's loss of innocence, whether literally so or not. Realistically, one cannot imagine a Greek male of that age still a virgin, but the poet chooses to establish this act of love as momentous for our hero, so that it acquires the symbolic value of that rite of passage in a boy's life. There are innumerable narrative parallels before and since Apollonius. The Lemnian episode is an analogue to the loss of innocence which Enkidu experiences after intercourse with the harlot, or the fall from Paradise which comes to Adam and Eve after eating the apple. Elsewhere in extant Greek epic, the motif of the loss of innocence is to be found in Athena's visit to Telemachus and in Agamemnon's depriving Achilles of his concubine.

One of the major flaws imputed to this poem is that Apollonius has been unable (more likely unwilling) to explore and exhibit Jason's feelings in his dealings with Hypsipyle and later with Medea. The effect is to show him as more passive than, judging by the symbols Apollonius employs, he ought to be. The problem is very likely cultural. In Western letters and Western culture a male's erotic passion, when it involves anything more than lust, has been difficult to express. Notice that two important exceptions are ancient Greek homoerotic emotion and medieval courtly love, both of which are perverse; the former has an unusual object, the latter celebrates adultery, although it usually suppresses the physical.

A male's commonplace feelings of love mingled with physical attraction for a woman are not often celebrated until nineteenth-century Romanticism helped to free males from their habitual repression. The misogynist streak in ancient Greek culture made love of a woman undignified because (presumably) it meant getting serious about something dangerous. Even in the Hellenistic age, when women appear far more valuable and less threatening, heterosexual love is best celebrated in comedies depicting silly young men impotent everywhere but in bed, and in pastoral poems—the Hellenistic invention—where thoroughly unlifelike rustics ineffectually moon over young women.

Epic poetry is male poetry. The *Iliad*, like *Gilgamesh*, focuses on the problem of death as it is experienced by males who have no obvious link with the biological means of achieving a kind of genetic immortality. The *Odyssey*, for all its implied celebration of Penelope, focuses on a man who enjoys the company of women and knows how to deal with them sexually or otherwise. There is never the slightest suggestion that he is anything other than master of every situation involving these women—except for that brilliant moment when Penelope tricks him with her lie about the bed. Love means having to submit, and the heroic ideology did not allow for that, except in the thoroughly narcissistic submission to one's own sex. Whether Achilles and Patroclus sleep together[16] is immaterial; they are completely committed to each other psychically. Apollonius, it may be assumed, is trying something radical in this poem when he tries to show a man in a heterosexual love relationship. His reticence in describing Jason's feelings make the hero seem unnecessarily wishy-washy, but the expression of love is almost a violation of genre.[17] Perhaps the poet's contemporaries would have read the minimal expressions of the male emotion as far more significant than we can understand them to be.

Following the sailing out, the poet contrives three major episodes, the one on Lemnos (609–908), another among the Doliones (936–1077), and finally the story of the rape of Hylas (1172–1357). Critics object to the episodic nature of Apollonius' narrative, arguing that in the first book particularly none of the incidents advance the plot. This is true, but Aristotelian profluence is not what the poet cares about, though he can manage that handsomely when he likes. Rather, we are given a series of disjunctive but internally profluent scenes which deepen our understanding of the character of Jason and the psychological values our poet endorses. Virgil's mastery of the symbolic episode derives from his having observed this technique in Apollonius' poem. One thinks of many episodes in the *Aeneid*—the funeral games, for instance, or the underworld scene, or the fatal expedition of Nisus and Euryalus—which do not advance the plot (whatever in fact that means) but which enlarge our understanding of the meaning of the events. Aristotle's standard of strict, scene-by-scene cause and effect is one good means of driving a narrative onward. Apollonius and after him Virgil are among those who prove that other effective means are available.

The Lemnos episode is erotic, humorous, ironic. The women of Lemnos are hungry. They pour out to the beach like raw-meat-eating Bacchants (*prokheonto . . . ōmoborois* [635–36]). Again, when the men leave for good, the women pour forth (*prokheonto* again [883]) like bees gathering the sweet fruit (*glykun . . . karpon* [881–82]) from the flowers. When Hypsipyle suggests that they provision the men on their ship but keep them away, her remarks are heard in silence. Her old nurse, Polyxo, a female Nestor figure, gets a different reception. She points out that the women of Lemnos need a younger generation and male warrior protectors. This she does by asking one rhetorical question after another, to which there is but one answer: men in bed. "So she spoke," the poet says, "and the meeting place was filled with the murmuring of the crowd. For they liked what she said" (697–98). Their urgency is underscored by Apollonius' startling description of Polyxo's companions: "Near her sat four virgins, unwed, with their white hair flowing" (671–72).[18]

No wonder Jason keeps his eyes fixed on the ground (784) as he makes his way to Hypsipyle's palace. We must remember his extreme youth, that he has got himself up officially with a spear which now, with no man in sight, must make him seem both pompous and ineffectual. Jason, the pretender to epic heroism, has wandered into the wrong poem. The women crowded in behind him "taking delight in the stranger"—no doubt audibly so—must make the lad still more vulnerable. His backside is no doubt as handsome as the rest of him; he becomes, in short, a cynosure, a sex object.[19] Again Apollonius has arranged a role reversal, forcing a man to walk a gauntlet which, in ancient Greek as in many other cultures, is usually set up for women. Lemnos becomes for Jason the site of a mock *athlos*.

The poet contrives an ironic heroic coloration to this *athlos*. There is the hint of a conventional arming ("now he fastened around his shoulders . . . a cloak" [721–22]; "in his right hand he held a spear" [769]). There is an *ekphrasis* highly reminiscent of the description of Hephaestus' creation of Achilles' shield in the eighteenth book of the *Iliad*. The poet describes Jason's progress in terms of a star (*bē d'imenai proti astu, phaeino asteri isos* [774]), an Homeric-like line which recalls us to Achilles charging across the plain toward the city walls of Troy (*pamphainonth hos t'aster epessumenon* [22.26]). The star, so baleful in the *Iliad*, gives a sinister cast to this moment, although it is at least superficially benign; as it goes through the dark sky, the sight of it charms the watching girl (*thelgei* [777]). The star's mesmerizing power is indicated, a power both pleasing and dangerous.

Erotic dialogue is complex, good and bad. The poet emphasizes this in the lengthy lie which Hypsipyle tells Jason when first they meet (796–826), a lie launched on the crescent wave of Hypsipyle's seductive charm: "Casting her eyes down, she blushed across her virgin's cheeks, and yet with all her shyness she spoke to him in flattering and seductive (*haimulos* [792], used later of Aphrodite [3.51]) words." She never does tell Jason the truth. However much Jason is faulted for loving and leaving, for coldness and indifference in his farewell to Hypsipyle, we must remind ourselves that she has founded their relationship on dishonesty. If it is not dishonesty, then it is at best indifference, like that of the woman in Theocritus' first Idyll, which describes two men, hollow-eyed with love, entreating their mistress, who looks at one and then the other, laughing (33–35).

That love is more than an amusing or pathetic human condition is signaled in the elaborate devices of Jason's cloak. The description, as we have said, recalls that of Achilles' shield. The shield which Hephaestus makes for Achilles shows scenes of peoples and societies in wartime and at peace, and scholars often suggest that the poet contrived his symbols very consciously— the city at war, the city at peace. Apollonius follows in this tradition, making scenes with a fairly clear allegorical ring.[20] In the section of the cloak on which is embroidered an image of Aphrodite examining her reflection in Ares' shield (742–46), there are several ideas combined: love and war, love *in* war, war in love, the narcissism which is love engendered by war. When Orpheus earlier sang a cosmology to tranquilize Idmon and Idas his theme was Empedocles' doctrine of creation by love and hate (*neikos*, "quarrel," compare 1.498, and *philia*, "friendship"). The cloak scene reiterates that idea. Just after the description of the cloak, Apollonius mentions Atalanta who wanted to come along but was prevented from doing so because Jason "feared harsh quarreling on account of [her? the crew's? his?] love" (773). The emotional career of Jason and Medea is in many ways a dramatization of the Aphrodite allegory on the cloak.

Just before the Aphrodite scene the cloak shows a scene of Amphion and Zethus building Thebes, the former with the magic of his lyre, the latter with the sweat of his brow. We recall the contrast between Idas and Idmon, and between the efficacy of brawn and the hypnotic magic of personal charisma which distinguishes Heracles and Jason. Amphion and Zethus also mark a distinction between the ways of Aphrodite and those of Ares. The subsequent scene of the bloody carnage of a war party's cattle raid reflects Ares; the scene which follows it, Pelops' deceit of Oenomaus because of his love for Hippodamia, describes the ever more subtle destruction inspired by love.

At the same time the poet uses this image to establish an interpretation for the future contest in which Jason triumphs before the astonished and baleful glare of Aeetes. When Apollonius describes the contest of Pelops and Oenomaus for the hand of Hippodamia, he makes Jason's forthcoming battle with the bulls on the Field of Ares what at heart it really is: more than a mere contest of strength, it is the triumphant suitor winning the daughter from her unwilling father. The cloak scene thus forecasts the interpretation which the reader must eventually place upon Aeetes' extreme anger and Apsyrtus' pursuit. Directly after the Hippodamia scene, Apollo is shown battling with the giant Tityos, and the reader is directed once again to make the equation between Apollo and Jason whose *aristeia* will be in battle with the earthborn men. In short, the cloak is freighted with scenes symbolic of events which are yet to transpire in Apollonius' narrative. Virgil may well have taken the notion of portraying Rome's future on Aeneas' shield from Apollonius' use of the cloak in this scene. Unlike the shield of Achilles, the description of which is a summation and therefore static, Jason's cloak and Aeneas' shield enter the action to become the future.

Dressed in his cloak, the proper amatory warrior, Jason advances in all his beauty upon the city, the palace, and finally Hypsipyle. It is a thoroughly erotic progression in which enclosures and their penetration are the dominant motif. He goes as the star, which causes the maidens to rejoice, shut up in their newly made chambers (*kalybē* from *kalypto*, "to conceal," hence a place or device of concealment, if only a veil), and the virgin seeing this star is in love with her man, who is far away. When they pass within the city gates, the women's enthusiasm mounts. When he reaches the palace of Hypsipyle, the maids open the doors, until finally he is in the presence of Hypsipyle, whose name means "tall gate." And why, she asks him immediately, have you waited so long outside our gates? Having urged in the very same words (659) that they be kept at bay, Hypsipyle has coyly performed a *volte face* true to her strategical rather than emotional hold on the situation. Notice that, like

Nausicaa and unlike Medea, she knows how to let go.[21] But then, she is not passionately in love or, for that matter, in love with a passion. She only wants a baby.

Clearly, Jason will not be an *exclusus amator*. For the first time in the narrative, Jason is completely successful, resolute, described in terms common to heroic endeavor. Ironic as these may be, they nonetheless confirm his achievement. Jason now has a glimmering of his true *aretē*. He is a love hero.

The rest of the poem's first book is designed to explore and define this notion. Heracles is the foil which illuminates Jason's special nature. From the first, when Apollonius positioned Heracles dead center in the catalogue, seventeen items before him, seventeen after, that hero has been the important alternative to Jason. Now at Lemnos he appears in opposition. He will not pay court to the women of Lemnos. While the city takes pleasure in parties and love-making, Heracles of his own will[22] stays behind at the ship. The poet says "with some companions who had been chosen out"; Heracles prefers male society. In disgust, days later, Heracles gathers the *Argo*'s crew together and lectures them on their duty and their frivolity (865–74). Properly chastened ("no one dared to look at him or say a word") they immediately make plans for departure.

Heracles, though less gauche than Idas, is just as impossible, just as anachronistic. Apollonius makes him depart from the narrative in an episode that marks his deficiency in exactly those character traits which this voyage demands, patience and politesse, both of which spring from humility. In a brief prologue (1153–71) to the Hylas episode, Heracles is portrayed as so surpassing his colleagues in a competitive burst of rowing that he snaps the oar. "He sat up in silence, glancing around, for his hands were not used to being at rest." With "glancing around," Apollonius betrays Heracles into the extreme of heroic vulnerability: he is made to appear as a fool in the eyes of the group (*paptainōn* here recalls *paptēnan* at 341 when the crew looked to Heracles as their leader). Clearly enough, in a story where magic and seduction are so powerful, violent physical exertion gets one nowhere.

The Hylas episode describes how a beautiful young boy—too young to row, hence no more than midteens—is snatched away, caught up literally in the clutches of a water nymph whose wits have been addled (1232–33) by her ardent desire for him. Like so many others, the nymph has been seduced by male erotic charms. The event presages Jason's capture by Medea, that is, the way in which he becomes submerged by her as she clings to him; initially seduced by his erotic charm, she becomes thereafter psychically dependent upon him.

Hylas' encounter with the nymph marks his entry into the adult world of heterosexual love relationships. While Apollonius does not say so outright—as Theocritus does in Idyll Thirteen—Hylas is Heracles' catamite, the *eromenos* every military gentleman from an earlier, more aristocratic and man-exalting era, acquired as a sop to his vanity and solace to his desires. Hylas' disappearance marks the end of that sort of relationship, the end of that sort of erotic performance in the face of the triumph of Jason, the new-found heterosexual love hero.

Apollonius emphasizes this idea. Hylas is *prōthēbēs* (132) in early youth, perhaps fourteen or fifteen, a boy whom Heracles carried off as plunder when he killed Hylas' father (1212). It is a commonplace rape, nothing more; Hylas is acquired as Iole was acquired. After the nymph has snatched the boy away, Heracles learns that Hylas is gone. His reaction is the extreme of lust and possessiveness, in fact bestiality—"quantities of sweat poured down from his temples; the blood boiled black under his viscera. Raging, he threw the pine to the ground, raced down the path on which his feet carried him in his rush. Just as when a bull, stung by a gadfly, races along . . . racing, now standing stock still, raising his broad neck, he bellows loudly, stung by the evil goad, so Heracles panting with eagerness, ceaselessly moved" (1261–71).

To reinforce the notion of bestiality, Apollonius has already described Polyphemus, Heracles' companion—also old and hence of an earlier style, and perhaps also Hylas' lover[23]—as wolflike. Polyphemus is burning with hunger (*limō d'aithomenos* [1244–45) and races about, beastlike, at the bleating of a "sheep"—that is, Hylas, as the earlier verb describing Heracles' tutelage of the lad implies (that is, *epherbe* [1211] meaning "to pasture," "to make to feed"). Polyphemus, like Heracles, roars incessantly when he hears Hylas' cry.

The similes are conventional expressions of highly distraught lovers.[24] Thus the poet has made the heroes' reactions humorous, or at the very least ironic, having set the tone with the scene of the broken oar, then describing Heracles' monstrous strength as he pulls a replacement tree from the earth, roots and all (1187–1206). Apollonius introduces the bestial eroticism principally through the notion of hunger, first in the picture of the toiler "who curses his belly" (1176), a reminder that we are slaves to our body's needs; hence Hylas goes for water, the nymph snatches him away, Polyphemus is like an animal burning with hunger—all of which leads to Heracles' mad raging, shouting dash out of this narrative.

Homosexuality was a socially acceptable, socially encouraged emotional form of male bonding found commonly in a number of ancient Greek city-states, principally at Sparta and among the upper classes at Athens. Greek male society was essentially so competitive that this physical, emotional relationship gave the males some way out of the generally pervasive tension between them. Likewise, it performed a valuable educative service. And, if the myths are any indication, where father-son relationships were freighted with so much ugly competition, the commonplace pederasty offered youths much needed caring and tender surrogate fathers. It differed very much from modern-day homosexuality. Since there was no stigma attached to but in fact approbation bestowed upon the man who took a male lover, he did not become categorized or ghettoized, that is, an exclusive homosexual, nor did he develop some of the neurotic patterns of behavior found among moderns who suffer from being despised and rejected by the culture at large.

The ancient Athenian upper class youth would normally form an attachment to an older male which would be one of the most important emotional relationships of his life. Adult males would have a teenage beloved and presumably expend far more emotional energy in that relationship than in the conjugal heterosexual one. Growing up for a male in Athens would mean, among other things, transferring one's sexual focus from the anus to the penis. Ancient statuary and the example of modern Mediterranean teenaged males suggest their remarkable androgyny. So this transference is a moving away from the feminine, the vaginal, and the passive to the masculine, the phallic, and the active. Hylas' entrance into the spring, a symbolical vaginal immersion, a baptism, is an accomplishment of this transference. If we connect it with Jason's immersion prior to his meeting the bulls on the Plain of Ares, we might say that Jason's sexual maturing is a prominent theme of the *Argonautica* as well.

One thing to be noted is that ancient Greek males of like age did not engage sexually, nor was there the promiscuity then which is so characteristic of modern times. Homosexuality was a very strictly defined emotional expression for males and thus must be considered as an institution, like marriage, which confers other benefits than the obvious ones of immediate physical and emotional solace. Viewed as a cultural phenomenon, pederasty could perhaps be called a male's preoccupation with regaining his youth, and in that sense the distancing of dying. But considering the narcissism seemingly inherent in homosexual love, we might remark that pederasty is the perfect expression of classical Greece's anthropocentric, parochial, city-state mentality. A male is nowhere safer, there are nowhere fewer surprises, than with his own kind. But then, too, we must remember that in a society which so highly prized the human male, nothing is more beautiful than the male youth just at the brink of manhood when his physique and his psyche are filled with the promise of strength, grace, and courage of body, soul, and intellect. Pederasty is an expression of what Wallace Stevens means with that memorable "Death is the Mother of Beauty."

If Apollonius emphasizes Heracles' more ridiculous qualities, it is not to ridicule pederasty so much as to mock the old-fashioned heroic, conservative, perhaps even Colonel Blimp-like cast of mind that accompanied it, seen from the vantage point of Alexandria a century and a half later. But, of course, Apollonius makes pederastry comical and therefore rather inconsequential in order to set the stage for the more serious, consequential heterosexual love

affair that lies ahead. Men *do* grow up. Even the Marschallin had to yield
Octavian to Sophie.

Heterosexual love for the ancient Greek demands that the male encounter
"the other," strain to know the unknowable, engage the unpredictable. We
do not understand this idea well anymore. In the late twentieth century the
sexes have merged in many ways, in dress, in occupations, in responsibilities.
Constant companionship and increased sexual promiscuity have made men
and women know each other well as never before. There are fewer and fewer
surprises although it is fair to say that a woman can never understand what it
is to be subject to involuntary tumescence and detumescence any more than
a man can understand what it means to menstruate or to grow a baby in one's
body. In classical antiquity, when the sexes were rather rigorously separated
and gender roles were thoroughly distinct, men and women were strangers to
one another.

Any number of reasons can be adduced for the growing freedom, impor-
tance, and respect in affection which can be called love of women in the
Hellenistic period. The tendency correlates with the ever-widening cultural
horizons which Philip and then Alexander brought about for the Greek world
by their campaigns to the East. Like Alexander's journey to the East, Jason's
voyage is a frightening trip into the unfamiliar land of barbarians and the
oddities of magic; at the same time, it is the encounter of a male in a com-
plicated emotional quasi-peer relationship with that other being, woman.
Nothing could be more Hellenistic.

As soon as Polyphemus hears Hylas' cry, he imagines that wild beasts or
pirates have taken him off, "an easy prey" (1252) as, of course, Hylas was
when Heracles took him as plunder (*apouras* [1212]) from the side of his dead
father. Polyphemus and Heracles are men of violent action; their imaginings
and wild behavior when they notice Hylas gone are in total opposition to the
soft, sensual, graceful, quiet, sinuous happenings which brought Hylas under
the water in the nymph's embrace. Was the cry which Polyphemus heard
(1240) Hylas' call for help or an ecstatic exclamation? We cannot know.

Though he probably knew the more recent fourth-century reinterpretation
of the mythological Heracles figure into a Stoic ascetic or a man of moral
strength who makes the choice between virtue and vice, Apollonius returns
to the classical conception of Heracles, the man of physical strength and im-
pulsive if not wanton action; in short, a brute. In the catalogue he introduces
him with the old-fashioned phrase "strength of Heracles" (122). The incident
of the broken oar and the subsequent reference to the pitiless (*nēleiōs* [1214])
killing of Hylas' father and the boy's rape enclose a detailed account of the
mighty man's huge feat of pulling a tree from the ground (1187–1206). Her-
acles goes for the tree as the androgynous adolescent Hylas, pitcher in hand,
goes for water.

No nymph, one suspects, would try to snatch Heracles; apart from the fact of his irresistible strength, he is not sexy. Shortly after his mad dash to find Hylas, the poet describes how he later killed Zetes and Calais in a fit of anger (1300–1308); at the poem's end there is a reference to his murder of his children (4.541); and when the heroes reach them, the Hesperides cry out to describe the monstrous behavior of Heracles when he robbed them of the apples (1436–48). Heracles, the brute, is an older fellow, an experienced hero before Jason's moping and indecision. But he is yesterday's man, the heroic has-been, meant to stay on the shore sulking as the younger fellows party with the ladies of Lemnos, content with a teenaged boy for his companion, still captive of his sudden strength and unbridled urges when the world calls for dialogue.

Not that all this makes Heracles a figure of absolute evil and Jason, by contrast, emblematic of good. There is something direct and honest about rape and murder, something missing in the more tortuous, often devious paths of courtship and seduction. Apollonius makes love as complicated and ambiguous as are those who practice it in his poem. Jason is often characterized by the adjective *amēkhanos*, "unsure." Heracles' typically Homeric self-assurance is in a way enviable, as the poet suggests at the close of the poem (4.1477–82).

> That day Lynceus thought he saw Heracles
> all by himself [so typical!] far off at the edge
> of the land as a man sees the moon or thinks
> he does through the clouds. . . . And he went back
> to tell his companions that no one would find Heracles.

The Heracles Apollonius has offered us until now has been as problematical as his Jason. It is significant that the poet has eschewed the more palatable conceptions of Heracles devised in the century or so previous to his writing, and instead returns to the traditional strong man who appears all the more to be a brute and bully when set beside so gentle and accommodating a person as Jason. Heracles has not thus far been condemned, but neither has he been approved. Like an older brother about whom one is not sure, he has been tolerated. Until this remarkable last notice of him. Here the tone is nostalgic and regretful. Heracles seems a force to be envied and admired but never retrieved, gone from Jason's world, not unlike the bargirl, a kind of madonna figure, who waves distantly and unobtainably as Fellini's *La Dolce Vita* comes to its close.

The physical strength and impetuousness of the traditional hero are not for Jason, nor can he aspire to their martial prowess. His *aretē* resides in other capacities—which is just as well, Apollonius suggests. The poet demonstrates the futility of war in the one traditional battle narrative in the poem. Jason and crew arrive among the Doliones, where two battles ensue. The one arises when monstrous giants of the region attack. Heracles brings them down one after another, fighting them alone until the other heroes arrive to help. "I think," the poet says, "Hera may have set them up to this as another trial (*athlion*) for Heracles" (997), reminding us of Heracles' worth in his natural milieu.

Again, as the poet notices (992–93), Heracles had been left behind, this time with some of the younger men, while Jason and the others pay a courtesy call, one might say, upon the local king, Cyzicus. Heracles, we may imagine, would be *de trop* in the setting of obligatory diplomatic politeness. Cyzicus, although only a recent groom, very young and yet without an heir, casts fear aside and leaves the bridal bed (972–79). All the more reason to keep Heracles to one side, being the overbearing sort he is, and not given to the sentimentalities of domestic life. Lucky, too, since Heracles is therefore at hand to resist the giants' sudden incursion.

But Apollonius has ironies in store. Jason's first triumph in battle, just immediately following his triumph in love (sealed by Hypsipyle's parting reference to a hoped-for child [898]) is about to come. The crew sails away, then is blown back to a shore they fail to recognize as that of their new friends the Doliones, who in the obscurity of night imagine hostile invasion. The two sides fall to. In the thoroughly traditional language of the Homeric battle (*androktasia*), Apollonius describes a general melee in which Cyzicus is the first to die at the hands of Jason. The Homeric phraseology "him the son of Aeson rising up struck as he turned toward him right in the middle of the chest, and the bone was shattered all about by the spear" (1032–34) and the syncopated victim-victor list which follows raise up strong images and impressions of the high-hearted, ambitious, and professional attitude toward fighting and killing which marks the *Iliad*. And it is only natural that this afraid, unsure young man would triumph ironically by killing—by mistake—his exact counterpart, equally young, equally vulnerable, as Apollonius describes him. It is absurd enough to be grimly humorous; the poet clearly maintains with respect to his narrative a distance which the older epic poets do not know. For it is a kind of mockery of Jason to expose him so, flailing away in that special language at a victim as innocent as himself.

By mentioning twice over that Cyzicus is a new groom, passing time in the bridal bed, Apollonius makes Jason's killing especially horrible, given the values of this poem, which we have begun to recognize in Jason's triumphant progress to Hypsipyle's couch. It is in fact ironic that, fresh from that couch, Jason kills a young man whose preoccupation, as Apollonius suggests, is in making babies. And the horror is compounded when Cyzicus' wife Cleite hangs herself in grief. Apollonius manages to make an *aition* of this event (1075–77). Some modern critics tell us[25] that the premature deaths of the newly wed royal pair signify the annual pause in the vegetation, and Apollonius follows the event with a supplication of the great Mother Goddess whose beneficence is duly recorded. "Trees poured forth fruit without end; at their feet the earth spontaneously bore flowers in the tender grass; beasts of the mountains leaving their lairs came fawning upon them" (1142–45). This passage is so brief as to be ambiguous; conceivably it is no more than description for description's sake, like the account of the Etesian winds (2.500–527). Set against the description of Hecate's coming in the third book, it illuminates another facet of womanhood. Yet at this point in the narrative, it seems a strong affirmation of life and fecundity, forces rising in triumph over the death principle evident in the desolation of a wasteful, senseless killing. Immediately preceding the supplication of the goddess, the winds blew for twelve days, halting the crew's sailing and casting the chieftains into the sleep of exhaustion (1078–82). Like the sirocco, these winds bring depression. The *primavera* scene signals the return of optimism and vital force; it also focuses the themes of love and war explored in one way after another throughout the poem.

The act of killing on the field of battle is narrowly defined in terms of the special victims, the bride and groom, Cyzicus and Cleite, and their hopes for progeny. In Homer killing on the battlefield is shown to be self-affirmation, power, and triumph; but here the importance of the victims makes it very simply a brutal nullification of life. The Doliones flee the Argonauts like doves (Aphrodite's bird) before hawks, says Apollonius (1049–50), a theme which returns in the omen at 3.540–43. The hostile winds which hold the crew in part force a cessation to activity, as if the life principle has staggered and cannot yet go on—as if, in Cyzicus' and Cleite's death, life and love have given way to death and war. Life is restored through the supplication of the Mother Goddess, the female principle. Aphrodite is an expression of this, as Jason's battlefield career is an expression of Ares.

4

The Voyage

The second book of the *Argonautica* is the one least accessible to the casual modern reader. There is little action, the hero seems at first glance inconsequential to what action there is. Episode succeeds episode, ("pearls set on a thread"),[1] but apart from the dubious passage of time and the discernible movement past one geographical point after another, there seems to be no real development of the plot.

The more notable features of the book are its catalogue construction and the several *aitia* and other informational bits and pieces which the poet takes great care to present. At first glance, it seems that the poet is demonstrating stylistic virtuosity more than anything else, engaging in the commonplace Alexandrian literary critical dialogue through the medium of his verse. If the first book is a kind of revision of the Homeric epic wherein a new sort of hero is discovered, then perhaps one may say that the second book is an Alexandrian adaptation of the catalogue poetry of Hesiod. Catalogues, after all, were an important feature of the Alexandrian aesthetic. Callimachus' major piece, the *Aitia*, which is a comparatively long poem by the critic who eschewed continuous narrative, owes its unity to the structural principle of the lists, or as the Alexandrian critics called it, the *katalogos*. And, we may remember, the poet whom Callimachus praises the most is Aratus, whose *Phainomena* is relentlessly informational and deliberately Hesiodic in style.

The problem with the list, at least in theory, is that it has little in it which will lead a reader forward, unless he is actively seeking information. This, however, may be a spurious problem, if the modern reader can put himself in the place of an Alexandrian. The Alexandrians may have grown so used to discontinuous narrative—and so sensitive to other aesthetic values—that they would not care. Already in his first book, Apollonius has arranged the self-contained episodes in his narrative so that they succeed one another solely upon the apparently arbitrary grid of chronology and geography. What happens in the first book does not matter at all to the story—except for its symbolic value.

Plot is only one of the two great forces that can keep a reader turning pages—in other words, can give a narrative suspense. Argument, explicit or subtle, is the other. And the Alexandrians were nothing if not subtle. Partly because of his fondness for irony, Apollonius' way of arguing is tricky; but once one catches on to the method, it is brilliantly effective. Let us begin with some general observations.

The departure scene, from the catalogue to the actual sailing out, describes more than anything else the nonheroic quality of Jason. The Lemnos scene establishes him as a hero of love in mock-heroic terms; the Cyzicus episode demonstrates his failure as a traditional fighter, and the Hylas scene validates Jason by mocking and then disposing of the archaic heroic attitudes of Heracles. For the story line, however, these events, other than the actual sailing out, are negligible. In the second book it seems at first more difficult to establish some other meaning for some of the events which Apollonius describes. One is therefore left to confront the list.

Those who castigate Apollonius for his deficiency in constructing a story are working from a too limited aesthetic. Just as they wish a satisfying hero true to the tradition of old epic, they want a story line. Even on their own plot-oriented grounds, their position is weak: they forget that narrative eventually takes many forms. Apollonius' second book has affinities with Menippean satire (one sees this most clearly in the discourse on the Etesian winds [500–527]); it is also like a picaresque novel in the succession of episodes or adventures, except that it lacks a unifying hero figure.

But plot, as we have said, is not everything. Even before one grasps the real principle of profluence in Book Two, one can see virtues. W. H. Auden has remarked on the importance of catalogues to poets; we forget, in our insistence upon plot, that poetry is in some of its manifestations a purely sensual experience, and that perhaps Apollonius here describes principally for the sake of contriving a verbal sensual perception. Consider in our own time the popularity which Huysman's *A Rebours* has enjoyed in its century of existence.

Although one thinks of catalogues as representative of Hesiod's poetry, the Homeric poems, we must remember, also had catalogues, the *Iliad*'s Catalogue of Ships and the *Odyssey*'s briefer Catalogue of Noble Heroines being the famous examples. In the narrative of the *Iliad*, the catalogue or list seems to be the underlying structure of the ubiquitous *androktasiai*, the stereotypic descriptions of men in battle killing and being killed.[2] Miniature as they are, the battle narratives of the *Iliad* are truly discontinuous and episodic.

A passage (930–1089) from the second book of the *Argonautica* is remarkably like one of these Homeric *androktasiai*. It commences with a generalizing statement which introduces the specifics which will follow, in this instance comparing the *Argo* to a speeding hawk (933–35). The passage closes with a relatively lengthy account (1030–89) of a visit to the island of Ares with an anecdote which expands into a small drama complete with similes. This is not unlike many of the *androktasiai* which conclude with a larger item such as the battle list of *Iliad* 6.1–65 which ends in the larger description of Menelaus' killing of Adrestus (37–65) where there is even direct conversation. Between these two points the poet mentions a series of place names to some of which he attaches anecdotal material exactly in the manner of an *adroktasia*. Other places he simply lists (940–942): "During the night they kept on going at great speed past Sesamas and steep Erythini, Crobialus, Cromna and woody Cytorus," which is the equivalent of "Ajax . . . struck down Doryclus, Priam's son . . . thereafter stabbed Pandocus, also Lysandrus, Pyrasus, and Pylartes" (*Iliad* 11.489–91).

The anecdotes attached to the names of victim or victor in the *Iliad* do not relate to the immediate circumstance of the narrative but, being about genealogy, marriage, or wealth, reflect the general concerns of the society which is being destroyed by this war or recall those values for which the individual men who die stand as emblems. Hence they provide a counterpoint of pathos to the exaltation and exhilaration which emanates from the often grisly details of the wounding and killing of human beings. Since Apollonius is so careful to tailor the details of his similes to the narrative line and is elsewhere so pertinent in his allusions, one searches the anecdotes of this passage for precise correspondences with his story. There are indeed anecdotes of love; Sinope's tricking Zeus and Apollo (946–54), both of whom fancied her, is a story of love, seduction, and beguiling which relates to the main themes of the *Argonautica*. There are anecdotes of persons associated in friendship or enmity with

Heracles (957; 967–69) which form part of the ever-present Heraclean leit-motiv which functions as a mirror image of Jason's progress, just as the Cly-temnestra-Agamemnon-Orestes story mirrors the main story in the *Odyssey*.

A larger space is given over to the description of things which have no obvious relation to the story, such as the Thermodon River with its extraor-dinary delta region, the iron-working Chalybes who forsake agriculture, the Tibareni in whose culture the men simulate labor pains at their wives' con-finement, the custom of the Mossynoeci (which Xenophon noted) of doing in public what other peoples customarily do in private. In short, Apollonius offers us strangeness, oddities; and as a consequence, one is tempted to sug-gest that these anecdotes augment the generally morbid and gloomy tone which the poet establishes at the visit to the Mariandyni and afterward. Other than that, they illustrate Apollonius' use of real, contemporary (to him) an-thropology which he plays against the fable of Jason's adventures. The Argo-nauts are acting out myth in the real world, taking on the legend and the voyage, the archetypal and simple action set into the peculiar facets of the historical-anthropological perspective.

And yet, to go further, the facts which the poet has chosen to introduce are, most of them, so extraordinary, so beyond the usual experience as to be fabulous in the less precise sense of the word. Hence, he manages yet another irony, that is, that the fabulous voyage of Jason and his crew is with its essential humanness less a fable than the anthropological facts displayed on the way.

Because the *aitia* describe scientifically determined truths, specimens of the art of geography, ethnography, and the like, the reader gains a special per-spective upon the travel story which accompanies them. The epic travel story set beside these truths becomes all the more a naïve narrative; the reader, as he participates in the story, becomes himself a naïf, in Hurst's terms. The traditional heroic travel story has a pattern of adventures which custom rather than observable logic motivates. An oft-told tale gains credence through fa-miliarity rather than through persuading the auditor of its veracity. The words "once upon a time" are an invitation to submit to the story, to accept its development as inevitable. One is reminded of a child's characteristic un-blinking gaze. Apollonius' *aitia* act to highlight this aspect of the legendary voyage. The *aitia* are explanations of how things came to be as they are, in sum, studies in cause and effect, revelations of the historical process, peculiar, special, and detailed. As the voyagers, with the reader in tow, sail past the *aitia*, evoking as they do a very different sensibility, the reader is made all the more aware of the surface of the voyage story. This is the way things are supposed to be. The *aitia* promise something other.

Callimachus did not like mechanical connections. "I hate the cyclic poets," he says, "who say, 'and then, and then.'" Hesiod's *Theogony*, the earliest extant triumph of catalogue poetry, coheres perfectly because several elements in its subject material create structure: for instance, the inherent chronological nexus of the divine succession (Uranus, Cronos, Zeus, the swallowing of Metis), the categories of natural phenomena, the sense of moral progression implied in Zeus' triumph over the Titans and then over Typhoeus. The catalogues of the *Theogony* taken together describe the birth and elaboration of the material world and the divine order which animates it. From material and moral chaos, the poet advances us to a realized, detailed natural order, and a moral order as well.

But despite what seems, in the second book of the *Argonautica*, to be a series of absolutely unconnected elements characteristic of the catalogue, the poet has managed to tie the narrative together in a number of ways. Principal among these is the lengthy prediction by Phineus of the future travels of the crew (309–407) which constitutes a rehearsal of everything which then occurs in the rest of the book, and provides a frame for it. Just as Phineus concludes with the prediction of the fleece in the grove of Ares guarded by the sleepless serpent, so finally, at the close of the second book, the poet describes the very same scene (1268–70) as the *Argo* sails up to Colchis. We observe the poet become Phineus, as it were. The poet begins the book with an elaborate description of the bogeyman Amycus and the boxing match which he demands of passersby; toward the end of the book, Argus describes (1202–6) a similar bogeyman, the dread Aeetes ("endowed with baleful cruelty . . . he could rival Ares in his huge strength and war cry"), and forecasts a grim battle with the king for the fleece. The Phineus figure is briefly repeated in the notice of Prometheus at the very close of the book (1256–59). Both are seers; both tell the route; both are punished and finally freed; their punishments involve extreme sadistic acts performed by winged creatures. The description of Prometheus is stark and grim, whereas Phineus, like Callimachus' Hecale figure, is described in homely detail.

Elements in this cataloguelike narrative have a continuing existence beyond their mention in the list. After the death of Amycus, while the crew fights the Bebrycians, Lycus, king of the Mariandyni, and his people take the occasion to ravage and pillage the Bebrycian territory (138–42) and later he becomes more prominent in the narrative (752–814) when he rejoices over the fall of Amycus and welcomes the crew. Events matter, therefore, beyond their mention. It is clear as well that Apollonius has some kind of grand scheme because so many items in the second book resemble those in the fourth. The complex description of the *Argo*'s passage through the Symplegades, which is paralleled in a kind of rococo manner in the description of the passage through the Wandering Rocks (4.924–63), is the best example. There are others, parallel deaths of crew members, for instance. Even the curiosities of the second book are paralleled by such things as Circe and her entourage of gargoyles in the fourth.

The reiteration of the voyage, first from Phineus' mouth, then from the narrator's, is a narrative device found frequently in this book. At the first the poet describes Amycus and his habit of demanding a boxing contest of everyone who crosses his path: "arrogant" (2); "most presumptuous of men" (4); "he killed many of his neighbors" (7). Amycus then appears to tell the crew of his habit, repeating the information which the narrator had told us. At the same time his manner of speaking (as the poet says, "in his overbearing way he disdained to ask who they were" [9], certainly the extreme of rudeness in this style of poetry) clearly portrays him to be arrogant and presumptuous. When the crew meets Phineus he has just been described by the poet (178–93), who tells the reader of his transgression of Zeus' command and of his punishment. When Phineus introduces himself in direct discourse (209–33) he described his miserable lot, and later, when the crew sets a trap for the Harpies, the poet describes (267–72) once again their noisome onslaught upon Phineus' meal. After the poet describes the Boreades' pursuit of the Harpies, they return and describe the event to the crew (430–34). When Jason meets Lycus he briefly (762–71) recapitulates the preceding events of their voyage.

A modern reader might perhaps like Apollonius to do something clever with these repetitions—after the manner of Lawrence Durrell, for instance, who gives us several views of the same action in his *Alexandria Quartet*. Apollonius was better at pleasing modern taste when he offered the amusingly contrasting accounts of Lemnian history from the narrator and from Hypsipyle.[3] Apollonius seems to be trying for the same effect, but more subtly, when he has Phineus describing the Harpies. Whereas the poet points out that the seer has transgressed, the old man evades the basic fact of his guilt (notice his very oblique reference to it at 215–16), only much later getting around to an admission (313–14)—in fact long after he has been prodded to it by the Boreades. "Why have you so much trouble? Did you as a prophet disobey the gods in fatal madness?" (245–47), they ask in a kind of straightforward Boy Scout innocence (as the poet notes, they first brushed away a tear at Phineus' plight, and Zetes took the old man's hand in his—charming, but not without a hint of sweetly comic stupidity). To this the prophet replies: "Be quiet. Don't think such thoughts" (they had been unwilling to help him because if he were being properly punished by the gods, they themselves did not wish to transgress) instead of repeating exactly the words of the narrator as a Homeric character would have done. In fact, Phineus only reveals his guilt in vague language and at that only when the Boreades are flown off in their pursuit of the Harpies.

The most obvious stylistic achievement in these repetitions is the variation in language, with its subtle implication of deviousness in the characters. While variations seem almost obligatory to a modern reader—and those in this part of the *Argonautica* are certainly innocuous at first glance—they may have had considerably more force with Apollonius' original audience, as they will for us if we recapture the original effect. The oral epic poet repeated exactly or, if he condensed—as Achilles is made to do when describing to his mother Thetis the quarrel between himself and Agamemnon (*Iliad* 1.370–80)—then what he retains is still lines exactly repeated. This probably made no great effect upon Homer's original audience, since they heard each line and then had—to some extent—to let it go. For a reading audience, however, exactly repeated passages tend to reinforce the sense that the saga material, the poem, has an existence of its own which resists manipulation. Here, however, when on three different occasions the Harpies are described in varying language, with minor differences in emphasis, what is sensed is that the event exists independent of the descriptions of it and that the descriptions in turn exist independent of each other: first for the narrator in an objective preamble; then, subjectively, for Phineus, as a horrible condition of his life; and finally acted out in the story for all of the participants including the reader to experience.

Note how the poet's initial description (2.187–93) is static. Except for the phrase *allote tuthon*—"at other times just a little"—which implies diverse behavior in the context of repeated action, the scene has no temporal perspective, no real connection with what precedes or follows, no psychological connections. It is like *ekphrasis*, a genre scene from a vase or a mural. Phineus' description, by contrast, is full of his misery. His account rings with emotion; perhaps, considering what we know and he avoids saying, we may add that it serves up a comic touch of bathos. The narrator had said (187–89) "suddenly swooping . . . snatched the food away." Phineus says, "snatch the food . . . swooping down" and adds "it is easier for me, longing for food, to escape from my own thoughts than to escape them" (225–27). The narrator says (191–93) "no one dared not only to put the food to his mouth, but even to stand at a distance, so much did the remnants of the meal give off a smell [*apepnee*, a rather neutral word]." Phineus says, "If ever at all they do leave me a morsel of food, it smells like rot [decaying flesh], and the odor is unendurable, and no one of mortals not even for a moment [*minuntha*, a tiny moment] could endure coming near, no, not even if his heart were beaten out of adamantine" (228–31). Phineus' account strains with the energy of woe.

When Jason and the sons of Boreas recapitulate their adventures, these truncated versions of what the narrator has described to us at such leisure and so fully, consign the action over to the participants who, because they can shorten, alter, and omit, make the action their own. The participants in the narrative become narrators themselves. Apollonius gives his characters the independence which tragic characters possess. In epic, the characters speak through the narrator, in drama they speak out independent of the third-person narrative which establishes the speakers in epic. The alternative descriptions which Apollonius introduces give the characters a certain autonomy. The action is clearly the invention of the narrator; the variant versions create the illusion that the speakers exist independent of the action and therefore of the narrator. They are like pop-up figures in children's storybooks, or like the freed, existential characters in John Fowles' *The French Lieutenant's Woman*. Each of them lives in his own story, his own version of events.

In one instance, Apollonius may seem to have lost control over the distance he places between himself and a character. A character takes extreme license in his narration. Apollonius, as we know, is so precise in everything—as the scholiast notes here he has Iris, rather than the traditional Hermes, halt the sons of Boreas because in Hesiod's account she is the Harpies' sister (*asteōs*, says the scholiast admiringly at 2.286). It is odd, therefore, that when he has described the sons of Boreas turning back after being halted by Iris at the so-called Floating Islands located in the Ionian Sea, he notes that the Harpies enter their den in Crete (296–99), but he then allows the sons of Boreas, in recounting their adventure, to assume a peculiar omniscience when they mention the Harpies going into their cave in Crete. How indeed could they know that? One is tempted to say that even Apollonius nods, but more to the point, we might say that Apollonius wants his reader to imagine a narrator who, if not nodding, has nonetheless momentarily lost control of his story which here as elsewhere assumes its own momentum.

When Phineus describes the voyage to Colchis which lies ahead for the crew, the poet again varied the information given from time to time. Phineus says of the Chalybes "most wretched men, who possess land that is rough and unworkable ["indestructible," when used as it so often is, of iron], hard-working men" (374–76); his description is short and neutral. The narrator, on the other hand, who is after all not giving a set of directions to an eagerly awaiting band of men, but in fact has all the time in the world, devotes seven lines enlarging Phineus' "rough land" into "plowing is no concern for them, nor is there any planting of honey-sweet fruit, nor do they pasture sheep in the dewy meadow" (1002–8), his "unworkable" (with its association with iron), into "they cleave the harsh iron earth exchanging their wages for food" (1005–6), and his "hard-working men" into "nor does dawn rise for them without toil but with black smile and flame they endure heavy labor" (1006–8). Likewise, Phineus' nondescript Homeric epithet "rich in sheep" applied to the Tibareni, is changed to a five-line discussion of birthing customs (1011–14). It is as if Apollonius the poet were making a scholarly commentary on Phineus' prophecies to the crew. One might also remark that the amplifications show that Phineus the seer does not know everything. Consider how full he is in his description of the Mossynoeci (379–83) and yet how much more material the narrator has to add (1015–29), which is in fact far more interesting as well. The narrator is again like Apollo, omniscient and in total control.

Apollonius' fascination with the narrator's disengagement from his narrative appears elsewhere in the second book. Amycus while fighting Polydeuces is compared to a wave (as befits the son of Poseidon) rising up against a ship which the clever pilot manages to elude; just so the clever Polydeuces avoids the blow of the king (70–75). Very shortly thereafter the *Argo* meets with a "real" wave, as it were, which rises up in just the same menacing manner and only at the last minute is avoided by the skillful steering of the pilot Tiphys (169–76). Herman Fränkel points out an adjacent concatenation of images. A simile compares the Argonauts to shepherds (130) who smoke out bees (the Bebrycians). When the Bebrycians are vanquished, the poet mentions that the crew is busy driving off their sheep (143–44). A little later dawn is described as the light which wakes the shepherds (165) and without any further specification the poet tells us that the crew put on board the booty they needed (167). Apollonius generally emphasizes the artificiality of the simile so that it is paradoxical to see the similes come alive into the "true" narrative. Here art is imitating nature so successfully that it becomes animate.

Apollonius' descriptive powers are unusually well illustrated in this relatively static second book. When the crew reaches the isle of Ares and the birds begin to drop their dangerously strong and heavy feathers, Amphidamas suggests a defence by holding up shields and spears and shouting, which the poet then describes in three similes run together (1073–89), another instance of alternative verbal accounts of the same event.

> As when a man roofs over the enclosure of his house
> with tile, to be an ornament and a defence
> against rain; and one tile fits to another firmly, in succession,
> so they roofed over the ship interlocking their shields.
> Just as a clang arises from the dread din of men
> on the march, when the phalanxes meet, such was the noise
> spreading up on high through the air from the ship.
> ....
> As when the son of Cronos sends down a thick hailstorm
> from the clouds over the city and its houses; and those who
> dwell beneath hear the noise above on their roofs and sit quietly
> for the storm season did not catch them unawares but
> before this they had strengthened the roof, so the birds
> sent against them a thick shower of feathers.

The clever handyman's contrivance of the protection of shields is appropriately described in domestic terms, in its whole history from the first tile laid to the smug satisfaction of hearing rain on the tiles. The account is broken to describe the warlike act of shouting, set into a military simile.

The storm which cast Argus, son of Phrixus, and his brother on to the island where they meet the crew (1098–1121) is another descriptive tour de force which achieves much of its power from the suggestive sound of the language. The poet begins, for instance, by mentioning an ominous rustling of the leaves during the day, followed by a heavy storm at night, "*autar hog' ēmatios men en ouresi phyll' etinassen/ tuthon ep' akrotatoisin aēsyros akremonessin*" where the dry rustling of the leaves comes in the repeated *-ssin* sound and in the repeated *a* and *t* sounds of the second line. Then the storm comes: "*nukti d' ebē pontonde pelōrios, ōrse de kuma,*" sensed in the kettledrum effect of *nt* and *nd*, and the heavy long *o*'s with the plosive *p*'s preceded by the voiced labial *b*.

The second book opens with its most stirring descriptive passage, which also establishes the main themes. The boxing match between Polydeuces and Amycus is also the subject of Theocritus' twenty-second Idyll. Again, as in the case of the Hylas story, there is no way of knowing which poem has priority. They are very different in any event and hardly seem to be a commentary or correction of each other. Theocritus begins the boxing scene with a physical description of Amycus, follows this with a twenty-line dialogue between Polydeuces and the ogre king, and then describes the boxing, rather carefully, paying close attention to strategy. When, for instance, the young hero has so bloodied and disfigured the king's face that he cannot see, he delivers the telling blow and the fight is over. But Amycus remains alive, whereas in the *Argonautica* he is killed.

In Apollonius' version, Amycus' initial challenge, "pick out your best alone from the crowd" (15), is answered by Polydeuces unbid: "he stood forth in front of the crew" (or champion of the crew, or first of the crew: *promos*).

Apollonius is indifferent to the technique of boxing; he concentrates on the contrast between the adversaries, the one an ogre force of nature, the other an emblem of humanity and civilization. Amycus, glaring at Polydeuces like an angered lion (26), seems to be a monstrous son of Typhoeus or Earth (38–39) standing apart in silence (48–49), waiting in repose, his eyes on the other (49). Polydeuces, on the other hand, is like a star whose rays shine in the evening sky (41), down on his cheeks, sparkle in his eye (43–44), exercising his hands to take the rower's cramp away (45–46). The young hero lays aside his cloak (*theto*), the gift of a Lemnian woman which the poet calls well woven (*eustipon*), delicate stuff (*leptaleon*). The king, by contrast, throws down (*kabbale*) his dark cloak, double thickness, with big clasps, and his staff made of mountain olive. The boxing match will be a contest with youth, beauty, grace, subtlety, and manners on the one side and harshness, heaviness, crudeness, and thickness on the other. Asked to choose his gauntlet from the two before him, Polydeuces with a slight smile selects, without considering, the set nearest his feet (61–62)—the perfect *beau gentilhomme*!

Once the match begins Apollonius eschews details but instead lets the images of three similes tell the tale: Amycus the giant wave about to engulf the ship, Polydeuces the nimble, clever pilot who steers free of the wave (obviously the clever one; he was testing his hands before the match while Amycus sat still trusting in his brute strength). Blow after blow raining on the two bodies is like the hammering of shipbuilders, teeth rattling like echoing pins; the furiousness of their coming together like bulls fighting over a heifer. The poet moves from human wit to the nervous power of the limbs to the brute fact of normal male violence. Only the death stroke is described, and for that reason is all the more impressive. Amycus rises up again:

> Rising up on tiptoe Amycus, like one who slays
> an ox, stretching, brought his hand down on the
> enemy, who bent to one side, ducking his head,
> taking a blow from the arm on his shoulder, then
> Polydeuces came near, and getting his knee past the king's,
> he hit him one behind the ear. The bones broke
> inside, the king fell to his knees in agony.

As Amycus is described here it could be yet another sea wave confronting the clever, nimble Argonaut.

The threat and the maneuver foreshadow the perilous passage between the Symplegades, described in another of Apollonius' purple passages. Here again the water rises up (580–87) and only Tiphys the pilot's quickness keeps them from the rocks. High up in the air the *Argo* rides, the rowers' oars, says the poet, are bent like bows (591–92), after Athena's assist the boat speeds on like an arrow (600). The scene has the quality of a Disney fantasy, and is frightening because of that same surreal, exaggerated quality. In the course of the description the poet's precision creates an image of perfect terror. Euphemus releases the dove which Phineus says must fly between the rocks as good omen; otherwise they are doomed.

> All raised their head to watch
> But the dove flew between the rocks, they
> rushed together, and crashed face to face.
> Foam flew up in a cloud; the
> sea roared fearfully; the great air roared
> all around. The caves beneath the cliffs
> boomed as the sea poured in. White
> foam from the crashing wave spewed up. The
> current turned the boat around. The rocks

snipped the tip of the dove's tail feathers, but
she made it through safe, and the rowers cried out.

Eleven lines of suspense and physical terror in that split second during
which the bird flies through the rocks are translated moments later into the
boat's birdlike passage, picked up in the air by the waves, held aloft by Ath-
ena's hand, only to have the tail ornament sheared off as the boat slips between
the rocks (601–2).

Phineus is the most important figure in the second-book narrative. The
270-line passage in which he appears (178–448) is by far the longest in the
book. The scene in which his prophetic speech of 99 lines appears (311–425)
equals almost all the preceding parts of the Phineus narrative, which has been
broken down into seven sections; 178–93, the poet's introduction; 194–208,
the physical description of Phineus; 209–39, Phineus' introduction; 240–61
the reaction of the sons of Boreas and Phineus' response; 262–300, the Bo-
reades and the Harpies; 301–425, the prophetic speech and aftermath; 426–
48, the successful return of the sons of Boreas and Phineus' response.

Phineus is special because he is so old while the crew is so young, again so
victimized and defeated while the crewmen are adventuresome, and then a
seer where they are all knowing. Apollonius creates his most brilliant portrait
when he describes Phineus (197–205).

> He rose from his bed like a lifeless dream;
> on shriveled feet he went to the door
> propping himself on a staff, feeling the walls.
> His joints as he went trembled with age
> and weakness. His dry skin was
> parched from the dirt, only the skin
> held bones together. Out of the house he
> came; at the threshhold of the courtyard
> he sat down, as his knees gave under
> his weight. Stupor from a rush of blood
> covered him; the earth seemed to
> move under his feet. Speechless,
> enfeebled in a trance, he lay there.

Phineus the old man says to the young men when he advises them on
passing through the Symplegades, "Don't bring death on yourself through
foolishness (aphradeōs), nor rush into this led on by your youth" (326–27).
Later, describing his neighbor Paraebius whose father brought down upon his
son the wrath of a nymph because he cut down the stump in which she lived,
Phineus says "he cut it down foolishly (aphradeōs) in the arrogance of his
youth" (480–81). True to the pattern of old men in epic narrative, Phineus
is generous with his maxims. "Reverence for the gods" (325), "it is better to

yield to the immortals" (338–39), "as things happen, so shall they happen" (345) are the words of wisdom which fall from the failing, desiccated, tormented man who in his youth misguidedly ("I was infatuated in my foolishness" [aphradia] 313) set out to tell everybody everything of the will of Zeus, and incurred that god's wrath.

Phineus' advice for passing the Symplegades must be followed exactly. It sets the tone for the entire prophetic utterance. Like Circe's directions for the ritual ways to speak with the dead, or like the Orphic sacred literature which gave instructions on where to go and what to say on the road to and through the lower world,[4] Phineus' list of way stations on the voyage sets up a kind of rite of passage for the young men of the crew. The catalogue quality of the narrative is exploited to establish what are a set of fairy-tale obstacles to overcome or labors such as Heracles performs seriatim or the adventures of Odysseus. What Phineus stresses, however, is the need to follow the rules. His life and his friend Paraebius' life are examples of the fate of delinquents. For the crew, however, the rules are more the rules of the game than anything else.

Even when Amycus menaces the young men with his brutal contest, the boxing event is called *thesmos*, a law or ordinance (5). He challenges them saying, "If you try to trample my decrees with no reverence (*apelegeontes emas pateoite themistas*) then harsh necessity will overtake you" (17–18). The moral authority of his vocabulary—Phineus will use "reverence" (*alegeontes*)—seems to be in ironic contrast to his brutal, crude way. And yet, though wild (*agrios*) anger takes them all (19), Polydeuces answers meekly enough, "do not display your harsh violence. For we shall obey your rules, as you say." The beast talks of rules, the polite young man represses bestial anger. Things seem topsy-turvy, but they are not. The narrator, Amycus, and Polydeuces are using the language seriously. The brutal contest is legitimate.

What is being played out is the grim game with brutal rules, the game of life itself. Again one has the sense of a portentous passage. Apollonius has located Amycus and his boxing contest as the first incident of the second book. Alone of the four books it begins without the conventional invocation which formally signals commencement. Apollonius has therefore boldly made the boxing contest a beginning; Amycus becomes a gatekeeper as it were who must be vanquished before the heroes can enter the narrative of the second book; Amycus, like Aeetes later on, has no familiar guardian or patron deity. We have entered another region where the Olympian gods do not hold sway. Literally, of course, this is not true: Athena helps, Apollo appears. But Amycus is a bogeyman, or the wicked giant, Polydeuces the fair knight. It is a battle between good and evil, between Horus and Seth, light and dark, youth and age.

Hereafter the youths must pass between the Clashing Rocks, which some scholars consider to be an entry into the infernal regions, or the other world, as it may be called.[5] Phineus himself is typical of the prophet whom the hero encounters in a *katabasis*, Tiresias in the *Odyssey*, or Utnapishtim in the Gilgamesh story. The poet suggests an infernal landscape. The *Argo* arrives among the Mariandyni who are ruled over by King Lycus. Phineus has prepared them when he says: "Here is the road down into Hades. The promontory of Acherusia stretches along high, the river Acheron, whirling along, cuts its path below right through the promontory and sends its waters out from a huge chasm" (353–56). Hades has been on the crew's minds. Before reaching there, but after enduring the ordeal of the Symplegades, Jason complains "now I am wrapt in overwhelming fear and unendurable anxieties, hating to have to sail this ship down the chilly (*kruoenta*) paths of the sea" (627–29). Other than Jason, the crew had been generally overjoyed to survive the Symplegades, since, as the poet says, "they said that they had been saved from Hades" (609–10). And his comrades cheer Jason up, so much so that he can say, "now even if I must go through the depths of Hades, I shall not be afraid" (642).

Finally they arrive at the land of Mariandyni which Apollonius describes this way: "there sloped down toward the mainland a hollow wooded valley where there is a cave of Hades roofed over with woods and rocks; here an icy cold breath, blowing out continuously from the chilly interior, continually makes shining bits of ice which melt in the noonday sun. Silence never takes over that grim promontory, but without cease there it murmurs with the sound of the echoing sea and the leaves rustling in the winds from the cave" (734–42). Here, in this deathly setting, a boar which is associated with the infernal regions fatally gores Idmon. A few days later at the very same site, Tiphys dies ("the story goes that Tiphys died here" 854).[6] Two expiatory deaths and the crew sails forth, freed of all obstacles now until the men reach Colchis.

Apollonius seems to be using motifs associated with a descent into the underworld,[7] but it would be nonsense to say that he is describing an actual descent. There are too many confusions, such as the way in which the Symplegades duplicate the Acherusian headland and the subsequent deaths; nor would Apollo appear in such a scene, although it could be argued that, if the arrival at the cave of Hades is, strictly speaking, the descent, then Apollo's epiphany directly before (669–719) is the last sparkle of sunshine before the surrounding gloom. In any case, the poet maintains the sense of an infernal setting, for instance describing the tomb of Sthenelus (911–29) whose ghost in tears appears before them, and then describing the sight of Prometheus chained in the Caucasus, like any one of the punished sinners in the infernal regions (1256–59). Phineus with all his prescience does not mention these two scenes, nor does he mention the deaths of Idmon and Tiphys, so that they're all the more emphatic when they appear in the narrative.

At the arrival in Colchis, Jason pours libations "to Earth, to the gods of the country and to souls of dead heroes" (1273–74). The prayer is curious. No Olympian deities are invoked, instead the gods whom he calls upon are ambiguous. Then, he calls upon the dead and upon earth in which they are buried. It is a prayer suited to the sense of the infernal which has colored the latter half of the second book.[8] Most of all, Apollonius has depicted a state of mind, of dread, of impossibly grim possibilities, a limbo of horrible potentials. When Tiphys dies, Jason in his despair at finding another to steer for them says, "I see an evil fate lying ahead for us *just like that of dead men*, if we do not make it to the city of Aeetes nor get through the rocks back to Greece; here sad fate will cover us over" (889–93; my italics). They will be trapped, entombed in this strange Hades-like landscape.

Jason is curiously inactive in this book, while Polydeuces, the sons of Boreas, Tiphys, and Peleus each have a brief moment at the center. Nowhere does Jason himself accomplish any special feat in a book describing obstacles or tests. But the poet registers Jason's emotions for us; for most of the book he is frightened and downcast. In the exultation of success at having got past the Symplegades, Tiphys forecasts easy sailing thereafter (611–18). But Jason, while sticking with his customary conciliatory tone (*meilikhiois epeessi*), replies in a speech whose violent exaggerations show him to be in the blackest of moods.

We see Jason still suffering the ravages of fear which gripped them all as they sped between the rocks (622–37).

> Tiphys, why do you try to cheer me up like this in my distress?
> I was a fool (*aasamēn*) and badly mistaken to my own ruin.
> When Pelias asked me I should have said straight out no to this voyage
> even if it meant dying hideously pulled apart limb from limb.
> Now I have laid upon me overwhelming fear and intolerable anxieties,
> hating the icy paths of the sea we must traverse, hating the
> moment when we must put in to the mainland. For everywhere
> there are hostile men. Always I pass the night in groaning,
> since first you gathered together for my sake,
> pondering each detail. It's easy for you to talk;
> you've only yourself to consider, whereas I, while I don't
> care a bit for myself, must worry about this one
> and that one and you and all my other companions
> whether I shall get you back to Greece safely.

Upon first reading, this is a curious outburst. More curious still that Apollonius appends, "He said this making trial of the chiefs." We are reminded, as surely we are meant to be, of Agamemnon's stratagem in the second book of the *Iliad*, when he gives a despairing speech to the assembly in the hopes of arousing the men's ardor in reaction. And in that scene Dream had said to

Agamemnon when he had counseled the speech, "a leader ought not to be sleeping all the night long to whom a people are entrusted and so many cares are his."

Apollonius, as usual, is being thoroughly ironic. Unlike Agamemnon, Jason *does* want some support from his crew; clearly his own morale has evaporated, having lost himself in his own sea of hysterical worries. His Homeric counterpart sleeps the night away; Jason, as he tells the crew in this self-pitying speech, cannot.[9] Jason's psychological bankruptcy at this point is perfectly illustrated in the way he mouths the words of Tiphys, once the chiefs have cheered him up. From the deepest despair he revives immediately to say, parrotlike, in almost the very same words which Tiphys used, that once past the rocks, it will be easy sailing, following Phineus' direction (644–47).

The death of Tiphys once more submerges Jason in a slough of despond, this time shared by the crew. But once Ancaeus volunteers to steer the ship, some optimism returns. Peleus adds his encouragement after Ancaeus' speech. And, as Fränkel notes,[10] Jason answers them in a speech which parallels the structure of their two, a parody done in irony and gloom. Jason foresees the failure of their trip, the utter incapacity of his crew ("those whom we once boasted to be the men who knew how to do things [*daēmonas*, 887], these are distressed and dejected even more than I"), this, despite the cool resolve of Ancaeus, who wants to be the new steerman, and the enthusiasm of Peleus. Apollonius appends laconically, "Thus he spoke, but Ancaeus immediately made plans to take over the guiding of the ship," and lists still others who were willing to steer. This is Jason's lowest point. His gloom, which parallels the atmosphere of the landscape through which they pass, is ignored by the crew, who take over the action. No more is heard from Jason until once more his formal role of leader is set upon him when the shipwrecked sons of Phrixus address their words of supplication to him.

In a curious reversal, Apollonius has assigned the timidity and despair of Odysseus' crew to Jason, and Odysseus' courage and resolution to the men around Jason. As Jason says, when the crew shouts encouragingly (641), "O friends, my courage waxes in your *aretē*." Jason, clearly enough, does not have an insatiable thirst for high adventure. He vacillates, doubts, and despairs. Some would say he whines, and is wishy-washy, and is thus a thoroughly unsatisfactory central character, even for a work which is presumed to portray an anti-hero.

One does not have to be so unsympathetic to Jason, though the element of ironic comedy is undeniable. It is doubtful that Apollonius is entirely unsympathetic. An author, though he may fail in the endeavor, generally tries to make his central character sufficiently attractive to hold his reader's interest. The second book portrays Jason's state of mind as he is borne along toward the events which will confront him in the third book. When Jason has heard

Phineus out, he still has the overriding question: How will I get home? and
he adds, "since I know nothing and my companions know nothing and Col-
chis lies on the edge of Ocean and the edge of the world" (416–18). Put
together with the many references to the youth of Jason and his crew, the
ignorance which he proclaims here is the ignorance and innocence of youth as
much as anything else. Apart from the *Odyssey* poet's sketch of Telemachus,
this portrait of Jason is the only developed depiction of youth in ancient
literature. The self-assurance of the older Homeric hero has not yet been
achieved by the more youthful Apollonian Jason. The irony cuts both ways.
If Jason is comical, if his youthful insecurities are comical, still, when he is
considered in comparison to, say, the wily Odysseus, Odysseus' cunning and
self-assurance suddenly seem a touch cold-hearted.

"Well, my friends," replies Phineus (423–25), "keep your minds on the aid
from Aphrodite which comes through seduction (*doloessan arōgēn Kypridos*).
From that source will emerge the glorious result of your labors. And beyond
that don't ask me anything further." Mysterious and abrupt as any other orac-
ular agency, Phineus can only excite nervousness in one so young, a male, as
well, who has not been trained to consult Aphrodite's repertoire of stratagems
when he must make his way in the world. At this point Jason has lost his
innocence in Lemnos, and triumphantly, too. Phineus is clearly pointing the
finger at him as the source for the future triumphs and ultimate salvation
which will come to the crew.

The crew can afford to be lighthearted and enthusiastic as they make their
way successfully across the unknown territory. For Jason, however, this is
another kind of trip. True to the peculiar quality of déjà vu which oft-told
mythological stories create, the reader may endow Jason with his own fore-
knowledge, invest in Jason some premonition, inkling of what he must do in
the future. (He has rehearsed it so many times before in so many versions of
the myth, how can there be surprises even for him?) The second book is an
entry, a fateful entry into a world which will eventually be a psychological
complication for Jason, a net which will hold him fast: love. The ogre at the
gates is killed, they enter, the rocks are parted, the ship goes through, an
infernal landscape emerges to evoke the sense of a fateful crossing into states
hitherto unknown. These events in fact parallel the later career of Jason: the
Amycus contest is his victory over Aeetes, entry through the Symplegades is
his conquest emotionally (and potentially and ultimately sexually) of the vir-
gin princess; the Hades atmosphere forecasts the despair as well as the foul
acts which fill the fourth book, which become the realization of what love in
fact means. We must not forget the rituals which precede Jason's triumph on
the field of Ares; for the poet makes it seem as though Jason were selling his
soul to Hecate. Through these scenes in the second book Jason grows more
and more terrified. Phineus has hinted that the challenge is his; the new and

uncharted experience of conquest through love will be his *athlos*. Read in this manner, Jason's apprehensions are altogether justified.

All the while allusions to the Heracles story inform the narrative as an ever-present paradigm, which has the quality sometimes of a reverse image. After Polydeuces' victory over Amycus some one of the crew says to another (145–53) that if Heracles had been present there would have been no boxing contest, no rules (*thesmous*), since his club would have decided the issue. In effect, Heracles is capable of the same kind of brute violence that Amycus represents, a very different person from the gentle Polydeuces. Lycus, king of the Mariandyni, reminisces (774–79) over a visit Heracles paid to his home in Lycus' youth ("he found me with the down just starting on my cheeks" [779]—what erotic memories does Lycus conceal in that line?). Heracles entered a boxing match against Titias "who shone out among all the young men in beauty and strength [another *bel ragazzo!*] and he knocked his teeth out to the ground." The king's anecdote reinforces the image of Heracles as an Amycus figure. Both allusions to Heracles must, however, also be humorous because Heracles is a sympathetic figure and the allusions thus ironically undercut the serious-ness of the beau ideal which Polydeuces is set up to be. The politesse which Jason and the other youths practice is always ambivalent. It is so easy to slide from "soothing words" (*meilikhiois epeessi*) to "fawning" (*hyposainōn*).

Heracles is not always the unattainable or undesirable alternative. Sometimes Jason is his peer. Lycus says that his people used to be menaced by Amycus and his Bebrycians because Heracles was far away (793), but now at last Jason and his crew have saved them. At the island of Ares where the birds rain down iron-weight feathers on the passersby, Amphidamas reminds the crew (1052) that not Heracles himself was able to drive the birds away with bow and arrow, but had to resort to noisemakers as the crew of the *Argo* also do.

When Heracles met the young Lycus he was on his way back from his encounter with the Amazons. One of the twelve labors imposed upon him by Eurystheus was to win the girdle of Hippolyte. The Amazons who live on the edge of the known world as it slips over into Never-Neverland are essentially *Märchen* figures, and the girdle is a magical charm. Heracles won the girdle by catching Queen Antiope in ambush, whom her sister Hippolyte ransomed with the girdle. The story is a counterpoint narrative to the quest which brings Jason into this part of the world. Whereas Jason has been told to stake everything on Aphrodite and will win the fleece by means of his erotic charm, Heracles as ever wins his counterpart object by brute force. The poet returns to the story of the girdle when he mentions Sthenelus (913) and the sons of Deimachus (955–57) who were in Heracles' entourage on the expedition, and then describes the event when Jason and crew pass the land of these warlike women (967–69).

Jason is beloved of Hera as counterpart Heracles is hated by the goddess. It is thought that in earlier versions of the Argonaut story Hera functioned as Athena does in the *Odyssey*, that is, a constant companion and helpmeet to the hero. Unlike Odysseus and indeed most other epic figures, Jason encounters no opposition on the divine level. It is unclear in fact what the poet means to say, if anything, in his portrayal of the Olympian deities whom he has inherited from Homer. It is not altogether clear in fact what the older epic poets are telling us either. The poet of the *Iliad* is particularly ambivalent about the deities, now taking Zeus seriously, now making fun of him.[11] Apollonius employs the conventional turns of phrase for describing the divine presence in his narrative. It could be argued that he fostered, rather anachronistically one would think, a conventional belief in these deities whom most students of ancient religion would claim to have become principally poetic conceits by the third century B.C.[12]

It has been said that "the [second] book is a vast homily on the nature of the relationship between gods and man."[13] Here it is that Jason learns piety. If so, it is a lesson he easily forgets when he evilly kills Apsyrtus, an affair that causes so little a ripple on the divine plateau that one can only imagine Apollonius to have been describing the Epicurean Mount Olympus, absolutely remote from the affairs of men.[14] Divine indifference at Apsyrtus' murder as well as the Apollonian caricature of divinity in the third book make the traditional potency of the anthropomorphized Homeric gods suspect. Apollonius perhaps catches their impotence in his description of the epiphany of the god Apollo in the second book. The god appears in all his beauty ("around his face the golden hair flowed down" [676–77]) and in his awesome might ("the island shook beneath his feet" [679–80]). In their awe, they bow their heads. The reader anticipates that the moment for contact is at hand. One thinks of Athena and Odysseus, Apollo and Diomedes, any number of colloquies in epic poetry which mark that special relationship between god and heroic man. But Apollo "far off proceeded to go toward the sea through the air" (683–84). A god from epic poetry seems to be more than usually indifferent to man.

But then what are we to make of Phineus and the lessons of recklessness, punishment, and endurance which he represents? Phineus is so thoroughly described, and the implications of his story are underscored by the brief notice of the fate of Paraebius who paid for his father's recklessness. And what of Phineus' divinely inspired prophetic art which, it develops, is absolutely true? Do not these events signal the triumph of divine will? Is this a world in which cause and effect, crime and punishment are in the hands of a deity anthropomorphized enough to feel at least the emotions of anger? The answers to these questions are bound up, here as in so many other acts of interpretation, in the reader's perception of Homeric practice.

The Homeric poets described worlds where the gods intervene directly and frequently into the lives of mortals. This does not necessarily describe any overarching moral order, since the deities are often in conflict with each other in their support or rejection of human figures. One is left with the idea that mankind is subject to arbitrary sudden and irrational forces which are more apparent and recognizable to heroes than ordinary mortals. Living closer to the throne, as it were, the heroes have fewer illusions. Finally, however, man is on his own. Achilles at the close of the *Iliad* says that Zeus rains down now evil, now good mixed with evil without, it seems, the slightest rationale. Zeus in the *Odyssey* objects to man's assignment of good and evil to divine whim; it is their human folly which does humanity in. The strength of the Homeric vision is that heroic man is alone, stronger, perhaps more perceptive, favored by nature, genes—call it god—but still alone when he creates his destiny.

Half a millenium later, Apollonius re-creates the Olympian deities. They are either indifferent (Apollo) or silly (Hera). What has supplanted the Olympian deities in Greek religious thinking is most of all the philosophy of Stoicism. Surely that great crushing inevitability of the second book as everything Phineus says comes true is the Stoic concept of Providence, that eternal rhythm of the universe, the Divine Mind, the Fire, Zeus—call it what you will—which moves all things along the path already known. The portrait of Phineus as the old man is a metaphor for this force. And so it is that Phineus' advice to the crew on youthful impetuousness is illustrative of the condition in which the second book is begun. It is a voyage of discovery in which all things turn out to be inevitable. The old age of Phineus, so amply described, is in fact mankind's experience of the penultimate inevitable truth of human existence. This voyage, then, is the lesson in growing up, the discipline and bondage to which all adolescents must submit. If we consider Jason, like the young Telemachus, to be learning while traveling, then we might say that as he becomes sexually aware he must also learn about the entrapment of life. It is a natural and easy passage from Lemnos to the instructions which Phineus gives. This is the lesson of Adam and Eve's Fall, this is the lesson Enkidu gains from his intercourse with the harlot. It is the underlying rhythm of the second book, one which, justifiably enough, can only contribute to Jason's dread and melancholia.

5

Sweet Talk

=====
‖‖‖‖‖‖‖‖‖‖‖‖

The second book began with a contest between a bully and a gentle young man whose boxing skills and strengths killed the brute outright. At the close of the book Argus, son of Phrixus, describes his grandfather (1202–6) as a similar bully brute who will not give up the fleece easily. The heroes sail into Colchis past the sacred grove of Ares where the serpent guards the fleece. Ancaeus says, "The time has come to consider whether we shall make an attempt on Aeetes with cozening ways (*meilikhiē*) or whether some other approach will be better" (1278–80).

Apollonius begins the third book by invoking the love Muse, Erato, asking her aid in telling the story of Jason's success aided by Medea's love. "For you share in Aphrodite's office; by virtue of the affections you excite (*teois meledēmasi*) you enchant (*thelgeis*) virgin girls." The story which fills the third book of the *Argonautica* tells of the success and failure of *meilikhiē*. It is also a story about love, which in Apollonius' view is fostered and sustained by enchantment and seduction. The story is told through many comings and goings and constant scene changes, and yet it is not action which holds our interest but rather talk, conversation, the psychological manipulation or attempts at it which animates each exchange. For this book Apollonius has fashioned a comedy of manners.

Longinus called the *Odyssey* a comedy of manners (*On the Sublime*, 9). This is particularly true of the episode which takes place upon the island of Scheria when the shipwrecked Odysseus is met by the princess Nausicaa and entertained in her father's palace. Because the poet makes so many close equations between his story and Odysseus' experiences among the Phaeacians (the sixth, seventh, and eighth books of the *Odyssey*), the reader of the third book of the *Argonautica* should have the Homeric episode well in mind. When Apollonius describes Aeetes' palace as seen through Jason's eyes as he enters it there are parallels between the architectural details at Colchis and Homer's Scheria (references to the walls, the coping stone), and between the way in which the heroes position themselves at the threshold in wonder at what they see. Whereas Hephaestus has made gilded statues of youths holding torches for Alcinous, he has made a brazen bull and plough for Aeetes. Apollonius, however, can be eclectic: Aeetes' four fountains with running milk, wine, oil, and water are a fancy version of Calypso's four streams of fresh springwater, next to which both Calypso and Aeetes have vines. The simile comparing Medea to Artemis (876–84) has several parallels with a simile comparing Nausicaa to Artemis (*Odyssey* 6.102–9); and Medea's visit to Hecate's temple (869–75), where she has her initial meeting with Jason, is very much like Nausicaa's clothes-washing outing to the beach where she meets Odysseus. There are the same handmaids, the cart; the game of catch is replaced by singing and flower-gathering. Odysseus, however, wakes from sleep and comes upon the surprised maiden all unsuspecting; Medea on the other hand is going to an assignation with Jason.

The economical character sketches and the rapid pace of the action of the episode at Scheria suggest that here if nowhere else the poet is making a fiction out of, to be sure, a number of traditional elements. The way in which the Telemachia prefigures Odysseus' travels and the Scheria adventure prefigures Odysseus' homecoming (remember the important repeated simile 6.232–34, 23.159–61) argues again that the poet foreshadowed the homecoming by making up this episode. It is essential, however, to the story of wandering. Just as Calypso's offer of immortality and sex, combined with a list of men destroyed in love adventure with female divinities, recalls to mind Ishtar, so the compelling tranquillity and security of Nausicaa and her parents remind one of the vineyard girl Siduri whose advice to Gilgamesh was to stop traveling and abandon his quest.

Put in terms of the *Odyssey* story, Nausicaa offers one of the greatest temptations to confront a middle-aged traveling man, the chance to start all over again, with a young virgin bride and a new kingdom. Odysseus, who is ever master of the situation, manages with his customary politesse to get what he wants from the Phaeacians without having to accede to their desires. Nausicaa hints at marriage to him. Alcinous, socially clumsier than the women—as is common in the ever so feminine *Odyssey*—takes up the marriage question outright when first he meets Odysseus. Odysseus competes with the young swains of the island and wins in a contest which is typical of those in which the princess is won by the victorious underdog. But he makes no declaration, and Alcinous realizes that he must be married (8.243). Nausicaa says goodbye in the coolest way (8.457–58), just as she had directed him to her parents' home so as to avoid scandal (7.255). All this is in contrast to the song of Ares and Aphrodite which Demodocus sings as evening entertainment, a story of self-indulgent lechery and public scandal, completely at variance with the tidy, almost bourgeois outlook of the Phaeacian court. ("Where did you get those clothes?" Arete asks the suppliant Odysseus, when she meets him first, recognizing her daughter's washing.)

The beach scene wherein Nausicaa gives Odysseus clothing to cover his nakedness is a charming blend of eroticism and military parody. Odysseus appears stark naked covering his genitals with a leafy branch. He comes forth like a hungry lion, says the poet (130–34). But he won't take Nausicaa by the knees in supplication as is the custom, nor will he let one of the girls bathe him. The hero is very aware of his nakedness. Nausicaa stands bravely awaiting him as he advances from where he had been concealed; the language suggests a battlefield. Once he is bathed and dressed, she wants him for a husband (244–45). The hungry lion of the simile suddenly confronts a predatory sheep. Many things are topsy turvy on Scheria. "We take our pleasure in running, sailing, feasting, music, dances, changes of clothing, and hot tubs," says Alcinous (8.246–49). For a military hero who is intent upon property and dynasty, Scheria must always be Never-Neverland. Like a traveling salesman from Hartford who has stumbled into Big Sur, Odysseus must know he would not be happy in the long run.

In Apollonius' day, the comedy of manners had evolved onto the dramatic stage in the New Comedy of Menander and his colleagues. Apollonius has disposed the events of the third book into an interlocking pattern which resembles comic theater. There are numerous entrances and exits carefully noted and motivated. The transitions from scene to scene which encourage the reader to keep in mind the situation in Colchis in its entirety anticipate, on the other hand, the novel.

At the beginning, the poet locates the heroes in their hidden cove (6), bringing their locale over from the close of the second book (2.1282–83).

After the divine colloquy at Olympus, the poet once more reminds us of the heroes' locale (168, repeating *lelokhēmenoi* from 7), returning us to it as events are proceeding (the imperfect verb of *ēgoroōnto*, 168, "were holding a meeting"). After meeting Aeetes, Jason returns to the cove (489) and after another parley the men decide to move the ship out of the cove and closer to the port (572–75). After the divine colloquy, Eros descends from Olympus to Aeetes' palace, and the poet manages the transition to the heroes in the cove by describing Eros first in the immediate vicinity of Zeus' palace (158–59), then high over the earth, so that the reader can refocus on the cove where the discussion is being conducted. After the discussion Jason goes to the palace where he stops to examine architecture, which serves as Apollonius' transition.

In the palace courtyard, Jason and his party find Medea ("going from room to room in search of her sister" [248–49]) and the rest of the family comes forth, exactly like the theater convention whereby action takes place before the house. Then the poet describes the bustle of the servants in this general area (271–74), which allows the reader to back away from the doors and the intimate greetings. And in the diffuse focus of the general scene, the poet introduces Eros once again, whose arrival converges with Jason's. We now focus on the sudden onset of love in Medea from Eros' arrows, after which the poet describes the general scene in the hall (299–301) so that the reader can shift his focus within the context of the general setting. After Aeetes' angry outburst, Jason and his party get up to leave. Medea gives the handsome stranger a covert glance. "Her mind, creeping along like a dream, flew after his footsteps as he went" (446–47). With this stage direction, Apollonius shifts the reader's concentration to Medea, whose emotional agony is described, though the poet also keeps in our minds Jason and Argus, engaged in conversation as they walk along the road away from the city (472–73)— which detail of locale Apollonius is careful to note.

When Argus returns to talk to his mother (572–73), the narrative is directed away from Jason and crew in the cove and toward the city. Thus, while Argus walks along, Apollonius describes Aeetes' council meeting, at the end of which Argus reaches Aeetes' palace and proceeds to talk to Chalciope about Medea (609–15). This prepares the reader to turn with the poet into some adjacent palace room where Medea lies sleeping. When she awakes, her anguish is so great that one of those ever-present theatrical servants (664–67) overhears and rushes to Chalciope. (Notice the magical way in which Apollonius brings the servant to life by means of the immediately preceding simile, 656–63, describing a newly widowed bride hiding her feelings from her attendants.) As in comic theater, the sister hurries from her room to Medea's. The plot is seamless here. Chalciope remarks that she has been talking to Argus (721–22), "I left him in my room when I came here" (723), and when she finishes speaking with Medea, she goes back to announce the news to Argus (740). The narrator is able to contrive a larger scene than is possible in the theater; it suggests a novelistic scene in which everyone everywhere is visually accounted for all the time.

The third book divides into five parts which Jean Godolphin Kurtz reminds me may itself reflect the tendency in later theater toward pentamerous construction. The first action (6–166) takes place on Olympus among Hera, Athena, and Aphrodite, reminiscent of the ubiquitous divine councils in epic and tragedy, particularly the two councils in Books One and Five which motivate the action in the *Odyssey*. The second part of the third book's story (167–608) is the embassy to Aeetes and his reaction to Jason's diplomacy, preceded and followed by group scenes of the Argonauts deliberating. The third (609–824) is Medea's passionate, anguished decision to betray her father and help the stranger. The fourth (825–1162) presents the meeting of Jason and Medea and shows them falling in love. The fifth (1163–1407) is Jason's *aristeia* in which he accomplishes the task Aeetes sets for him.

The third book is often treated as though it were an independent whole. It alone is the truly popular book of the poem, sometimes printed separately as an individual story.[1] As such it is unusual among the surviving pieces of Greek literature since it builds to a climax at its conclusion. Yet of course the third book is not independent; the story continues, the traditional description of the action's outcomes fills the first part of the fourth. Apollonius again demonstrates his amazing complexity in balancing the various elements of his story. The third book *seems* complete until we enter the fourth. Not only is the grammatical carry-over decisive in bonding the two narratives, but our hero has yet to get the fleece as well. Again Jason *seems* to be the hero, the only hero, the true traditional centerpiece of the action, until Medea commences to debate her great moral choice. Suddenly all that is crucial is hers. She begins to emerge as Jason's equal. So that again, while the conventional *aristeia* with which the third book concludes *seems* to be also a conventional climax, it recedes in our interest, becomes the traditional post-climax or outcome, giving place to the love scene between the two principals, an *agon* moment of far more tension and movement from which Jason's *aristeia* proceeds as a foregone conclusion. What is truly remarkable throughout the third and fourth books is that the poet manages to contrive a narrative in the third book which has a theatrical beginning, middle, and end, is complete in itself, and yet when extended into the fourth book easily dissolves into a larger unity which culminates in the murder of Apsyrtus whereupon again the poet brings his reader into a still larger narrative structure which reaches back into the second book until, when finally we arrive again on shore at the very close of the poem, we are once more at the poem's beginning and the still greater and overarching unity has been realized.

The poet calls upon Erato, the Lovely One, to help him with this narrative. He has undertaken to describe what the ancients considered the most fearful and devastating emotion, love. Apollonius introduces a dialogue of goddesses to explore this very human emotion. In this respect, he is of course similar to Homer who was inclined to describe human psychological states in terms of divine intervention—Achilles' decision not to kill Agamemnon, for instance. Unlike Homer, here in the third book he mocks the seriousness of human action, though he will treat it seriously later on.

The divine scene with which the book commences presents a cynical portrait[2] of three society ladies who happen to be goddesses. The extent to which they have any real function as divine beings is debatable. Hera replicates the thinking of Ancaeus (compare 2.1278–80 with 3.12–15) in the initial stages of planning, and later on Argus comes up with the same scheme which Hera proposes of enlisting Medea's magical skills to help the Argonauts. Some critics read this scene as expressing that peculiar dual agency in human affairs—conscious will and inner voice, one might say—acted out so tellingly when, for instance, Athena takes hold of Achilles and stays him from killing Agamemnon (*Iliad* 1.197–98).[3] But one could also say that the plot has no apparent need of the goddesses.[4] The parallel with Homer does not, in fact, prove much. Homer has other kinds of overhead action that cannot so readily be interpreted in this way. For instance, the divine marital quarrel (*Iliad* 1.536–600) between Zeus and Hera, brought to truce by Hephaestus, is, among other things, a parody of a scene which took place not long before this moment, the argument between Agamemnon and Achilles, brought to truce by Nestor. What the overhead domestic comedy does for the *Iliad* is emphasize the banality of invulnerable immortality (gods can bicker and whine, but they cannot die).

Apollonius' view of life is different from Homer's—perhaps more religiously optimistic, in the end—but it is no less serious. But however religious Apollonius was or was not, there is no reason to consider his treatment of the goddesses in this scene as anything but literary: the goddesses afford him an opportunity for comic literary allusion (to Homer), social satire (the fakery of genteel ladies), and one thing far more precious to the sophisticated Alexandrian heart, psychological analysis through the dramatized projection of forces that confuse and complicate human emotion. But unlike Homer, here in Book Three the poet presents the divine royals as a mythically inflated version of normal human foolishness; that is, he mocks the high seriousness of human action, though, without real contradiction, he will treat human action very seriously indeed later on.

On the surface, the conversation of the goddesses presents a comic vision of the scheming behind love affairs. On closer reading, we see that something more interesting is involved: allegorized psychology. Watching the love goddess and her agent or erotic desire at home, we are in fact watching a kind of objective—or dramatized—analysis of the emotion which is about to play so momentous a part in the story. The tone is amused, slightly cynical. Apollonius is not creating tragedy; the amused detachment helps to distance the reader from the characters, rather in the manner of Trollope, who was so deplored for this by Henry James. The effect need not be viewed as entirely comical. The distancing places the author (and the reader as well) in a position like God's. The pressure of sentiment has no place in his view of the scene. We must not forget that after Anna Karenina jumps under the train, Tolstoy recounts for us a number of Levin's agricultural reforms.

The words which Apollonius uses over and over again in connection with love have roots of *thelk-*, *dol-*, and *meilik-*: enchantment, deceit, and seduction.[5] These are weapons of love in the Hellenistic world which should remind us that love for the pagans—young, romantic love—was erotic and not altruistic. This is the Apollonian view of things. It is instructive in this regard to read Theocritean Idylls and compare them with Apollonius' poem. The Theocritean lovers keep the emotion light and the sex minimal, because the erotic appetite violates the Epicurean dictum that serenity is an absolute good.[6] Though the frivolous tone of the Olympus scene has sometimes led critics to imagine that a comedy of manners after the fashion of Oscar Wilde is about to be played out, one sees at once, when comparing Apollonius with Theocritus, that the Apollonian vision is darker than that, more serious and urgent.

The prelude to the scene in Aphrodite's chambers presents the two traditionally most powerful female deities in the universe, claiming they haven't the power to help Jason. A thoroughly domestic scene, it takes place in a chamber (*thalamos*) rather than on a peak of Olympus where Homeric deities were wont to converse. At a loss the goddesses stare at the ground, brooding, a gesture Apollonius will repeat when Jason despairs at Aeetes' demands (422), when Medea wishes to avoid direct eye contact with Jason (1008), and when the two lovers are overcome with shyness (1022). Like a symphonic theme, the gesture registers the ebb in the flow, the pause in the forward movement of the action.

Finally Hera suggests Eros. Athena, the mighty strategist, whose skill created the *Argo* and whose strength got it through the Symplegades—Athena the intellectual—has to admit failure. Having already admitted (18–21) to having thought hard about the problem (*meta phresin hormainousan*), and found no adequate scheme (*noeō; dolon*) although weighing numbers of ideas (*boulas*), she now replies, "Hera, father bore me to be ignorant of the weapons of love and I don't know any enchantment which awakens desire" (32–33). Set against the ensuing scene, the confession captures the Apollonian Athena perfectly: forthright and intelligent, she is no match in this particular narrative for the insinuating, smiling, duplicitous Aphrodite (51: "and smiling she addressed them with wheedling, flattering [*haimuloisi*] words"). The most telling image comes, however, when Eros gives Aphrodite his dice for safe-keeping before he descends from Olympus, "gathered up his dice, *counted them carefully*, threw them in his mother's lap" (154–55; my italics); no trust there! Somewhat later, when Argus also suggests enchanting Medea with love for Jason, a dove falls from the sky into Jason's lap (541–43) and its pursuer, an eagle, falls impaled upon a stern ornament of the ship. Mopsus recognizes the *meilikhos* bird (550) to be Aphrodite's. The omen, which is a kind of refrain of Athena's capitulation, is clear; it is time to make love, not war.

Apollonius describes Aphrodite at toilet, a time of self-glorification for any beautiful person as the love goddess is (white shoulders, long hair). She is in the process of combing her hair, one of the more narcissistic of human attitudes; the poet emphasizes this in describing her self-indulgently gathering it up in her hands (50). The three goddesses talk like elegant versions of the two vulgar parvenu women whom Theocritus so perfectly catches in dialogue in his fifteenth Idyll. Aphrodite is overcome that the two reigning queens of Olympus should come to her begging. When she hears their request for Eros, she commences a petulant mother's tirade against the ill-behaved disobedient teenager (which recalls Herondas' third mime "The Unruly Schoolboy") to which the other two smile and glance at one another (100–101). Aphrodite, annoyed at their condescension, replies in Apollonius' most naturalistic style: "To others my pain is a joke. Why do I have to tell everybody? It's enough I should know it myself." Hera takes her hand, and smiles to placate her. True to life and amusing as the banal scene is, several important psychological truths about love have been established: its narcissistic quality, its insinuating quality, the luxury of it, and most important the wayward, uncontrollable nature of desire (Eros) as it wars with the more intellectual, other-person-oriented emotion of love (Aphrodite).

The scene in which Aphrodite talks with Eros is one of the most splendid of the entire poem. Apollonius recalls every sensuous detail, every psychological nuance. Put together, it is the grand portrait of the emotion of love. The poet seems to want to treat Desire more as the emotion than the anthropomorphized figure, since after Eros shoots Medea and departs, references to Desire thereafter (for example, 452, 687, 765, 937) are in the plural, which encourages the notion of a characterless divine entourage or a psychological state. Eros and Ganymede are at dice; Eros, in the first roseate blush of post-pubescent sexual boyhood (121–22), holds his hand full of dice—he's winning. Greedy, the poet calls him, a natural attribute of desire. Beautiful Ganymede, silent and dejected, loses the last throw, stalks off in anger at Eros who laughs at him (the same word for Eros' laugh will be found 162 lines later when Eros laughs at the wounded Medea), victim and victor, seduced and seducer, one who gives, one who takes. Ganymede goes off, empty-handed and helpless (*amēkhanos* [126], the epithet so frequently applied to Jason). "Why do you smile?" asks Aphrodite of Eros. "Did you cheat him, overcome that innocent boy unjustly?" Love understands Desire.

Aphrodite offers Eros a beautiful ball. "Hephaestus will never make any-thing better" (135–36). Since lines 42–54 recall the shield scene in the eigh-teenth book of the *Iliad*, we are to understand that this ball is greater than that shield. Apollonius reinforces the irony as we involuntarily compare a second time, now more fully realized, the circumstances (tragic, cosmic) of Thetis' embassy and of this lovely lady in her pretty garden offering this darling, difficult child the ball. The irony does not ask us to dismiss this scene; rather, it reminds us that "real" life does not operate on the level of performance which Homer depicted.

The ball is the lure. With her description of it, Aphrodite enkindles eros in Eros. "He threw down all his pleasures (*meilia*) and took her gown in his hands on both sides without letting up, [and] begged her to give him the ball right away" (146–48). The important truth which Apollonius imparts is that Desire is an utterly self-serving emotion. Harsh and uncompromising, cynical, some will say, it is a conception at variance with the commonplace erotic attitude not only of Theocritus, but of the epigrams in the anthology as well. Love is the great discovery of the Hellenistic age; Apollonius has found its psychological measure.

The self-aggrandizement and bargaining of this scene are repeated in the minuet of muted passion in which Jason and Medea engage later in the book. Jason is Medea's golden ball. The poet never tires of telling us how handsome the lad is, how Medea's eyes cannot take him in sufficiently. As he goes to meet her the poet's eloquence becomes feverish. "Never yet among men of old, or those sprung from Zeus or from any of the other gods was there such a one to look upon or talk with as Hera had endowed Jason that day. Even his companions were amazed as they looked at him glittering with sexual attrac-tion (*lampomenon charitessin*)" (922–25).

Aphrodite needs Eros to enchant Medea. Jason needs Medea to enchant the bulls. His glowing sexuality suggests one thing, but he offers her fame in his statement to her (990–95). That is his idea of the golden ball. But Medea with her eyes fastened on Jason has other ideas. The subsequent dialogue is thoroughly amusing and, though touching, gently cynical. When he offers fame, Jason introduces the example of Ariadne (997–1004), who won eternal fame and divine favor for her aid to Theseus. The example, of course, has highly ambiguous implications. Jason mentions Ariadne's coming on board ship with Theseus and leaving her homeland, but omits to mention that Theseus callously left her on Naxos when he was able to give her the slip while she was sleeping (a fact of which Apollonius pointedly reminds us at 4.433–34). It would clearly not do in the present moment. Medea, who knows nothing of Ariadne's subsequent betrayal, naturally fastens on Ariadne's accompanying Theseus. She has been dreaming and worrying about betraying her father and what would happen to her.

Medea, like Eros, is greedy. Instead of fame, she wants a different golden ball. Unlike Nausicaa, who hints and then defers before the masterful, resistant Odysseus, Medea presses her point until she wins. The development of the passage implies that Medea is at the beginning unconscious of what she is doing. Apollonius like all of antiquity's masters of irony has established the truths in prologue, that is in the divine colloquy, so that the reader may discover the young girl's desires which are more or less veiled from herself as she speaks.

"Take the fleece and go away. Go *nevertheless* where you will" (my italics). That tell-tale "nevertheless" (*empēs*) marks her own opposition to his departure. She acts it out with tears, thinking of him gone, and then speaks to him face to face (*antēn*) and dropping all *aidos* takes his hand. Passive Jason must be trembling, but we do not know. This is Medea's great moment.

Remember me, she continues (1069) just like Nausicaa, enkindling no doubt some guilt in Jason's breast. For when he replies, he is fervent. "One thing I know all too well, I shall never forget you night or day." (1079–80). She had asked about his country, too, and also more about Ariadne, taking up homecoming and an accompanying maiden as a means to maneuver the conversation in the direction of her goal. Pressing her point still further, she points out to Jason that Aeetes is not the same as Minos, being untrustworthy and then ambiguously says (1107–8), "I can't compare myself to Ariadne"— which of course she has indeed done if only in negation. The persuasive rhetoric of these speeches is formidable. Then she hints more forcibly. "May a little bird come with a message to you when you forget me [planting a seed of guilt in Jason] or better still would that a swift wind would carry me across the sea to Iolcus so that I can reproach you for having forgotten that it was my aid which saved you [more guilt!]. Oh, if only I could be sitting in your great hall, a surprise guest!" By this point, we will have to admit that she knows exactly what she is doing.

She bursts into tears, and Jason is lost. "Forget winds and messenger birds! If you were to come to Hellas." So far, he is in the subjunctive mood and it is hypothetical, but he is clearly testing the water. He falls back on the subject of fame. Then suddenly in the indicative mood he takes the big plunge. "In our bridal chamber you will prepare the marriage couch. Nothing shall take our love away 'til death envelops us" (1128–30). No doubt Theseus gave similar assurances to Ariadne. For the moment, Medea has won. The victory, however, is bittersweet, darkening the humorous passage with somber overtones. "Her soul melted at what she heard him say. But then she shivered when she saw in her mind's eye what hideous deeds lay ahead" (1131–32).

These have been difficult days for Jason, for he has already had to try out his diplomatic skills on Medea's father; and father, just like daughter, had struck a hard bargain. The previous day had begun pleasantly enough, with an address by Jason to the crew (171–93). It is remarkable for its naïveté. He begins by emphasizing his reliance on them. "I'll tell you what I think best, but it's up to you to make it happen. We're in this together; everyone has the right to speak. He who keeps his ideas and plans to himself is only canceling out our chances of going home." Like Hera and Athena at a loss and staring at the ground, Jason is insecure. He is no leader from the traditional epic mold. One thinks of Odysseus' stern injunction to the reluctant warriors in the *Iliad* (2.190–205) when he talks about Agamemnon's primacy or Nestor's beginning his speech in council, "In thee Agamemnon I make my beginning and find my conclusion" (9.96–97). Part naïveté, part civilized behavior, young Jason is a very different person. If Aeetes refuses, then "we shall consider war or some other plan if we refrain from war" (183–84).

"Let us not try by force to take *his* fleece before we try with words. It is better to go first and placate him with speech" (my italics). Jason evidently chooses to ignore or has forgotten what Argus said about his grandfather (2.1202–6), although his emotion and that of his brothers (*estygon* [1196], *atembomenos* [1199]) must have been apparent. Even easygoing persons are generally loathe to give up trophies such as this fleece, which in fact Jason acknowledges to be Aeetes' property.

Jason launches into platitude. "Ofttimes you know, a word achieves easily what force can only accomplish with difficulty, soothing (*prēunas*) in whatever way it seems right." It was what he was doing (*kateprēunen* [1.265]) when first he appeared in the story. And he trusts to civilized convention. Aeetes received Phrixus pleasantly enough; everybody abides by the law of Zeus, god of hospitality (192–93).

Behind the naïveté stands the jingoist Greek, the heir to Isocrates' belief in the supremacy of Greek culture, which Alexander's armies brought throughout the East, or tried to bring. Alexandria, the city, was a Greek transplant in the vast, ancient Egyptian land. How little of Egyptian culture even penetrated the Greek consciousness! Jason, who will shortly be offering himself and the crew as a mercenary army to do Aeetes' fighting in the Hellenistic tradition, is like any Greek captain stranded in barbarian land. Xenophon's experiences are very much to the point. The civilized act, as Menander proclaimed, is Hellenistic.[7] When you are among wogs, keep your values. That is what Jason seems to be doing. Fränkel is charitable. "[Jason's plan] war moralisch korrekt, aber unrealistisch."[8] Apollonius makes clear just how silly the plan is in the laconic: "So he spoke; the young men approved the speech of Aeson's son with all speed. Nor was there anyone outside of the consensus (*parex*) who could urge another course." It is the young who approve. The old-timers keep silent just as Jason anticipated when he began speaking. And there is no one with the moral authority of Heracles to speak out.

But of course things go badly. Argus in fear speaks to his grandfather on behalf of Jason. The speech (320–66) delivered as usual *meilikhiōs* is a model of diplomatic persuasion. Aeetes reacts with insane, paranoiac rage, which Apollonius describes in five beautiful lines (367–71), then speaks. "If I'd known this before you were a guest at my table [you see, he *is* civilized; he reverences Zeus, god of hospitality, just as Jason imagined] I would have cut out your tongues, cut off your hands." The effect is hilarious, more so Jason's response, again with soothing words (385). In essence he says that he has been forced into it. He offers his services as a mercenary, and, curiously enough, promises that he will make Aeetes famous. "To the whole of Hellas I shall bring a marvelous report of you" (391–92). As we've noticed, Jason offers Medea fame as well. It is of course one of Jason's arguments in Euripides' *Medea*; presumably Apollonius is playing on it. Or the Greeks' obsession with their own superiority causes Jason to imagine that anyone in a backwater like Colchis wants a larger stage—but Chalciope, we remember, asked her errant sons, "Why should you go to this city of Orchomenus, whoever this Orchomenus is?" (265–66).

Jason spoke to the king in mild words, fawning, says Apollonius (*hypossainōn* [396]). The young prince's proud civility and gift for words has come to this. Polydeuces, we feel, had an easier time of it with Amycus. Aeetes meanwhile broods over his response; it is a parody of Jason's speech to the crew on violence and words. He ponders whether to kill Jason on the spot or make some test of his strength. Settling upon the latter course he delivers an ultimatum that is altogether honorable, however tricky: if Jason is really of divine descent, and for that reason intends to take others' property, then he must prove himself. Aeetes throws the idea of mercenary soldiering back at Jason. He has an *athlos* for Jason, and he describes the bulls and the pasture. He would not, he explains, become angry at noble men. For as Jason can plainly see, it would not be fitting for a man who was proved to be a fine man to yield to a weaker figure (*kakoterō*).

Throughout the narrative, Apollonius has managed to preserve the perfect balance between his ironic overview, his humorous perception of human action, and his sympathetic portrayal of human aspiration and failings. This passage is an example of that discretion. For the poet balances Jason's little-boy naïve pretentiousness with the hysterical paranoiac outburst which makes Aeetes a buffoon. In his last speech, however, Aeetes has spoken reasonably so that Apollonius is able to describe Jason's emotional and verbal response to it altogether sympathetically.

"He sat in silence just as he was, staring at his feet, without a word, helpless in his own weakness (*kakotēti*). For a long time he turned strategies around in his mind, but there was no way he could take up this contest with courage, since it seemed a big job. Finally, he made a reply and said with the hope of gaining some advantage (*kerdaleois*):

"'Aeetes, you know you've got me totally cornered with your argument about justice. So I will dare this contest—although I believe it to be over-whelming—even if it is my fate to die. Nothing which befalls a man is scarier than dread necessity, which in the form of a king's command was what made me come here in the first place.'"

At the crucial moment, Jason has simplicity and honesty. As he leaves the gathering, the poet notes that he shone out among all the assemblage in his beauty and sensual charm. He deserves saving and the poet is ready to introduce the plan of Medea's assistance. With that he begins his portrait of the princess.

The old myth told the story of the king's daughter who gave the fateful aid to the prince who was compelled to do her father's bidding. Betrayal such as that sent her out from her father's home, forever after forced to follow another's fortunes. What was this prince like who commanded such devotion? Who was this maiden who risked everything upon the newcomer to her father's house? Myths never tell, only the poets make human beings from the action of myth. By the third century, five hundred years of poetry had described the hero, the wandering man, the adventurer. However idiosyncratic or special Jason may be, he remains nonetheless a variation on a theme. Where Apollonius triumphs and is most daringly original is in his creation of Medea, the first fully realized, complex, utterly sympathetic and—finally and most importantly—heroic female figure to appear in Greek literature.

The first and last times (3.27; 4.1677) when the poet affixes an epithet to Medea's name, it is *polypharmakon*, "versed in many drugs or charms." That is how the poet of the *Odyssey* describes Medea's aunt the witch Circe (*Odyssey* 10.276). Medea is in the service of the dread infernal goddess Hecate (compare the association between Medea and Hecate in Euripides' *Medea*, 395–98). This deity is another version of the common Great Mother Goddess figure so ubiquitous in the Mediterranean area. The description of Nature lavishing her treasures when the goddess Rhea is propitiated in the first book (1140–45) is a common manifestation of the Mother Goddess figure. In many areas of Greece, Hecate's worshippers credited her with every manner of life-saving skills beyond the central fact of her importance for reproduction and fertility. These last make her important to the earth; hence, she became associated with the dead who, like seeds, are laid into the earth.

She is therefore a counterpart of Artemis, with whom she is often associated; in effect, she is the other face of Artemis. Crossroad statues often had three faces which are taken to be Hecate, Artemis, and Selene (the moon, with which she was also associated). She is queen of the ghosts who congregate at crossroads, where she was thought sometimes to appear looking like one of the Erinyes, dread female figures of wrath and revenge, with whip and hounds. Medea's association with this figure lends mystery to the little-girl innocence of the virgin princess. It poses an unpredictable and potentially frightening side to her nature, as though she, too, were Artemis and Hecate combined. She has powers and presumably with them attitudes which do not properly belong to a teenaged girl. The poet underscores the association by reminding us of it often, when it is otherwise unimportant to the plot. When Jason first meets her, for instance, they come upon Medea going from room to room in search of her sister; and the poet adds parenthetically that Hera had kept her at home away from the temple of Hecate, where as priestess she usually busied herself (250–52). And considering the terms in which Argus first describes Medea to Jason, it is a wonder that the young man has the courage to meet with her alone ("she can stop rivers . . . stay the course of the moon and the stars" [532–33]).

This seeming Dr. Jekyll-Mr. Hyde complexity of Medea is a problem for critics who wish to maintain the princess in their imaginations simply as an innocent, as love's victim.[9] But Apollonius has done the same thing with Jason, setting him up as heroic, giving him the phrases and some of the actions required for heroism, but at the same time showing Jason's utter incapacity for the heroic. He means neither to make Jason a weakling, nor Medea a witch; rather, he is exploring stresses and capacities, conflicting tendencies in the two major sympathetic figures which deepen and complicate their personalities and hence their interaction. Because Apollonius also has a sense of humor and a well-developed sense of the absurd, he delights in startling juxtapositions of the kind we find in such modern novelists as Nabokov.

By Apollonius' day, the traditional, epic manner of creating monolith character through stereotypes had effectively collapsed, together with the formulaic manner of narration characteristic of the oral period. The tendency toward caricature which extends from tragic personalities through Theophrastus' *Characters* is a legacy of the epic way of building from type. The only really subtle portrayal of personality before the third century is to be found in the pages of Thucydides, whose Cleon, Alcibiades, and Nicias, especially, are complicated, as we know human beings to be.

But Apollonius goes far beyond this, creating something truly new. He builds opposing conventional types and combines them into one person. The effect is to portray more probable human beings, fluid personalities in a state of tension. Read by the conventions of traditional Greek narrative, the ambivalence, indeed ambiguity, which proceeds from these figures is completely upsetting. More than anything else, the portrayal of character is a departure from the literary tradition from which Apollonius springs. Virgil was clearly impressed by this experiment because he attempted to imbue Aeneas with equally powerful ambivalences, making him both an impetuous, high-hearted warrior and an unwilling melancholic servant of a burdensome destiny. Apollonius is the more successful, because he has managed to distance himself from his characters by his irony, his humor, his perversities. Virgil, by contrast, believes so fervently in Aeneas that he makes it almost impossible for the reader to accept Aeneas' shortcomings.

The complicated personalities which Apollonius has contrived prepare the way for the great psychological truth of the fourth book, that is, the disappointment of love. As modern psychologists often point out, love relationships go sour when either or both partners begin to feel cheated because their mate does not fulfill their expectations. It is also often noted that a person tends to marry the kind of personality which will complement and make complete his or her own. Here in the *Argonautica* we have, on the face of it, a conventional hero and a conventional young princess but, as we know, the other side of Jason is inordinate insecurity and weakness, whereas Medea has unusual power and strains of temperament. The latter is not demonstrated in the third book, but we may extrapolate it from the Hecate association. Read Theocritus' second Idyll, which is the monologue of a woman whose lover has forsaken her for another. Its extreme passion is atypical of Theocritus. Burning with the fury of the betrayed, the woman calls on Hecate (12), mentions Medea, and delivers a ritual incantation accompanied by magical rites and potions which will draw the errant creature back to her side. From the point of view of a male whose sexual allegiances are in the best of times tenuous, the grim determination of this female speaker is frightening. And indeed Medea's ferociousness in her arguments to Jason in the fourth book betoken a violent temperament. The young princess consciously wants the strong young prince to ride in out of nowhere and snatch her up. That's what Medea thinks she has got. But unconsciously the dominant woman wants a manipulable male. When Medea discovers that *that* is what she has got, it's too late. Jason wants a pretty young thing *he* can dominate. That's how he behaves toward Medea in their love scene. Only later aboard ship does he discover she is the powerful, inherently domineering woman his subconscious sought against his will.

The Hecate aspect to Medea works with the Hades associations in the voyage of the second book. Jason is going on a momentous voyage in this poem into another realm, a portentous place. That is what the poet means to say about love, not pastoral love which only scratches the surface itch of eroticism, not homosexual love which merely reaffirms the mechanisms in the lover, but deep self-abnegating passion for the other sex. Where it may start as attraction and move on to desire, there comes a moment when one can lose oneself, just as Hylas literally lost himself, pulled into the pool. This is a male's point of view, particularly one who has real fear of women.

Epic poetry in particular, Greek culture in general, at least as it was limned by males, was misogynistic, or in any case fearful of women. The voyage into the Hades-like environment, the infernal princess waiting in the castle of the dread king (we must not forget Jason's walk to the palace past the rows of hanging corpses, 200–203), these are mysterious, frightening elements which give to Jason's progress the sense that it is irreversible, like death itself. There is no way for Jason to turn back. We may note his obsession with going home. For instance, instead of asking Phineus about the fleece, he only wants to know about the *nostos*. Going home will have to be different, for on this voyage Jason is coming to know a woman.

Once his virginity, his innocence, is gone, Jason cannot have it back again. This is equally true for Medea, but the poet is presenting the story from Jason's point of view, partly because he is nominally the central figure. A woman's marriage and departure from home is obviously irrevocable, another rite of passage, already an irreversible process on the physical level; the male's union with a woman is only irrevocable psychologically.

Still Apollonius gives Medea one of the great scenes of the third book, in which she wrestles with and overcomes her feelings of guilt at betraying her father for a lover. The passage is important, because Medea is shown to be more active and decisive than Jason is anywhere. The result is to constitute her as a hero, at least equivalent to Jason in the narrative. Jason does not have a shadow figure companion like Achilles' Patroclus on this voyage. Even Hera does not accompany him as Athena accompanies Odysseus. The crew does not interact with him as Odysseus' crew does. Peculiarly enough, for all the vivid characterization of his crew, Jason is quite alone. Into this void emerges Medea who develops in the fourth book into Jason's absolute equal, if not superior, in power, energy, and daring.

The instinct to domesticate heroism is a distinctly Hellenistic attitude. Apollonius gave the tiniest hint of things to come when he added Chiron's wife, holding baby Achilles, next to the traditional tutor of heroes in the first book's departure scene. Who ever considered the possibility that Chiron was married? Who ever paused to give credit to the anonymous female who must have been changing Achilles' diapers and feeding him his porridge?

Medea's moral travail is expressed in the three monologues of this book. Like Achilles' three great refusals in the ninth book of the *Iliad*, which grow increasingly equivocal in their denunciation of the request made of him, Medea says no while she means yes, gradually weakening until she finishes by agreeing to aid the stranger. That there are *three* monologues gives the passage the fairy-tale sense of having made the enchanting, transforming decision. Medea begins by telling herself that she does not want to get involved, but that she does not want to see the stranger hurt (464–70). The second monologue is provoked by a dream in which she sees what is indeed the underlying truth of the poem, that the fleece is somehow symbolic of her virginity, and Aeetes' anger at losing the fleece is a father's anger at losing his daughter to another man (619–31). The poet dramatizes this by describing Aeetes' agitated speech in council held because of his suspicious nature far from the palace (577) in which the king reiterates the Oedipal theme of his grandson's betrayal (594–97) and ends by proclaiming that he had not the least fear of his daughters, typical of all those comic theater fathers whose daughters are plotting with their lovers on the other side of the stage.

In the second monologue (636–44), Medea determines to remain a virgin, hoping that the stranger will woo some Greek girl—entirely ignoring the fact that Jason has not yet cast a glance in her direction. We may remember however the steamy sexuality of very young persons which no doubt operated that day in the great courtyard in Aeetes' palace when Eros drew his bow and shot the arrow. In the third monologue (772–801) she wishes he would die and asks for her own death. Once having divorced action from its consequences by allowing herself the luxury of suicide, she proceeds to contemplate helping the stranger, betraying her parents, and losing her reputation in a series of rhetorical questions which have no answer.

This internal struggle is accompanied by physical and emotional behavior which Apollonius describes in considerable detail. The poet uses Medea's bedroom as the place of her virginity. She cannot leave the room to offer aid to Chalciope's sons. Three times—again the magical three!—she tries and then falls crying on her bed. It is her sister who must come to her. The poet compares Medea to a newly widowed bride whose husband has died before they have had intercourse (660–61), whose embarrassment over her manifest newly aroused desire causes her to shun her companions. Medea herself is aroused by the stranger and fearful that he will die. The simile probes further; it is Medea's subconscious that contemplates the gratification of her aroused carnality. Finally after the third monologue, she takes the casket filled with magical charms and deliberates whether to destroy herself. When she tells herself no, the decision has been made. In effect, then, she is offering herself to the stranger, since helping him will cause an irrevocable rupture with her father. In ancient Greek culture, a woman can only pass from the protection of one man to another. So it will be the stranger, and she will lose her virginity. Apollonius describes her constantly unbolting the door of this virginal chamber as she awaits the dawn (822).

The physical agony of desire (well described at 761–65), the vacillations (compare the simile comparing her heart to dancing light reflected from a pail of water, 756–59), together with the burden of decision, are the outgrowth of that poignant moment (284) when first her heart was struck with love for Jason. And Eros laughed. Apollonius immediately (291–95) compares Medea's growing love to a flicker of flame growing from enkindled twigs. What adds poignancy, however, is the detail that it is a woman who lights the fire—"a hardworking woman who starts the fire in the darkness, for she has roused herself very early"—in effect, the poet draws attention to Medea's plight, which now begins as it does for any woman who falls in love, namely, a life of dependency and bondage. The poet returns to the image in a simile in the fourth book (4.1062) where the woman is now toiling at night. Medea's burden of love which began in the dawn of that innocent day of Jason's arrival is still with her as she has to fight not to be rejected by the very man for whom she gave up her own life (4.1031–52).

Before Jason can enter the field of Ares to master the magic bulls of Aeetes, he must subdue Medea to his will. It is almost a preliminary *aristeia*. Apollonius suggests it in the lines (919–26) describing Jason's setting out. They convey the grandeur of any traditional epic hero's entrance into battle, except that *kallos* and *kharitas* replace *menos*. As the young man closes with Medea, the poet likens him to Sirius (957–59), the simile which describes Diomedes' entry into battle in the *Iliad* (5.5). Past associations from the first book convert Jason's arrival for the assignation into a military advance. Then, too, the *Odyssey* poet has elevated the tension of that electric moment when the young innocent Nausicaa stands her ground as the naked Odysseus advances upon her by employing formulae typical in battle narrative.

The poet describes Medea's preparations for this event so as to be able to present the fundamental ambiguity of the young girl. She dresses herself and calls for the horses (829–43), then draws the charm from the cask, which Apollonius describes in detail (844–66). The charm derives from the blood dripping from the liver of Prometheus which the ravening eagle carried from his body. Medea gathered it after taking ritual baths and calling on Brimo the night wanderer, queen of the dead, in the middle of the gloomy night as she goes garbed in dark clothing. This grim item "she then places in the perfumed band which encircled her body just under her ambrosial bosom" (867–68).

There ensues a drive to the temple distinctly reminiscent of Nausicaa's drive to the beach, including the simile comparing Medea to Artemis. Her girlish pleasures and those of her companions are spiked by her revelation to them finally that she has a meeting with the stranger. "Girls, I have made a great mistake and completely overlooked the fact that we ought not to be out abroad today with all those strange men who are wandering around. The whole city is turned upside down. You notice no woman who ordinarily comes to the temple is here today" (891–95). With those words, Apollonius shows that Medea in her own way has the courage of Nausicaa. In a society where

virgin girls are kept in virtual seclusion, naturally none would go out un-
chaperoned, unprotected with fifty sailors on shore leave. Jason speaks to that
the minute he opens his mouth (975–78). "Why, young lady, do you stand
in such awe of me when I am all alone?" Which is to say, he will not hurt her
or rape her; there is no gang here. He continues, "I am not one of those nasty
braggarts, never was even at home," by which he must mean the kind who
force unprotected girls and then talk of it in the tavern. It is amusing and at
the same time sad to note, however, that Apollonius describes Medea going
home in a daze and saying nothing to Chalciope, whereas Jason goes imme-
diately to the waiting Argus and Mopsus, "telling them each detail" (1165).
What Medea treats so seriously, what is so momentous to her, seems less
consequential to Jason.

Medea continues to manipulate her attendants. "Since we're here and no
one approaches, let us take pleasure in song. . . ." Without preamble, she
then proceeds to bribe her attendants shamelessly. "You will take home many
gifts today, if you are complacent with this desire of mine" (900–911). She
then tells them of the meeting, and alludes to the gifts again. The only gift
Jason will bestow in fact is a marriage proposal. She in effect is lying to her
attendants to gain their compliance; we are reminded of Nausicaa's entirely
contrasting candor.

Jason goes to the temple in the company of Mopsus and Argus, in a kind
of parody of the embassy to Achilles when Odysseus, Phoenix, and Ajax went
along the beach to the isolated hero's tent to get him to return to battle and
save the day. But this is not heroic epic, nor oral poetry where everything is
expressed externally and before witnesses.[10] Apollonius introduces a talking
crow who like any yenta on the block gives advice. A seer ought to know
what any child knows, that no young girl will say a word of love when there
are others present.[11] The talking crow was a feature of the *Hecale* of Callima-
chus; the language here has affinities with Callimachus' *Hymn to Apollo*. It
would be nice to believe that Apollonius was paying homage to his teacher
here, acknowledging him as the grand master of propriety in the Hellenistic
literary scene.

The scene is indeed an erotic one beginning with the immediate sensual
reaction which two young people provoke in each other. This Apollonius
captures in the most elegant simile of the poem, a Sapphic reminiscence (frag-
ment 47 [Lobel and Page]), its very simplicity suggesting the *elemental* erotic
forces being set in motion. "So the two of them stood there face to face
without a word uttered, like oaks or tall pines which are rooted in the moun-
tains side by side, still, when there is no wind; but then when the wind
comes, stirred by it, they murmur, ceaselessly" (967–71).

A little bit later (1008–25), Apollonius has a description of the lovers'
physical reaction to each other's presence, in the tradition of Sappho's cele-

brated description of her body's reaction to seeing and hearing her lover. In the midst of this ecstasy, Medea withdraws the charm from her bodice and hands it to Jason (1013–14). The exaggerated pleasure with which he receives it, the love which it excites, her mounting ecstasy and wish to give more transform this transaction into some metaphysical sexual intercourse. In this way the poet manages to achieve the combination of a number of important ideas. The charm is given in seduction; Medea loses her virginity (figuratively, of course) which makes her slightly veiled marriage demands all the more cogent.

Jason again meets, in intercourse, with the woman who will overcome him. For directly after this scene, Medea gives him instructions on how to use the charm, and shortly thereafter he is described preparing himself. Granted, the ostensible purpose is to charm the bulls; still, the preparations suggest a momentous transformation in Jason. He strips, and in the very dark of night immerses himself in a pool. Thereafter Hecate appears, described in her entourage with many of the same details encountered in the Artemis simile (876–80), as though she were the true infernal counterpart to the Medea-Nausicaa-Artemis concatenation. The passage reminds one, too, of Hylas' nighttime disappearance into the pond. Jason's immersion is a kind of baptism which changes him forever. The presence of the charm in this powerful description of sexual excitement endows the erotic scene with something menacing and fatal.

Like Odysseus, who approached Nausicaa speaking soothing words which would gain him his ends (*meilikhioisi, kerdaleon* [*Odyssey* 6.146, 148]), Jason took his glamour to the temple of Hecate and spoke as a practiced courtier, as Apollonius remarks, "fawning" (974). He got what he wanted, but he paid a price. And that is what love is all about.

Jason's meeting with Medea has the climactic tension of an *aristeia*. But the poet gives him yet another, truer to the epic tradition. In the nineteenth book of the *Iliad*, Achilles makes his peace with Agamemnon, girds himself up for battle (19.364–98), takes up the new shield which his mother Thetis had besought Hephaestus to make for him, and ascends his chariot, ready to return to battle. His *aristeia*, the longest in the *Iliad*, fills the ensuing three books, ending in his killing of Hector and the Trojan lamentation over that fallen hero. In the manner of oral poetry Homer has rehearsed this event many times in the poem, but particularly in the *aristeia* of Diomedes in the fifth and sixth books of the poem. Now at last comes the fulfillment of the heroic promise of Achilles' *aretē* while at the same time he reaches out for his own death. His mother had told him that he had the choice of peaceful but inglorious old age away from the battlefield, or a glorious youthful death while fighting the foe. Now by returning to fight he has made his choice. It is a solemn and fatal moment. As in a fairy tale, his immortal horses disclaim responsibility for saving him any longer from the fate which surely lies before him (408–17).

Jason's *aristeia* begins with Telamon and Aethalides going off to Aeetes to secure the dragon's teeth which he must sow to produce the monster men whose cutting down is half the contest imposed on him. Apollonius seems to have combined a story of physical strength—yoking the bulls—with a story of the dragon slayer. For the motif of the dragon's teeth comes from the Theban saga in which Cadmus came to the site of Thebes and slew a dragon who guarded the well. At Athena's command he sowed the teeth, and there sprang up magical men. The Scholiast at 3.409 tells us that Antimachus, the fifth-century author of *Lyde*, had mentioned the bronze bulls. Apollonius probably introduced the dragon's teeth. What was his motive? They are the teeth of the dragon of Thebes, slain by Cadmus. Yet they associate Jason with the killing of the serpent at Colchis, although in fact the serpent is subdued by Medea's magic. Here in the *aristeia*, as Jason sows the dragon's teeth, the reader's knowledge of the prototypical dragon-slaying story makes him anticipate a similar feat with the serpent-monster guarding the golden fleece. Jason's battle on the field of Argus gains a kind of extension by association into that episode. Furthermore, the reader associates Jason with Cadmus. It makes Jason's *aristeia* the more momentous and decisive, for Cadmus' victory had to do with gaining a throne, founding a city, a great marriage, a divine friendship. [12]

Of course, it is magic and a woman's help that wins the *aristeia*. From the start, some of the crew are opposed. Peleus had been ready to sacrifice himself in a fight (511–14), and several others had volunteered. But Argus suggests Medea, and with his customary tact urges patience, not exactly an heroic virtue (523–28). The omen of the dove and hawk silences the opposition, however, except for Idas. "To hell with you all," he shouts sarcastically (562–63). "Just ignore war, and turn all your attention to pleading with defenceless girls and seducing them." Apollonius, as before, makes Idas tell the truths. The ensuing response is amusing, as Jason fills an awkward silence with a fictive show of martial valor.

"So he spoke passionately; there was lots of mumbling from the comrades, but no one spoke out a word in opposition to him. So he in his fury sat down. Then Jason in an attempt to encourage everyone suggested this plan, 'Let Argus proceed from the ship, then, since it seems like a good idea to all of you [he continues by suggesting that they move the ship from the cove] for surely it is not fitting for us to hide it any longer, cowering here in the face of battle.'" Now that nothing will be decided by simple human strength, Jason can introduce this braggadocio as a sop to their vanities.

The conventional Homeric *aristeia* begins with a stereotypic description of arming; the items donned, their order, and the language used to describe this do not vary from passage to passage. Apollonius only alludes to the conventional pattern, but not in fact for describing the arming of Jason, but King Aeetes. He follows this with a simile comparing the king as he comes out on the field of Ares with the god Poseidon (1240–45). The simile is unusual for the *Argonautica* since it is a commonplace Homeric type without the customary Apollonian details of space or grouping which give visual perspective. Poseidon belongs to the older, sterner generations of gods; his was the anger which blocked Odysseus' return for so many years. These associations are part of this scene. Although Aeetes is not actually come to fight, these two Homeric reminiscences establish the king as the conventional force or power to whom Jason has been contrasted so often in this poem.

Jason's arming, or what passes for it, indeed, very much in contrast, has already been described by Apollonius. In addition to the fateful and mysterious bath, the invocation of Hecate, and her epiphany, the poet says that Jason went through the night like a thief (1197), and after his bath, wrapped his naked body in a cloak given him by Hypsipyle, "a reminder of their constant lovemaking (*hadinēs mnēmeion eunēs*)" (1204–6). The reference to the thief acts as some kind of judgment upon the proceedings, and the mention of the cloak defines the aspect. It is as though the nighttime preparations were that moment when Jason sells his soul to the Devil to gain the victory he so desperately needs.

The literature of the classical period did not emphasize free will; therefore, the matter of moral choice was to some extent problematical. But later, explicitly moral formulations such as the choice of Heracles, between Virtue and Vice, or the deliberations of Socrates as they are presented in the *Apology* and the *Crito*, or the decision of Orestes and Electra to kill Helen in Euripides' *Orestes*, show a turn to the morally fateful choice, the act of free will. The second and third books of the *Argonautica* show this later perspective, posing matters in terms of good and evil. That is the sense of the Amycus-Polydeuces contest, the triumph of light, goodness, and youth which gives a thematic coloration to subsequent events such as the pursuit of the Harpies and the freeing of Phineus by the Boreades, and then the frightening journey past the land of the Mariandyni. Here in the third book, Jason's alliance with magic becomes less innocent. In contrast to the description of conventional arming and the conventional simile applied to Aeetes, the poet turns Jason's alliance through the allusions to thief and the love cloak into something sinister, dangerous, perverse, morally dubious. It echoes the rebuke of Idas so many lines earlier.

The rebuke serves to point up the alternatives from which Jason must choose. Trapped as he may be by Aeetes, he deliberately chooses to solicit Medea's aid. Apollonius does not emphasize the workings of fate or gods. True enough, Jason and Medea's compact comes about as a concomitant or consequence of their love; and mankind is a slave to love. Yet the poet does not describe Jason as passion's thrall, and he so thoroughly depicts Medea's interior struggles at making a decision that we believe her to be capable of choice. This is surely one of the most powerful features of Apollonius' narrative. He has chosen to create complicated major characters, bestowing upon them any number of undignified weaknesses; but he makes them strong by giving them far more free will than classical literature generally acknowledged in human character.

6

Love Affair

In every book of his poem, Apollonius has experimented with the narrative form. In the fourth book, once again, he is innovative and perhaps at his most original. Within the first sixty-five lines, the poet manages to establish Medea so firmly into the center of the narrative that the poem thereafter becomes the adventure story of the couple rather than Jason's enterprise. Epic adventure stories traditionally featured the hero and his friend. This shadow figure, analogue, alter ego, whatever we call him, is unmistakably the hero's inferior, in physique (Gilgamesh pins Enkidu when they wrestle), in psyche (Achilles gives instructions to Patroclus), in imagination (Odysseus has to force his crew, a kind of composite companion figure, to go with him to investigate strange places). In no instance has the hero had to share the audience with his companion. Male traveling companions display this character-istic disparate valence throughout Western literature. Apollonius' male-female couple is a change from that, introducing a new relationship of absolute equality which, too, has had its successive reincarnations down into our own time.

The change in the balance of the action in the *Argonautica* was begun by the poet in the third book's initial meeting between Jason and Medea. Whereas the demonstrably impassioned girl might have been conceived in the simplest conventional terms as another female figure, the victim of innocence, of love, and finally of Jason, the poet chose to represent her daring in the way she went to the assignation at the temple, her courage in willingness to betray her father, her power as a sorceress, and finally her strength of character in negotiating a marriage for herself with Jason. If we compare that scene to the wrestling match between Enkidu and Gilgamesh, it is fair to say that Medea emerges from that exchange with Jason very much his formidable equal.

As we have noted before, the poet fashions a seamless fabric of narrative between the third and fourth books by continuing the story line by means of the most intimate and instinctive of connections, the pronoun. He last mentions Aeetes at 3.1404–6. Seven lines later, at 4.6, the poet identifies him only as "he" ("he all night long was pondering"). At the same time, this narrative monolith is fractured by the simple, conclusive line—"The day closed, and his contest was ended"—of the third book and the apostrophe to the Muse which fills the first five lines of the fourth. Here the poet asks the Muse to tell him of Medea and explain her motives for leaving Colchis. In this way the poet carves out from his story line the form of a book at its beginning.

The principal achievement of the formal fact of the fourth book, defining as it does a part of the narrative, is to bring the focus squarely around to Medea. It is suddenly her going out, her voyage, her adventure. To underscore the new importance of Medea, the poet returns to her powers and courage in the Talos episode (1638–88), the last adventure, the last test of strength in the fourth book, the last, for that matter, of the entire poem. And as these sixty-five lines reveal, Medea is an exceedingly complex person. What emerges is the presentiment of the tragic figure, hints of the woman who Medea will become in the Euripidean conception of the betrayed wife.

"Tell me, Muse, of the Colchian maiden's travail (*kamaton*) and of her plans/ counsels (*dēnea*)," asks the poet, thereby immediately establishing the duality of his conception of Medea. She will suffer, but she can also manipulate and command. "Was it the pain caused by this unfortunate love affair which confounded her (*atēs pēma dyshimeron*)," continues the poet, reinforcing her passion and victimization, "or did she turn face and flee (*aeikeliēn phygan*)?" This latter, however undignified, is nontheless the act of a strategist.

The phrase for retreat in the Greek has a military connotation. Apollonius continues the idea into the next line (6). "Aeetes was plotting with men of his country, the best men (*hossoi aristoi*)." This last phrase recalls us to the epic military mentality, foreshadows the long pursuit by the Colchians, and the eventual strategic necessity which compels Medea to murder her brother. Medea's eventual significance in the action is focused here in the smallest ways, in, for instance, Apollonius' clever progression in "Aeetes was plotting against *them* [the heroes]," "nor did he imagine that these things had been done without his *daughters*," and "into *her* heart Hera put fear" (in this instance the fear is prudence, the restatement of her instinct to retreat).

"She trembled as does a swift fawn secreted in a deep thicket whom the uproar of dogs frightens" (12–13) perfectly evokes the still of the night in which the young girl lies terrified in her *thalamos* (women's room) listening to the sound of angry men's voices floating in at the window. Men will hunt her down, too. Although she is a victim, like the fawn, Apollonius chooses this moment to recall us to her earlier daring—"She feared the knowledge which her maiden companions possessed"—and we remember that they were witnesses to her secret meeting with Jason, made accomplices by her false hints of gifts (3.891–911). Again, she contemplates suicide, as she had when love first came to her (compare 3.806), but, as the poet declares (20), Medea will not be allowed to thwart the plans of Hera. Suddenly this passive, suffering, vulnerable, would-be suicide becomes the malevolent agent of Hera. The overarching motive, the grand purpose of this entire narrative, surfaces here for a brief moment. Pelias was to beware the sandaled man, Jason, but it is not that Jason will be an active agent in his destruction, but because he will return with Medea, the naïve girl child turned adventurer, murderer, and desperado. Whatever feelings this may arouse in the reader, the poet will bring Hera back into the narrative again in this book with the forecast of Medea's marriage with Achilles, a kind of poetic absolution for our heroine.

Medea rejects suicide and prepares to leave the room. Like the suicide itself, the leave-taking is a doublet of her action in Book Three (645–55) as she anguished over helping the stranger. The poet repeats details here from the third book, as though to emphasize that the future which she there foresaw and which caused her such torture and self-doubt seems now to be coming to pass. The description—kissing the bed, the doors, stroking the walls—is a tragic *topos* of departure, usually for married women, not maidens.[1] Alcestis leaving her room (Euripides, *Alcestis* 175–95) is a particularly memorable scene of this genre. It invests Medea's departure with a tragic foreboding. The girl herself senses it. "Would that the sea had smashed you before you got to Colchis, stranger," she says, echoing her sentiments at 3.774–77. Now wiser, she asks for his death whereas before she yearned for her own. The description is a splendid farewell to girlhood; the event and its description are so momentous that the reader is invited or instructed to place it beside Jason's leave-taking, and hence to see it for what it is, Medea's embarkation, a going out which parallels Jason's, making her his equal in adventure.

Thereafter her progress to the waiting ship again parallels his own, except that it is all ironic. She flees under cover of the night. Apollonius compares her to an indentured servant fleeing a cruel mistress. The image will come back the moment when Apsyrtus has closed upon Medea, and Jason raises the spector of her being led back as a captive (400). With swift strokes, Apollonius sends the reader back and forth between the two strains in Medea's rich and complex character. "She rushed along on bare feet . . . holding a veil over her pretty cheeks with her left hand . . . holding up her hem with her right" (43–46). The delicacy and pathos fade in: "she had hitherto wandered this way in search of corpses . . . as sorceresses are in the habit of doing" (51–53). In the very same line (53), as if to emphasize the complexity of his heroine, he adds, "her heart (*thymos*) shook with quivering fear."

No crowd of onlookers murmurs at her advent such as Jason and his Argonauts had encountered. Instead, the moon looks down, solitary witness to Medea's excursion; the poet in his most ironical manner gives the moon a conventional speech on love agony. It is terror which grips Medea now, not love's pangs. The agonies which she will suffer in the days ahead are the pangs of love betrayed and love dulled. Silly moon, she belongs in the erotic poems of the *Anthology*.

The parallelism continues throughout the fourth book. Principally, there are parallels with the cataloguelike travel narrative of the second book. For instance, the seer Mopsus dies bitten by a venomous snake (1502–36), paralleling the death of the seer Idmon who was gored by a boar. The poet even contrives doublets in each instance. Tiphys dies directly after Idmon in the second book, victim of some undescribed sickness. Here Canthus dies directly before Mopsus (1485–1501) of a head wound from a stone thrown by a shepherd whose sheep he was rustling—as undistinguished a way for a hero to die as in his sickbed.

Argus is a parallel for Phineus in the fourth book. The old man had told the Argonauts that the return journey would be different from the one coming out (2.421). Directly after a sacrifice to Hecate and perhaps by her divine prompting, Argus starts up with a detailed account of this *nostos* or homecoming (257–93). Since Argus is not a prophet, Apollonius has to establish his *bonae fides* first. This he does through a long account by Argus of an early time when an Egyptian king, much traveled, left records which generations maintained of various voyages throughout all the mysterious parts of the world. Since the Colchians are descendants of Egyptian colonists, the writings were preserved there and known to Argus. At the same time, the vision of this prehistorical time (261–71) when Danaeans did not exist, when there were only Arcadians eating acorns, who lived, as Argus says, before there was a moon (264–65) and Egypt was mysterious and called Ēeriē, "Morningland," has that faraway quality which is consonant with the vague geography of the distant lands through which the Argonauts will travel. It fits also with the notice of the passage of the *Argo* past peoples who have never seen a ship before (317) and the description of Circe's creatures, who are monster animals only just starting on the path of evolution.

The voyage across the Euxine to the Ister River, as the Danube was called in antiquity, is clear enough. The Ister was thought to rise from the Ocean which encircles the world and go through subterranean passageways until surfacing in present-day Romania where it divided, one branch emptying into the Euxine, and the other crossing above the Balkans and issuing into the Adriatic at the peninsula called Istria. It was only through the conquests of the Romans under the Empire that any accurate knowledge of the Danube was acquired.[2] Hence Apollonius was relatively free to be as fanciful as he liked, but only relatively, since the Hellenistic world spawned a host of geographers who had definite ideas about the route taken by the Argonauts.

The Scholia to our text show how radical Apollonius was.[3] Although Argus does not tell them, they will subsequently enter the Po (called Eridanus in the *Argonautica*) until they reach the Rhone. Today we know that this is not actually possible, but then Apollonius could play freely with the uncharted regions. The Rhone deposits the Argonauts in what is now the Italian Riviera where they proceed down the coast of Italy through the Straits of Messina and east to Corcyra (modern Corfu), thence to the area of Africa which is present-day Tunisia and finally back north to the place from which they started.

It is not that Apollonius has created an absurdity; rather, by using very little-known, little-understood places in his itinerary, he makes the voyage fantastic. The voyage of the first and second books is mostly through well-known territory. The ever-present *aitia*, the descriptions in the present tense, establish the veracity of the narration. The *nostos* of the fourth book, on the other hand, is altogether mysterious. On the voyage out, Apollonius plays real places against fantasy heroes. By fantasy, I mean that the poet makes them act out or respond to the epic conventions of heroic endeavour and to the traditional Argonaut myth. On the voyage back, Apollonius plays fantasy places against real people, a man and a woman who have been made to step forth from their myth after the fashion of Euripides' seriocomic plays to act out the implications of their initial archetypal behavior.

There is a formal departure scene (190–240) which recalls the initial departure from Iolcus (1.519–79). It contains a peculiar exhortation by Jason which marks it as a beginning: "now we hold the fate of our children, our aged parents and our dear country in our hands; all Hellas has a stake in our venture, either to be cast down in failure or to win great fame" (202–4). The anachronism of the utterance makes it hard to understand. The Alexandrians had well-developed historical imaginations. It is hard to believe that they would not have reflected that the heroes came from a wide range of places in the Greek mainland; that they were not part of a common country which was just beginning to be understood in Apollonius' time. No epic hero ever thought of country, of Hellas, although one might argue that Hellas is simply meant to be an anachronistic reflection of the fact of Greek civilization as opposed to the barbarian world which Aeetes must represent.

One is not sure of Apollonius' tone here.[4] These brave and bold words can be read as vainglorious and ridiculous when once it is clear that no battle follows them.[5] The Argonauts simply set to and row down the Phasis River and out to the sea, past Aeetes waving in impotent rage upon the riverbank. Again, it seems to be a parallel to the first book where Jason's heroic stance does not match heroic action. But it is not clear that Apollonius means to be amusing here, since in general he keeps to a serious tone in his narration throughout the fourth book. Perhaps the seriousness with which he treats Medea does not extend to Jason.

Jason, when he has finished what amounts to preliminary remarks to a battle charge (and the word translated as venture, *ephormē*, is better understood as "charge") is said to put on his armor of war while the crew shouts eagerly, full of wonderful enthusiasm (206–7). He then draws his sword to cut the ship's cable. However modest the act relative to the inflated preparations, it has important symbolic value.

The passage formalizes the conflicts which will dominate the narrative until finally Medea and Jason are married. In a sense, the battle is joined. For Aeetes is also described as appearing at the water's edge in full battle dress. The Colchians are there, countless as leaves falling from a tree, a ghostly image used by Bacchylides (5.65–67) which Virgil took over to describe the spirits of the underworld (*Aeneid*, 6.309–10) and Dante used again (*Inferno* 3.112–16). The menace of their numbers is increased in the simile which closes the departure passage. The Colchians set sail in pursuit, to which the poet says that "one would not say that this great expedition was a fleet of ships, but rather a flock of birds in flight endless, sounding out over the sea" (239–40). The image of birds in migration again conveys the sense of commencement as well, so that the passage marks an important turn in the narrative.

This marks the beginning of the *nostos* for which Jason has yearned throughout the narrative. Events have changed him, too. Jason, fired up as leader and ready for whatever challenge Aeetes offers, is a different man from the lad who left his native shore in tears in the departure scene of Book One. Yet his role in the fourth book is again ambiguous. He does not have much to do in this narrative after the wedding scene, except to call Apollo himself back to the narrative briefly near the end. The crew is lost and in distress. Jason calls out, once again "tears running down his cheeks" (1703−4),[6] and Apollo appears. Thereafter Jason interprets a dream for Euphemus (1749−54). The act endows Jason at the poem's very end with the clairvoyance which is marked in others in this poem and claimed by the poet himself at the very beginning. Otherwise, Jason's virtual disappearance from the fourth book narrative, while in itself paralleling his minimal role in the second book, perhaps represents an accommodation to the increased importance of Medea's role. As the invocation to the Muse with which the fourth book begins has prepared us, Medea has the strong, passionate scenes in this book which are nowhere paralleled by any action of his own.

Toward the very close of the poem (1400−1484), Heracles comes back into the narrative indirectly, as though this were one of those musicals where all the principals appear in the last number as a kind of exaggerated curtain call. Heracles appears indirectly when the heroes reach the Hesperides. Desperate for water, they throng around a spring which the Hesperides tell them Heracles had caused to flow just the day before. He had come for the golden apples. The serpent which guarded them lies almost lifeless before the crew's eyes, struck by Heracles' arrows. The Hesperides sadly report that there came a most beastly fellow (*kyntatos*, most doglike), "baleful in his violence and the way he looked . . . eyes flashing under a grim brow . . . without pity . . . rushed in thirsty, smote a rock with his staff; out came water." This accords with everything we know of Heracles. Brutish as ever, taking advantage of vulnerable women, with an uncomplicated view of things, he moves fast, deliberate, kills the snake, steals the apples, strikes the rock, gets water. By contrast, we are reminded of Jason's fear when he confronted the snake (149) and his need of Medea. All his inadequacies of the first book return in this reference to Heracles.

Apollonius emphasizes Heracles' importance when he has one man say to another that Heracles has saved them even though he is not with them. Ah, the fellow sighs, would that we could meet him coming along. Moments later (1477) Lynceus thinks he sees Heracles—maybe it is a mirage—at a great distance. The immense and untraversable distance which lies between Heracles and Lynceus is Apollonius' way of describing the reader's and Jason's new understanding of things. All that has transpired in the intervening books make the events of the first so far away, a kind of innocence never to be regained. It is at once both sad and satisfying. The peculiar melancholia, futility, and failure aroused by the idea of Heracles both there and not there, repeats the effect of the scene in the first book, when the priestess of Artemis reaches out futilely to touch Jason as he goes by.

The most telling parallel is between the murder of Apsyrtus and the killing of Amycus. The murder has the brutality of description and the appropriate temple setting which make it a ritual slaughter like that at the sacrifice to

Apollo in the first book (427–28).[7] It becomes an ironic sacrifice performed in the presence of Hecate's priestess at Artemis' temple to assure the successful voyage home. There are two verbal parallels, however, which emphasize a perverse connection between it and the boxing contest. Amycus rises up like the killer of an ox (*boutopos* [91]), but Polydeuces eludes him and lands in return a fatal blow. The king falls to his knees (*gnyx ēripen* [96]). When Jason kills Apsyrtus, Jason is *boutopos* (468) and Apsyrtus falls to his knees (471). Thereafter, at a signal the Argonauts fall upon the Colchian followers of Medea's brother who are slain in numbers like the Bebrycian followers of Amycus. The second book's victory of light over darkness, good over evil is ironically compared to a brutal and unheroic murder. What in the second book had seemed to be an obvious and instinctive identification of Jason with Polydeuces falls away before this new ruthless manslayer Jason has become.

The fourth book has a formal structure which derives from the many parallels between the travel narrative here and Jason's initial departure and voyage up to Colchis. But what pulls the reader along is the suspenseful tale of pursuit. Two similes establish this at the beginning. The comparison of Medea to a fawn in a thicket as the hounds surround it without (12–13) sets up images of the hunt which later appear in the narrative (109–13). Dawn is described as it affects the early rising hunter, who trusting in his hounds, never sleeps through the night to dawn. At this point, Medea has just thrown herself upon the mercy of the crew in extreme anguish after fleeing from Aeetes' fierce wrath. The dawn scene portrays the tension in them all, which causes them to hasten to the site of the fleece. At the same time Jason is the hunter, the fleece his prey, and Medea his trusty dog. When he exults in the fleece a little later, the fleece is compared in size to the hide of a kind of animal for which, Apollonius tells us, hunters have a special name (175).

The other simile (35–39) is longer and securely establishes the theme of pursuit in its social context. Medea is compared to an indentured servant or slave (*leias*) who flees a rich home, a maid who is separated from her homeland; as she sets out, she is inexperienced in the struggles on the road ahead, but, still unaccustomed to being maltreated, she shrinks from her mistress's harsh hand. Medea the princess is fleeing a rich home, estranged from her father but not her homeland, ignorant of the hardships ahead, but so unused to the rage she has excited in her father that she must leave. The reader remembers the simile when Jason says to her that the residents of the land will aid Apsyrtus to lead her back to her father like some captive girl (*leisthe-isan* [400]), or when she tells the crew "with men who are not kinsmen I wander, a hated creature" (1041). Like a runaway slave, Medea can never find anyone who will take her in. The fourth book is the sad tale of a princess turned vagabond for love.

While the tale is indeed sad, if not tragic, certain details of the story seem to be conceits of the comic theater which Apollonius has taken over into his story. This is not to say that the events of the narrative thus become comical—not at all. But rather the comic elements provide a social coloration to the events. Marriages, family standing, public reputation, propriety, property are important values in the minds of the participants in comic action. These become implicit in the action of Apollonius' characters. They are clearly sensed; some critics, such as Brooks Otis, have responded to them intuitively enough to worry literally about Medea's virtue and reputation while alone on the *Argo* with so many men.

Aeetes explodes with rage when he realizes Jason has won. Immediately he suspects Medea's complicity in the victory. Thereafter Aeetes wants Medea back home, he does not care about the fleece. The plot turns on the young maiden who falls in love and flees her father who will not give her to her young suitor. This is a conventional plot from the comic theater. Menander's *Perikeiromene*, for instance, deals with a young maiden in love who flees her father's cruelty.

The comic situation of the eloping daughter results in two domestic scenes unlike any other in the poem. The first is the couple's visit to Circe, the second their stay with Alcinous and Arete. Jason and Medea visit her aunt Circe to receive ritual cleansing of the pollution which they incurred by murdering Apsyrtus. Apollonius' keen sense of the perverse has touched the scene with humor. The description of Circe's nightmare of death and destruction and her entourage of grotesques give an initial gothic flavor to the scene. The poet then proceeds to a comedy of manners. Circe, in her "insincerity (*dolophrosynē* [687])," which term Apollonius uses here for politesse, greets the heroes. She is being duplicitous in the sense that the horror of her nightmare has made her unfit company for anyone, so that she has to strain in falsehood to be gracious. She directs Jason and Medea to seats, "absolutely undone by their arrival (*amēkhaneousa kiontōn* [692])." They can say nothing, cannot even look at her. Circe, no fool, immediately realizes that they are suppliants, guilty of murder. After the ritual cleansing, Circe questions them. She wanted to hear the voice of her kinswoman (725), for of course she had recognized her from the shining eyes, a genetic characteristic of the Sun's descendants. They talk in Colchian, Medea tells everything except for the murder, but of course Circe knows all (737). Circe pities the girl, but nonetheless she replies:

> Poor thing . . .
> I don't expect that you will escape Aeetes'
> wrath for very long . . .
> Since you are a suppliant and kin to boot
> I won't harm you and now that you've come.
> But get out of my house along with that stranger;

take him away whoever he may be . . .
Don't come kneeling as a suppliant at my hearth
I shall not approve of what you are doing
nor your shameful flight from home.

Circe the witch sounds more like an outraged middle-class matron drawing herself up in indignation at her scandalous niece. Love is all very well, but not when it insults the family. "Anguish such as no one could want overcame Medea. She threw her gown over her eyes and a groan fell from her until finally the hero took her by the hand and led her from the house shaking with fear." Apollonius concludes the episode starkly enough in the laconic "They left the house of Circe" (752). Apollonius keeps the visit to Aea in two perspectives, the *Märchen* and the comic. The romantic couple found absolution with the sorceress but no forgiveness from the aunt. And Medea the witch who never trembled before the serpent guarding the fleece quakes in fear at having become outcast from her family. The social values of the bourgeois comic theater prevail over those of the heroic mythic world.

Traditional epic emphasizes the sacral, the supernatural, the mighty, and the awesome. Odysseus' encounter with Circe is based on the commonplace fairy-tale threat of a witch who may destroy the hero. She is much like the witch in *Hansel and Gretel* down to living in a cottage in the forest. Circe the witch appears like a fairy-tale creature in the *Odyssey*; there is never the slightest hint of her personality, of her motives. Her singing and working the loom establish her only as a woman and a siren-figure. She replicates Helen, Calypso, and Penelope.

Purification for murder is serious business in epic and tragedy as well, again involving the sacral, the ritual, the awful, and the holy seriousness. It has to do with the change in a person's status, nothing more, freeing him from remaining a taboo figure, capable of bringing pollution.

Apollonius charges these matters with a new consciousness. He gives purification a social setting, a domestic setting. We see Circe as a family person and a social person, see her nervous politesse, see her talking in Colchian. No one in epic talks in a foreign tongue, certainly not when it must exclude the hero! Her disapproval of the poem's hero, when she says, "get him—whoever he is—out of here" is domestic and social where absolution in epic is simply religious and noncommittal. The tone which the disapproval imparts to the narrative is reinforced in the murderous couple's silence which betokens not only guilt but also shame.

The important fact is that these are distinctly separate modes of depicting action which are being amalgamated here. Apollonius is deepening and enriching epic narrative, building up the surface of the canvas, as it were, with marvelous pigments to get real depth and complexity in the action. Again it is suggestive of the narrative which eventually we encounter in the novel.

Is Apollonius being funny? Certainly Circe's grotesque entourage undercuts the seriousness of her person. Homer's Circe turned men into swine, Apollonius' Circe has misshapen beings, gargoyles, unearthly creatures which establish an aura of surreal mystery about her. Because it contrasts so strikingly with her commonplace social behavior, it is amusing. This and certain other details hint that Apollonius accomplishes an emotional purification for his reader in the Circe episode. The murder scene previous to this moment went as far as the narrative goes to the point of tragic seriousness. Beginning with their meeting in the third book the narrative has gathered force, has darkened, has moved from climax—marriage proposal—to climax—Jason's victory—to climax—Medea's escape—to climax—getting the fleece—and finally to this, the most powerful of them all, the murder of Apsyrtus. The humorous or ironic tone in the onset of the love affair returns in ever diminishing doses in these subsequent climactic moments until the murder scene which is altogether horrible. Even the Cyzicus episode is ironic while being horrible. The murder of Apsyrtus lends a new and distinctly ominous tone to the proceedings, a tone from which the poet must retrieve himself and his reader so as to achieve some neutrality before the so-called happy ending, Medea's future with Achilles, Jason's arrival home with the fleece.

The absolution scene absolves the couple of the pollution of murder. By introducing the domestic comic mode with even comical details, the poet absolves the reader from the deadly seriousness which the murder scene imposed upon him. No one will forget the murder; Jason and Medea's love affair breaks up in the shipwreck of that event. But Apollonius is writing a story about love and not about murder. The latter exists principally as a metaphor; he does not want his reader to linger over it and be deflected from the truth of his story.

At Drepanē it seems as though the wandering couple's luck will change for the better. The Argonauts are met with the Phaeacians' characteristic good cheer. ("You would say that they were rejoicing over their own sons.") But soon another band of Colchians arrives to demand Medea back. Negotiations proceed, creating a suspenseful scene played out by three distinct personalities thoroughly domesticated and bourgeois. As in the third book, Apollonius moves the reader from one room to another, the comings and goings reflect the comic stage.

Medea is ready to try everything in her desperation. As she pleads her cause to Arete, Medea makes herself sound like an innocent. Lucky for her the Colchians came straight from her father on the route which the Argonauts had used to go to Colchis and therefore know nothing of Apsyrtus' murder. Naturally Medea does not mention it herself. "Identify with me," she says to the queen, "if you belong to the human race whose mind runs swiftly into disaster because of every minor peccadillo (*kouphesi* . . . *amplakiēsi* [1017]).

My solid common sense slipped. It was not crazy desire (*margosynē*)" she declares to Arete, although when she had been pleading with Jason earlier she had said "you might as well cut my head off with your sword so that I can have the reward that comes from crazy desire" (374–75). True to life, Medea must exonerate herself to strangers, but cannot stop being self-pitying and bitter as she talks to her reluctant lover.

"I didn't want to leave home," she continues, "Fear overcame me, and there just wasn't any other plan" (just what Jason told the crew when he had agreed to Aeetes' contest: "Nothing better came to mind" [3.500–501]). She ends by swearing that she has kept her virginity, which is to say she may be an indifferent daughter but she is not a slut.

To the crew of the *Argo* she pleads for her life as though she would assure herself of armed support in case Arete were ineffective on her behalf. She pressures them with obligation: bulls, harvest of earth-born men, fleece they owe to her (1032–35); with guilt: they will see their parents again, she wanders with no kin (1036–41); and with fear: they must fear the Erinyes who avenges suppliants if they do not heed her (1042–45). She is successful, for they swear to defend her if the king's judgment goes against her. Apollonius in one powerful image reveals how much the effort of defending her position is telling on Medea. He likens her to a widowed woman with orphaned children for whom she must labor through the night, all the while crying over her wretched lot (1062–65). Medea, barely supported physically and not at all emotionally by Jason, is like a widowed woman. The simile looks ahead to the Corinthian tragedy when Jason will have walked out for good. The truth of it is that the strong are always doomed to be lonely. Medea and Jason began their relationship upon the assumption of her vulnerability and manipulability. The events of the fourth book have changed all that.

But Arete saves Medea when she is alone with her husband in their royal bed. The domestic scene where Arete pleads with Alcinous reverses the strengths of personality which the *Odyssey* poet gives to the couple. Nausicaa tells Odysseus to supplicate Arete; it is the queen who notices that Odysseus' clothes are from the palace; Alcinous on the other hand has to be reminded by his courtiers to offer Odysseus some common courtesy (7.159–60). Homer's quick, perceptive queen and the bemused king are a doublet of all-powerful Helen and ineffectual Menelaus. Apollonius situates his couple in a typical middle-class household.[8] In this domestic scene, Arete pressures Alcinous with personal arguments which are traditionally held to be the product of a woman's domestic way of seeing things. The cosy relationship of Alcinous and Arete is consonant with the fervent prayer with which Medea ends her apologia to the queen. "May god grant you a perfect life, beauty, children, and the glory of a city which is never sacked in war" (1026–28). It is what Medea herself would like to have someday. The poet throws into relief the dubious prospects of the romantic wanderer's marriage by contrasting it with the boudoir dialogue of the Phaeacian royals, who are a contented married couple.

Arete's arguments are charming: we must help Jason and Medea because the Greeks live near us. Aeetes comes from far away; we don't know him, all we know is his name. Medea's hardship makes me want to cry. She made a little mistake, and tried to resolve it—as we all do—with yet another [if Arete had only been privy to that butchery at Artemis' temple on the island of the river Ister!]. Jason will marry her and in any case fathers are too jealous.

Arete's speech, like Medea's before it, picks up a theme which runs through the *Argonautica*, that is, the frailty of human morals. It is in the word *amēkhanos*, in the argument of acceptance, in the melancholia of Jason's approach to things. The attitude is absolutely at variance with the Homeric conception of human strength and will. Homeric heroes may be thwarted or perverted by the gods, but they do not mistake what they do through a kind of indifference, nor do they comply with events from timidity or weakness. Apollonius' world is a sadder place, its occupants wiser people or in any case considerably younger people upon whose frail shoulders the harsh blows of events rain with greater impact.

Alcinous' response is characteristic of what traditionally is considered to be the masculine point of view. The sentimentality and emotion of Arete's conception of things gives way to a political and legalistic analysis of Jason and Medea's position. The king's logic is impeccable, he touches every factor in the conflict. The verdict: if she is married he will not give her up. "Thus he spoke and straightway sleep put him at rest" (1110). Again the poet contrasts the Phaeacian royal couple with his hero and heroine. The mental state of Jason and Medea, whose anguish, doubt, and confusion make them like rats in the research lab scurrying around desperately seeking the solution to the maze, is far away from the uncomplicated and magisterial view of things which imparts to Alcinous so serene a sleep.[9]

At last there is a wedding. One of the minor suspenseful themes of the fourth book is resolved. Medea's respectability is restored. Note how Arete gives her a retinue of female servants for the rest of the homeward voyage (1221–22), how the women of Drepanē bring her linens (1189) and gold ornaments (1190–91). Medea is no lost, vagrant flower child anymore, but a proper young lady. A long description of the city festival held in honor of the wedded couple (1170–1200) points up the social and political validation of their love. Jason and Medea pass their wedding night lying on the fleece which at last fully reveals its symbolic value, why Jason has been so amazingly protective of it. Shortly after acquiring it, Jason lays it out in the prow of the ship and sets Medea upon it. From that position, he officially proclaims to the crew his marriage plan. Much earlier as the lovesick Medea lay asleep she dreamt that it was she who won the fleece for Jason and angered her parents in doing so. Just as Aeetes' political suspicions and masculine ego tensions were replaced by a jealous father's anger, so Jason's masculine adventure of retrieving the fleece has evolved into a male's conquest of a woman. Apollonius manages to align the fleece and Medea so that they become the same, and the wedding bed made of the fleece is an entirely logical outcome of this.

Jason's response to the fleece is one of the fuller revelations of his generally repressed character. As he and Medea approach the fleece, it appears like a cloud which glows red in the fiery rays of the rising sun (125–26). Once he has snatched it, he takes it back to the *Argo*. "Just as a young girl catches the glitter of the full moon rising on high over her bed chamber on her delicate gown, and her heart is pleased as she watches the beautiful moon, so Jason in joy lifted up the great fleece in his hands and on his cheeks and brow there sat a rosy glow like a flame from the clusters of wool" (167–73). Striding along, Jason drapes it down the side of his body and worries that some man or god will try to steal it. Dawn breaks as he rejoins his comrades, the glow of nature in symphony with the fleece which "glowed like the lightning of Zeus" (185). When the crew tries to touch it, Jason keeps the men away and puts a protective covering on it.

Apollonius makes Jason react to the fleece with a pleasure and desire stronger and more obvious than that which anything else in the poem has been able to excite in him. The taking of the fleece occurs between Medea's initial reception aboard ship which accompanies her virtual surrender to Jason and his public declaration of marriage to Medea whom he has seated upon the fleece. The roseate glow which emanates from the fleece and colors Jason as he gazes at it, enthralled with the emotion of a young girl (who reminds the reader of her lovesick counterpart watching the star from her chamber at 1.779), is a hue which often describes sexual excitement in the poem (compare 3.122; 298; 963; 1018; 1020; 1024; and the cloak Jason wears on the visit to Hypsipyle was also like the sun, 1.726). Apollonius, in short, conveys Jason's sexual excitement at finally possessing Medea through the conquest of the fleece. Epic tradition is unusually discreet about erotic passion; masculine arousal seems to have been especially difficult for ancient poets to describe, perhaps because the poet must always and immediately confront the erection, that obvious, true and inevitably slightly ridiculous love offering which only an Aristophanes could set in its proper perspective. As a metaphor for sexual passion, the encounter with the serpent could not be better, for Jason is at first afraid, and once the conquest is achieved he wants only to get away, whereas Medea continues to stroke the dragon as though mesmerized. Ironically, the red of the fleece returns to haunt the two in the stains of red blood of Medea's brother spattered on her gown. There in that murder scene the bloodstained gown betokens a loss of innocence twice over for Medea who

will soon lose her virginity as she at that very moment is losing the illusions
of youth.

The preparations for the hurried-up impromptu wedding include the con-
ventional music of Orpheus, flowers, nymphs in attendance preparing the
fragrant bridal bower. The joy which the pastoral setting should inspire is,
however, missing. Instead the Argonauts carry their spears like guests with
their automatics at Rhodesian weddings. Jason and Medea are both disap-
pointed that it is not a conventional wedding at the palace in Iolcus (1161).
It was necessity that made them marry at this time, Apollonius reminds us
(1164), underscoring the sense of helplessness in the face of the inexorable
which has governed the action since first Pelias ordered Jason off on the voy-
age. As though indeed the wedding were the culmination of the events of the
poem, Apollonius bestows upon the scene the observation that life's pleasures
are mingled with pains (1165–67). Apollonius manages to make this notion
seem trite and the opposite of consoling by denuding it of theological context.
At the end of the *Iliad* Achilles was really saying the same thing when he
described the jars of Zeus. But here it sounds like nothing more than the
weary remark, "life is a bowl of cherries; you've got to take the bitter with
the sweet." And Apollonius leaves the wedded couple with the notice that
they were on the one hand lost in sweet love, and on the other possessed of
fear (1168–69).

Medea's defence of herself to Arete, in which she passes over the murder of
Apsyrtus, shows how far the innocent maiden has come since that fateful day
when Eros aimed an arrow in her direction. The range of experiences and the
decisions she has made in consequence of them have transformed the naïve,
expectant maiden into a determined, wiser, and immensely sadder woman.
This is not exactly character change, perhaps, because Medea's association
with Hecate foreshadowed her capacity for ugly actions and the emotions
attendant upon them. But certainly she never expected such unhappiness or
believed she would have to learn to deal with it. She has evolved in a manner
almost unique in ancient Greek letters.

If one considers the person of Odysseus or Achilles as either appears in the
very last of their respective stories, both are pretty much the same persons
they were at the beginning. Their experiences, particularly Odysseus', have
left them relatively unchanged. Patroclus' death has made Achilles a wiser,
more tolerant person. When the reader considers Medea, on the other hand,
how she appears at her wedding compared to her first appearance, she is much
changed in the sense of having acted and experienced. To be sure, she lied
from the start, at first to hide her growing love for the handsome stranger, as
now she lies by omission about the death of her brother. One suspects that
life's ironies and sorrows came as no surprise to Odysseus and Achilles; one
does not have that feeling about Medea. Principally, Medea is a changed

person because she must confront her personal relationship with Jason. He is an added element in the sum total which is Medea's personality. Male heroes in classical antiquity do not ever become involved with a spouse in the way that the necessarily dependent Medea does, so that this opportunity for growth and change in character is unique to this poem.

It is sometimes claimed that Apollonius' narrative is seriously flawed by the fundamental disunity of the character of Medea, her good girl–bad girl aspects, that she is the good girl in the third book and the bad girl in the fourth. This is an objection without foundation. The events of the fourth book call for desperate measures; Aeetes' rage, then Apsyrtus' pursuit; and Medea responds in kind—flight, murder. One should not imagine that Medea's role as a priestess of Hecate is emblematic of her so-called "bad side." Hecate is not a satanic figure. A developed notion of evil as an operative force in the universe is very infrequently found in the thinking of the ancient Greeks. Hecate's role is meant to convey the idea that Medea has a mystery, a power, a connection with frightening uncanny forces which make her latently if not obviously a figure whom a man, a suitor, a husband, a father cannot easily dominate and control. She is the unexpected, someone to love and admire but also dread.

In his creation of Medea, Apollonius plays upon his reader's expectations which are built up from familiarity with other myths and other narratives. Some of the major epic and tragic associations are: 1) Ariadne, the girl who helps and is abandoned on Naxos; 2) Penelope, the wife who waits and helps by keeping the house intact, who is in effect abandoned by her husband and the narrator of the *Odyssey* once she and Odysseus have gone to bed upon his return; 3) Euripides' Medea, a tragic female figure on the one hand, who must destroy her living issue, which is almost herself, who is yet on the other hand a witch and malevolent figure because she survives her evil deed, unlike the purely tragic Sophoclean Deïanira who dies; 4) Homer's Circe, who enchants men to their doom, a malign witch goddess figure who is sexually dangerous for males on the model of Aphrodite (Adonis perishes in his relationship with her) and Artemis (Actaeon perishes in his quasi-sexual relationship with her) as well as many others; 5) Aeschylus' Clytemnestra, who seduces Agamemmnon into entering a warm bath where he is stabbed to death, the paradigmatic threatening mortal woman whose power to kill is directly related to the intimacy of the matrimonial chamber. Very rarely in extant Greek literature does one find a male-female relationship which is explored in depth. Males either seek a woman to exploit and discard, or are drawn into a woman's power and destroyed.

Apollonius is brilliant and original in narrating the aftermath. Pindar, we may remember, omits describing the return voyage (4.440). Its essentially anticlimactic nature would have weighed down the lyric expression of Jason's adventure. An aftermath is always hard to portray. Lines are drawn in crisis situations from which the plot unfolds with an inevitability that can be tedious. The fourth book of the *Argonautica* is particularly interesting therefore because it deals with perseverance, that singularly bourgeois quality devoted to upkeep and maintenance rather than opening the gate onto the last frontier. It seems fair to say that of the many features of the *Aeneid* which Virgil owes to Apollonius' inspiration, not the least is the *pietas* of its hero Aeneas who endures indomitably one obstacle after another. It is endurance not charged with the enthusiasm of an Odysseus whose curiosity converts all setbacks into a mysterious challenge, nor with the overwhelming animal vigor of a Heracles whose megalomania gives exultation to whatever he does, but instead with gritted teeth and misery in his soul Aeneas carries on like the fundamentally unhappy Jason.

More unusual, of course, is the fact that Apollonius is chronicling the grim aftermath of love's sweet beginning. Almost without exception, ancient literature depicts the ecstasies of love's blossoming or the agonies of unrequited love—subjects particularly popular with Apollonius' contemporary, Theocritus. But Apollonius is doing something quite different. He is describing the quotidian experience of lovers who stay together past the initial night of ecstasy into an exploration of the meaning of eternal love.

The aesthetic of antiquity dictated that the author resolve his plot in the narrative rather than leave the audience with a crisis. Odysseus proceeds to war with the suitors' kin, Oedipus comes forth to make the necessary arrangements for living as a taboo figure, blind and rejected. It would have been harsh and contradictory if Apollonius had left his narrative right after the capture of the fleece. In some way—even if in the very compressed, allusive manner of Pindar—Apollonius has to get the Argonauts home. What is novel is that the resolution is done in terms of emotional and psychological evolution.

Notice that once Odysseus has secured Penelope in bed, she leaves the narrative forever. Medea scarcely reappears after the wedding. But the poet, by giving their first meeting so many intimations of a physical consummation through the emotional effects, has allowed himself a large canvas on which to paint the fading and darkening colors of love's first passion. Love ends in two people turning into different sorts as the love works upon them. Apollonius, of course, has made the love story painful. Love ends either in pain or boredom. The fourth book shows Medea's growing dissatisfaction with Jason as a mate.[10] More to the point, events conspire to put strains on the emotion of love, which came into being when the beautiful young couple first met by the temple of Hecate. The couple despairs, perhaps, of ever capturing again the fleeting aura of that evanescent moment.

What seems brilliant in the fourth book is that Apollonius takes the situa-

tion of the Ariadne story and the Penelope story, notices the strong emotion
enkindled in a man and woman as he adventures and she assists, and then
keeps the woman in the story when the adventure is over so as to portray how
the male has compromised his heroic "aloneness" in becoming an element in
a partnership. Then, too, Apollonius takes the Circe story, showing us a
powerful witch who seduces a traveling man into marriage and commitment.
But the poet will not let him escape her charms; there is no magical *moly* such
as Odysseus flourished. What then does Apollonius show us? A strong woman
who must struggle against being victimized and submerged by the dependent
man upon whom finally she must become dependent.

But, of course, dangerous woman remains dangerous woman. Greek males
were fundamentally misogynist; the literary tradition is imbued with this
attitude. The fourth book shows Jason caught in terrible trouble because
Medea brings on the pursuit of Apsyrtus and thereafter his murder. It would
have been better for Jason if he had jettisoned Medea. The power of Apollo-
nius' version is that we see these events from Medea's vantage as well. Instead
of the fairy-tale story of a witch who cuts up her brother to stop pursuit—
altogether morally neutral—the poet portrays a warm-hearted, naïve girl of
strong temperament caught and cornered in a relationship that grows more
dreadful until it is sealed forever in the murder of her brother, an event which
has metaphorical value for a love gone sour and debased.

In the comedy of manners which is played out in the fourth book, Medea
is still very much the young girl. Her flight from Aeetes' palace where she is
compared to an ignorant innocent runaway slave (despite the characteristic
Apollonian aside referring to her corpse-hunting expeditions) sets the prob-
lem for the subsequent narrative. The resolution for this comes finally in the
marriage and the gift of the retinue of maidens. It is difficult for us to exercise
our historical imaginations to the necessary degree so as to conceive how
frightening a voyage would be for a woman alone with men. The vulnerabil-
ity, the exploitability of unprotected young women was limitless. That is why
the crew was amazed to hear her call out to them on the banks of the Phasis.
"The crew was struck dumb in amazement when they realized that it [her
calling out] was really true" (73–74). The *thambeon* of 74 recalls the reader
the *ethambēsan* of 1.322, part of Jason's beach arrival scene, thereby strength-
ening the parallels here between the experiences of the two lovers. Medea
calls upon Phrontis, the youngest of Phrixus' sons, because he is cousin. Only
the extremest necessity would have allowed her to drop all her acculturated
defenses to call upon the strange male Jason. Is it Phrontis upon whom she
calls and not Argus because as youngest he will be less judgmental?

We must understand what extraordinary courage Medea exhibits in board-
ing the *Argo*. Nothing more becomes her, and yet present-day social condi-
tions obscure the dangers which Apollonius took so much for granted that he

passed over them. This is why Jason sets her upon the fleece and declares formally to his crew that she will be his bride. "Preserve her," he says (197), "she who is our savior and savior of Greece as well." He means, protect her from her enemies, but also do not try to violate her. Apollonius long ago told us how Jason prudently refused passage to Atalanta because he feared ugly quarrels on account of her love (1.769–73). One woman and fifty men on a long sea voyage does not ever augur well. Now that Medea's father is estranged from her Jason assumes the role of male protector.

Because he is her official protector, her anguish in the speech to him (355–90) when Apsyrtus wants Jason to hand her over is all the keener. She is absolutely at Jason's mercy, abject, defenceless. "Now am I borne along all alone far from home with the sad kingfishers" (363). When she tells him what Andromache tells Hector (*Iliad* 6.249–750), that she has lost her home, her family, it may be a rhetorical commonplace of the Hellenistic period,[11] but nonetheless it is glaringly true. A woman without a family has nowhere to turn. The seduced and abandoned woman, a pathetic figure of the comic theater, lies behind the sarcasm and anger in this speech. For the young girl in love has become the cynical and sarcastic woman. "Has the glitter made you forget, are you indifferent to what you promised out of necessity?" (356–57). I hope you remember me" she says in a bitter parody of her love-drenched speeches in the third book (compare 3.1069–71; 3.1109–11) "when you are wrung out by your troubles."

Before that, she had pleaded to be taken aboard the *Argo*, kneeling before Jason and her cousins, and whatever sympathy she might command was considerably enhanced by her offer to get the fleece. "Let us flee aboard ship. I shall put the serpent to sleep and get you the fleece" (85–88). "She spoke in deep anguish; the mind of Jason was overjoyed" (92–93)—presumably to be getting the fleece so easily. Nowhere does Apollonius make a more stunning revelation of Jason's indifference than in those lines. Medea's loneliness and desperation, which appear in all three speeches of supplication in this book (see also 1031–52), are not fancied but true perceptions or at least intuitions of her situation. So it is that the Medea of the third book, defenceless and exposed by her love for Jason, is the same Medea of the fourth book.

Just as she had the daring to meet Jason alone at the temple of Hecate, and the occult powers to stop the moon in its rounds, so in the fourth book she manifests the same courage and energy. Apollonius wants the reader to be left with this impression of Medea since almost the last notable episode of the poem describes her killing by magical means Talos, the almost invincible man of brass. Invoking the spirits of death, the hounds of Hades (1665–66), she grinds her teeth in anger against him, furiously raging, sending out deadly phantoms. But much earlier, from the moment when Jason accepts her aboard ship and clasps her hand in a symbolic gesture of the matrimonial bond which he is assuming, the poet says, "she then directed them to sail" (100). In the presence of the serpent which is described frighteningly in its hugeness Medea goes forward, whereas Jason "follows, already completely frightened (*pephobēmenos*)." When the great creature is stupefied by Medea, Jason snatches the fleece "at Medea's command" (163). She continues to stand before the snake unflinching, rubbing the charm on its head, until Jason urges her to return to the ship. The disparity in their reactions to this moment of high adventure is amusing, but also enlightening.

The test occurs in their colloquy as Apsyrtus waits to take Medea home to their father. Medea's sarcastic, cynical, and finally angry, vengeful speech (355–90) reads as though Jason had already given her up. The many rhetorical questions do not demand answers; it's as though the time for deliberation is past and no answers are needed any longer. Medea ends her speech in a series of threats. Apollonius says that she wants to burn the ship and break it apart. Jason replies in fright (*hypodeisas* [394]) with his usual *meilikhiois epeessi*. When he finishes, the poet describes his manner as fawning *hypossainōn* (410). Jason has not been this terrified since Medea's father threatened to tear out their tongues, to which the young man also replied with fawning speech (3.396).

Jason's reply to Medea is so ambiguous that interpretation is difficult.[12] He defends the truce by saying "the treaty will create a deceit whereby we can make him [Apsyrtus] walk into destruction" (404–405). He continues saying that there will be no opposition "with their chief not around" (406). Jason means that Apsyrtus will die, be killed. Did Jason plan to murder Apsyrtus from the start, as some suppose? This seems unlikely since Jason would have no access to him when he was not protected by bodyguards. The point is made when Medea ponders whether she can get the heralds to bring him alone (417–18). He might only drop his guard, if then, for his sister. Indeed he does, coming—as the poet says, to emphasize his psychology—as a child crossing a river swollen in the winter rain. The comparison makes him her sibling, not the Prince Royal, makes him seem naked and vulnerable as a child. Unthinking as a child, we might add.

So Jason as he speaks to Medea does not necessarily have a plan. The truce was to buy time. Medea's relentless bitterness and rage motivate him to speak of Apsyrtus' destruction; or perhaps he has all along delicately touched the notion, but cannot bring himself to speak the words, formulate the thoughts lying nebulous in his brain. We are witnessing, so to speak, the Hellenistic equivalent of Lady Macbeth and her timid consort.

"*Phrazeo nun*, consider this then," says Medea in answer as she begins what Apollonius calls a speech of death (*oulos mythos*). *Phrazeo nun* was the phrase with which she began her speech to Jason about the way in which to conquer the bulls (3.1026), a speech wherein Medea described the rituals of Hecate that Jason had to perform, rituals symbolic of his passage into yet another stage of transformation from the ineffectual naïf who left Iolcus. Now the last step is about to be taken. One thinks of Carmen and Don Jose. It is a persistent idea in Western culture which begins in Apollonius' poem, although it is implicit in the aftermath of Enkidu's intercourse with the harlot.

"Consider this, then," she begins. "For it is necessary to plan as follows, as the next addition to the rotten deeds already done, since from the first I was beguiled in error and the gods let me fulfill my wicked desires. Now you protect me from the Colchian spears in the general melee. But I shall try to cozen him into coming into your hands. You pay him court with shining gifts. If only I can persuade the heralds as they go off to send him to get together with me alone. Then if this deed pleases you, I don't care. Kill him and wage war with the Colchians."

"If this thing pleases you, I don't care," are the very words with which Jason answered to Argus (3.485) when first he suggested getting Medea to help them in their contest with bulls. From that fateful careless reply Jason has come a long way, now deeply into Medea's debt and under her spell. Fränkel conjures up[13] all the subtleties of the psychological novel to show that Medea's mind has finally snapped. But no; it is more the person who has gone beyond the barrier of any convention she knows who decides that she might as well be hanged for a sheep as for a goat. Medea's speech has all the key words of their love affair: *dolon, meilixō, phaidrois dorois*. The shining gift which Jason prepares for Apsyrtus is yet another perversion of love; a gift of Hypsipyle to Jason.

As in the ekphrasis of Jason's cloak in the first book (725;765–66), the poet enthusiastically draws us in: "you could never get your fill of touching it or feeling it" (429). It smells of sex, wine, and nectar. The drunken Dionysus once made love upon this very cloak to Ariadne after she had been abandoned (430–34), echoing the male attitude toward sex which Jason exhibits in casually employing the cloak as a snare for the murder of his current lover's brother. She does her part, talking to Apsyrtus in seductive fashion, passing out beguiling charms (*thelktēria pharmaka* [442]), "which would bring a wild beast down from the mountaintops" (444). She, too, will someday make the gift of a garment in order to kill someone. Love's cloak now cast off reflects the irony embedded in the subsequent apostrophe to Eros (445–48), "great pain and abomination for all mankind from which spring disastrous strife, groans, sorrow, and infinite woe." For Jason and Medea are now caught in a compact forged so long ago in the initial fires of their desire—fires which their speeches to one another now, in the fourth book, show to have since cooled down.

The same irony colors the speech of the Moon as she looks down upon Medea running barefoot toward the banks of the Phasis (57–65). The Moon, a common element of love poetry, contemplates Medea's flight and fondly misinterprets it as the hurried lover going to an assignation. All the conceits of erotic poetry spring from her mouth—"Now you are caught in destruction," "Some god has given you Jason to be a source of woe and grief for you," "be brave . . . take on the pain which will give you many a groan"—but the reader understands that Medea runs for fear, not love, and soon the reader will see that the miseries which Medea will come to know are far greater than the aching of awakened desire.

The description of Apsyrtus' killing reads like a scene from an opera. All the horror and guilt of murder lie there. As Jason lifts his sword to strike, Medea turns her face away and covers her eyes with her veil so as not to see the blood of her brother. "In the entry way to the temple he fell to his knees; there as he breathed out his life in his one last act the hero took the dark blood at the wound with both his hands, and he made red his sister's silver veil and her gown as she tried to dodge away" (471–74). Apollonius treats this murder as a completely personal act. There is no reaction from the crew, from Apsyrtus' family (except Circe, and then not as aunt), nor from the gods. Apollonius is only interested in the effect which the murder has upon Jason and Medea. Obviously he is depicting a well-developed guilt culture rather than a shame culture. (This peculiar focus may be found as well in Callimachus, for instance in the hymn known as the *Bath of Pallas*. The poet describes the occasion when Tiresias sees Athena nude and is blinded. Of the many ways in which one may view this action Callimachus characteristically centers upon the fact that Tiresias' mother Chariclo and Athena are close friends [57–67] so that when the goddess has blinded the youth, the poet can turn to the interesting reaction of Chariclo to her erstwhile friend's ugly gesture and the goddess's subsequent response to Chariclo.)

Just as the poet uses the fleece to concentrate the various emotions and attitudes which love inspires—desire, possessiveness, seduction, joy, and glitter—so he uses the landscape in the fourth book to express the couple's state of mind. This seems to be an innovation in narration which crowns the fourth book, making it into a literary statement to be set beside the other three books. The necessarily fantastical geography of the fourth book makes the journey immediately metaphysical in a way that the second book's landscapes could never be, except for the Hades-like atmosphere at the land of the Mariandyni. Two long passages, one following the murder of Apsyrtus (594–626), the other a pendant to the melancholic marriage of Jason and Medea (1232–44), are brilliant portraits of mood. They are so like the descriptions in Dante's *Inferno*, and seem to serve so similar a poetic purpose, that one would like to believe that Dante had had access to the manuscripts which were lodged in his native Florence in the thirteenth century.

As they speed along to Circe's island in search of absolution, depression holds the heroes (594–95). They enter the Po. There they see the lake into which Helios' son Phaethon fell, still giving off steam from that fiery accident. Is it coincidence that Apsyrtus is sometimes called Phaethon (3.245, 1236) and that Apollonius should introduce his nominal doublet at this point? "No bird is able to cross the water, spreading out its fragile wings. Mid-course it falls into the flame, fluttering." Daughters of Helios enclosed in poplar trees stand around the lake crying, a sad lament; from their eyes fall tears of amber. Celts say these are the tears of Apollo when Zeus was enraged at Apollo for killing his sons, the Cyclops (a doublet of Aeetes-Apsyrtus-Jason/Medea). "No desire for food or drink came to the heroes, nor did their minds turn to joyful thoughts. All day they were strung out, exceedingly weak, weighed down by the dreadful smell, intolerable, which the streams of the Eridanus sent forth from the burning Phaethon. All night they had to listen to the shrill cry of the daughters of Helios wailing in a sharp voice. As they cried, their tears were borne upon the waters like drops of oil." This is, at one level, a description of the insistent pressure of choking guilt.

The heroes' hopelessness at being lost to the world of moral order—for they wander polluted—is dramatically conveyed in the poet's description of their near-mishap at the entrance to the Rhone as it flows into the Po (627–634). It is another infernal setting.[14] "The river, rising from the ends of the earth where there are the gates and palaces of Night, pours forth on the beach of Ocean on one side, the other goes into the Ionian Sea." They in their ignorance are floating down a branch of water toward Ocean from which they would never have returned save that Hera in a thoroughly un-Homeric stance jumps down from heaven and shouts directions.

The second landscape expresses depression. The impotence and cyclic nature of the depressed state are also caught in some repetitions (*pante, pante* [1237]; *oude ti keise herpeton, oude potēton* [1239–40]; *ēera, ēeri* [1246]; *oude, ou, ouk* [1247–48]). "Everywhere shoals, everywhere thick seaweed from the bottom, the foam of the wave lightly flows over them. Sand stretches out until the eye mistakes it for air. Nothing creeps there, nothing flies . . . pain overcame them as they gazed at the air and the broad expanse of earth looking like air, stretching far away without end. No watering hole, no path, no shepherd's enclosure could they see anywhere. Everything was held in a dead calm."

Jason's next to last appearance in the poem finds the Argonauts lost in what Apollonius tells us they called the Pall of Darkness. "No stars pierced the deadly night nor beams from the moon. A black yawning void came down from the sky or some other darkness it was, rising up from the depths. The Argonauts knew not whether they were borne along in Hades or on the sea." Only an appeal to Apollo saves them from the utter slough of despond in which they are marooned, and the sunlight returns. Here at the very close of the poem Apollonius must remind the reader of the Hades-like atmosphere, sometimes physical, more often atmospheric, which has pervaded so much of the narrative. Jason had confided his fears that he and the crew would never return (2.885–93). In a sense, they never can; too many events have occurred to change them from the persons they were when they set out.

Curiously enough, one thoroughly lighthearted passage pierces the persistent gloom of the fourth book (930–64). It is the parody of the passing through the Symplegades. Here Thetis marshals the Nereids to lift the boat on high. And they hike up their dresses to keep them out of the water. They are first compared to dolphins at play around the ship; later they are compared to frolicking girls at play with a ball which they pass from one to another. As they succeed in their task Apollonius describes Hera's joy as she throws her arms around Athena. We could be at a soccer match. Once past the Planctae Apollonius devises a charming pastoral landscape to go with the euphoric mood. The daughters of Helios here are not amber-crying poplars, but two shepherdesses, one with a silver crook, one with a crook of an even more exotic metal. The cows are as white as milk, with horns of gold.

The wandering twosome have just been shown the door by Medea's aunt, and there is little cause for joy. But the unexpected passage is an imagistic outpouring of the comic resolution to Medea's plight which Hera has just announced (810–15): someday all her troubles will be over and she will be in the Elysian Fields married to Achilles, a man as bold and overbearing as herself and hence finally her own true mate. The prophecy is followed by the narration of the marital career of Achilles' mother, Thetis (866–79). A strong woman, a goddess, she was married to Peleus, who was incapable of understanding her attempts to render their son immortal. In wrath she left him. Here in the narrative, at Hera's command, she communicates with him as briefly as possible (touches the tip of his hand, and leaves the minute the message has been delivered [865]). As we all know, someday Aegeus will offer Medea sanctuary, and she will leave Jason and Corinth in a skyborne vehicle. She, like Thetis, like the Nereids, will be in control. True to the comic vision—more in Dante's sense of that phrase than in Aristophanes' sense— Appolonius is reminding us that perils, problems, and tears are only here for a moment; finally over even the Pall of Darkness Apollo sends light.

Bibliographical Essay

Notes

Index

Bibliographical Essay

The nineteenth century made love over into the chief metaphor for the human condition, akin to a religious principle by which to live and die; something to which a person could be eternally faithful, for a woman by dying into eternal chastity true forever to her lover, for a man by surviving into a celibate's eternal graveside yearning—what is called today "survivor guilt." One thinks of Count Vronsky and Anna Karenina, or Marguerite Gautier and Armand Duval. No wonder then that Apollonius' *Argonautica* received its first modern and enthusiastic reappraisal in Paris in 1845 in the pages of *Révue des Deux Mondes* when the celebrated critic, Charles Augustin Sainte-Beuve proceeded to rehabilitate the poem from its centuries-long obscurity.

The essay is entitled "De la Medée d'Apollonius" (reprinted in *Portraits Contemporains*[3] [Paris, 1874]). Sainte-Beuve begins with a comparison of Dido and Medea, remarking that Dido is *the* tragic lover heroine of antiquity, as well-known to his contemporaries as Medea is obscure. Passing over the early part of the *Argonautica* with distaste ("Le poëte-narrateur semble préoccupé, chemin faisant, de ne rien vouloir oublier"), Sainte-Beuve moves to the third book and the ensuing first lines of the fourth, which he conceives to be the real poem. When the fleece is won and Medea has been seated upon it on the ship, there for unity's sake, says Sainte-Beuve, the poem should end. After that point, Medea "cesse d'être l'interessante jeune fille qu'on a vue." What's more, "au moment qu'elle a été obligée d'aider et d'assister au meurtre de son frère, Apsyrte, elle est odieuse."

Some interesting attitudes are revealed in this essay. Like nineteenth-century choreography, reminiscences of which we can still see today in the corps de ballet created by George Ballanchine, in which the men partner the women whose role it is to dance out the meaning of the music, so Sainte-Beuve sees the role of Jason to be altogether secondary and supporting in the presence of the great emotional drama of love which Medea lives. She it is who becomes *odieuse* by virtue of her brother's murder. Jason is not judged, in essence not counted or valued. Like a couple in a nineteenth-century waltz scene, Jason is nondescript in his tails, Medea is in a glittering ball gown. Sainte-Beuve either wants Medea to go on dancing or to be buried in that ball gown; he does not want her to get it dirty. That is why he insists that the poem should end when he does. Whatever the poem's fundamental failures, the character of Medea, at least in the earlier parts "la Medée avant tous les crimes" as he calls her, is a brilliant portrayal; she is a love-sick heroine thoroughly contemporary, a sister of the many heroines the critic names from the literature of his time.

The implications of this exciting debut into epic poetry of the magic and devastating power of love is first seized upon by J. W. MacKail in an essay entitled "Apollonius of Rhodes and the Romantic Epic." (*Lectures on Greek Poetry* [London, 1911], pp. 239–72). MacKail places the poem in the ancient Greek epic tradition and imagines the literary cricumstances of Apollonius. The Alexandrian was young, a rebel. Setting himself up in opposition to the strictures of his teacher Callimachus, he wanted to do a long poem and, what is more, a romance. But the young impetuous fellow had not the maturity nor the singularity of purpose to shake off the enormous weight of the inherited epic form. What he created was a failure, a contamination of forms and styles, where nothing succeeds in coming together.

J. C. Wordsworth's essay on Apollonius (pp. 153–213) in his *Adventures in Literature* (London, 1929) more or less sums up the consensus of the early part of the twentieth century. The poem has no hero, there is no unity of action, there is too much unintegrated encyclopedia knowledge. Only the few individual scenes so perfectly realized and the influence of the poem upon Virgil's *Aeneid* redeem Apollonius from the obscurity of the closet of literary history's rejects. Upon reflection, one is not sure in what way Mr. Wordsworth managed to see the poem as an adventure.

The later twentieth century has found the *Argonautica* far more congenial. It is not hard to see why. We have experienced the experiments of Ezra Pound, of James Joyce, of Picasso, of John Cage, to name only the very obvious. Instead of condemning Apollonius for what he does not do—condemnation being a major piece of artillery in the nineteenth-century classical scholar's critical arsenal—critics have begun to try to understand what he does do. It is as if classicists have begun to read Northrop Frye's polemical introduction to his *Anatomy of Criticism*.

G. Lawall's "Apollonius' *Argonautica*: Jason as Antihero," *Yale Classical Studies*, 19 (1966), 119–69, is the perfect expression as the title indicates of the decade in which it appeared. The particular excellence of this essay is the allegorical interpretation of the crew as being representative of various human qualities all of which eventually fail in the poem. Set against this is the weak and essentially unattractive Jason, who stands as the Hellenistic world's answer to the supremely confident "good" Homeric hero—and of course the perfect representation, as any good twentieth-century novel displays, of the failure of mankind in this post-Christian century of the Holocaust.

Lawall's essay appears in the journal in which years earlier was published J. F. Carspecken's "Apollonius Rhodius and the Homeric Epic," *Yale Classical Studies*, 13 (1952), 33–144. This is the first essay to confront the peculiarly vacant quality of Jason and see it as the poet's design. The result is the thesis that the hero of the *Argonautica* is the ensemble, the group, rather than the individual. The equally powerful members of the crew are the Hellenistic world's acknowledgement of the obsolescence of the extreme individualism which marks the Homeric hero. Like Lawall, Carspecken is particularly eloquent on the bleakness of the Hellenistic world view.

My own interest in the poem came about from trying to incorporate the figure of Medea into the masculine hero formula. Both Lawall's and Carspecken's essays had, it seemed to me, neglected her importance to the poem as Sainte-Beuve had ignored Jason a century or so earlier. The result was "Jason as a Love Hero in Apollonios' *Argonautika*," *Greek, Roman and Byzantine Studies*, 10 (1969), 31–55. I tried to establish Jason as a radically new hero figure, an erotic yet epic hero, a heterosexual hero, to whom Heracles acted as a foil, representative of the traditional and now obsolescent masculine eroticism of pederasty. G. Zanker's "The Love Theme in Apollonius Rhodius' *Argonautica*," *Wiener Studien*, NF 13 (1979), 52–75, expands the range of examples from the text which illustrate the centrality of love to the entire narrative. D. N. Levin's "Apollonius' Herakles," *Classical Journal*, 67 (1971), 22–28, recapitulates the role of Heracles in the poem, endeavoring to show that the poet regards Heracles as a desirable alternative to Jason. Zanker says that the distinction which I draw between pederasty and heterosexual love is unimportant to the poem. Levin ignores its possibility in his evaluation of Heracles. Moderns who consider pederasty as a deviant psychological phenomenon overlook its philosophical and spiritual importance in a society where it is approved and indeed encouraged. Pederastic love represents a range of attitudes, values, and feeling markedly distinguishing it from heterosexual love. The present book which is in part an extension of the implications of that essay is, as one can see, equally a product of its era when the philosophies of gender and of eroticism are about all that is left in the final bankruptcy of Western culture.

In contrast to my use of Heracles as the major alternative to Jason, H. Fränkel's "Ein Don Quixote unter den Argonauten des Apollonios," *Museum Helveticum*, 17 (1960), 1–20, offers the figure of Idas as a symbol for Apollonius of an heroic stance that has become so anachronistic as to be vain, if not silly. While this seems to be true, it is also nevertheless the case that the heroism which Idas represents in its decadence is not so crucial to the poem as the emotional and spiritual contrasts suggested by Jason and Heracles juxtaposed.

Carspecken's essay, as the title indicates, has a great deal to say about the difference in style between the Homeric poems and the *Argonautica*. He is particularly good at bringing out Apollonius' use of detail, perspective, and dramatic formulation in his similes. It may be said that Carspecken was one of the first to accept that Apollonius is a master in his own right, always in control, simply using the Homeric exemplar as he chooses to serve his own ends, rather than self-consciously "standing in the tradition" as the proverbial dog in the manger. What conspicuously shines forth in this essay is the acuity of Carspecken's critical perception.

Naturally the relationship between Apollonius and the tradition occupies the attention of every critic who examines the poem. P. Händel, *Beobachtungen zur epischen Technik des Apollonios Rhodios*, Zetemata 7 (Munich, 1954), examines the origin and transformation of a number of his themes and narrative devices. In particular, he talks of the inheritance from the Homeric epic and in such a way as often to imply that Apollonius was compelled to do certain things in a certain way. But there is no evidence that the exigencies of genre were so extreme, and nothing to suggest that Apollonius was enthralled. Händel is especially good in his remarks on the third book (pp. 93–114) discussing the coloration which Hellenistic erotic poetry has given to an heroic narration, for instance, the glimpses of the interior person and the domestic details, itself another kind of interior, as it were. The best book in English on the background to Apollonius' poem is J. Bacon, *The Voyage of the Argonauts* (London, 1925).

Two important essays for understanding the poet against the tradition are G. Giangrande's "'Arte allusiva' and Alexandrian Epic Poetry," *Classical Quarterly*, 17 (1967), 85–87, and "Hellenistic Poetry and Homer," *Antiquite Classique*, 39 (1970), 46–77. Giangrande is marvelously sensitive to the way the Alexandrians brought their scholarship to bear on their poetic diction, and we are fortunate that these and other essays on Hellenistic literature have been gathered together and recently (1980) published in Amsterdam under the title *Scripta Minora Alexandria*, vol. I.

In the same way E. Livrea's commentary to the fourth book of the *Argonautica* (*Apollonii Rhodii Argonautikon Liber IV* a cura di Enrico Livrea [Florence, 1973]) is particularly valuable for his noticing every play upon a Homeric verbal usage, as well as assembling every instance of Apollonius' usage in order to establish meanings. This superlative commentary, which is to be followed by those on the other three books of the poem, is the most complete introduction to Apollonius as a poet.

G. W. Mooney's commentary on all four books (Dublin, 1912; reprint ed., Amsterdam, 1964) is the only one in English and for a long time was the only commentary. It is useful, for it contains all the more obvious Homeric allusions made by Apollonius as well as the important scholia which indicate Apollonius' use of and relationship with the contemporary literature and learning. The notes and introductions to E. Delage's French translation of the first two books of the *Argonautica* for the Budé series (Paris, 1974) by F. Vian are an important supplement to Mooney, presenting among other things excellent remarks on the variant traditions from among which Apollonius chose his narrative. For of course to a reader who knows the variants the silence of the rejected option speaks almost as loudly as the version said. We are fortunate to have copious further instances of Vian's excellent perceptions in the many references to letters written by him to Livrea about details of the text of the fourth book as printed in Livrea's commentary. D. N. Levin's *Apollonius' "Argonautika" Re-Examined* (Leiden, 1971) is a full explication of the text of the first two books of the poem. There is considerable reference to Valerius Flaccus' Latin adaptation of the *Argonautica*, valuable for those who see poetic adaptations as an act of criticism.

The great commentary is Hermann Fränkel's *Noten zu den Argonautika des Apollonios Rhodios* (Munich, 1968). Here is the record of the thoughtful and imaginative progression of a great mind thoroughly steeped in the poem and its scholarship as it moves across the text. Fränkel is selective, pausing where he will as long as he chooses, handling points of grammar, textual problems, narrative techniques, and literary themes lovingly and intelligently. Curiously enough the story has impressed itself so deep into him that from time to time he begins to psychologize as though Jason and Medea were real people or at least characters in a nineteenth-century novel—this is clearly the most important literary frame of reference for him.

Parenthetically, there is a suggestive essay on the *Argonautica* as a prototypical novel in A. Heiserman's *The Novel Before the Novel* (Chicago, 1977). Working from B. E. Perry's *The Ancient Romances* (Berkeley, 1967), Heiserman has much to say about suffering and star-crossed love in its relationship to the romance and the novel. There is a particularly interesting Freudian interpretation of Jason's symbolic patricide as he overcomes the obstacles set for him by Aeetes.

The *Noten* are to be read together with the text which Fränkel made for the Oxford Classical Texts series in 1966. He had a free way with emendations and other textual problems to which most would object. See the intelligent objections here and there in Livrea's commentary. But Fränkel's profound knowledge of and feeling for the Homeric texts allows him to demonstrate again and again the newness of the Apollonian narrative, particularly how it leaves things unsaid so as to draw the reader into the narrative. Here is Apollonius developing narrative foreign to the Homeric manner, which has been so well described by Erich Auerbach in *Mimesis*.

Fränkel's strong emphasis on psychology in the *Noten* inhibits him from looking at how very much the action and the characters are symbolic or emblematic, as he had seen in his Don Quixote essay. Again Lawall's essay is instructive for this. T. M. Klein's "Callimachus, Apollonius Rhodius and the Concept of the 'Big Book'" (*Eranos*, 73 [1975], 16–25) is instructive for understanding how self-conscious Apollonius was as a narrator. We await the publication of more of Klein's dissertation. One would like to see published the 1967 Columbia University dissertation by J. F. Collins ("Studies in Book One of the *Argonautika* of Apollonios Rhodios"). Likewise one hopes that the particularly brilliant dissertation of Mary Margolies will be published ("Apollonius' *Argonautica*: A Callimachean Epic" [Diss. Univ. of Colorado, 1981]). Margolies has constructed an elaborate, yet thoroughly believable allegorical interpretation of the poem which demonstrates that the *Argonautica* is essentially about the art of poetry, most of all the aesthetics of making epic narrative. Her interpretation tells us more about the nuances and sensibility of Alexandrian poetry than we have hitherto been able to see.

The present-day trend in Apollonian studies in the United States is toward discovering the narrator presenting himself and his narrative problems in his narrative. See E. V. George "Poet and Characters in Apollonius Rhodius' Lemnian Episode," *Hermes*, 100 (1972), 47–63, which is an excellent example of this sort of study. A. Hurst's *Apollonios de Rhodes: Manière et cohérence* (Rome, 1967) has excellent discussions of the poet's self-consciousness, his use of the naïve style balanced against his insistent learning, the symbolic value to be attached to the narrative. Unfortunately Hurst also has a scheme whereby he tries to attach the narrative entirely to the underlying rhythm of going out and returning. For me at least rigid schematizing and charts defeat the essential ambiguity which marks all art. Still Hurst's schematization places emphasis upon the importance of arrangement rather than chronological development in the narrative as well as elevating style to its proper place in our criticism of the poem.

The acute self-consciousness of the Alexandrian literary scene is a major factor in Apollonius' development. For this one can read R. Pfeiffer, *History of Classical Scholarship from the Beginnings to the End of the Hellenistic Age* (Oxford, 1968), and look up the appropriate sections of P. M. Fraser's vast *Ptolemaic Alexandria* (Oxford, 1972). One can review the relationship between Theocritus and Apollonius in reference to the passages wherein one seems to have copied the other in A. Köhnken, *Apollonios Rhodios und Theokrit, Hypomnemata*, vol. 12 (Göttingen, 1965), to be read in conjunction with Fränkel's customarily elegant exposition of the narrative values in the Amycus episode in his article in *Transactions and Proceedings of the American Philological Association*, 83 (1952), 144–55.

We will end as we began, with Medea. She has found less favor nowadays than before, as a literary creation, but more surprisingly as an ethical proposition. For instance, A. Hübscher, *Die Charakteristik der Personen in Apollonios Argonauten* (Freiburg, 1940), declared (p. 36) that Medea is morally inferior to Jason, and more recently B. Otis, in *Virgil: A Study in Civilized Poetry* (Oxford, 1963), takes her to task for her presumably easy ways. But she has her defenders. E. S. Phinney, "Narrative Unity in the *Argonautica*: The Medea-Jason Romance," *Transactions of the American Philological Association*, 98 (1967), 327–41, has good words to say about the nature of Apollonius' construction of the Medea character, as well as the Alexandrian use of assymmetry, and the problem of the narrative as a whole versus the independence of the episodes. G. Paduano's *Studi su Apollonio Rodio* (Rome, 1972) is mostly concerned with Medea. See particularly "Le due Medee e il problema della personalita nella *Argonautiche*" (pp. 63–239).

H. Herter has recently completed the article on Apollonius for Pauly-Wissowa (Supplement vol. 13, cols. 15–56). E. V. Rieu has made an excellent English translation for the Penguin series. At this writing, M. Campbell at St. Andrews is completing or has completed a fine lexicon to Apollonius.

The following works have been cited in the notes by the surname of the author. Where there is more than one by the same author, the publication date has been added. For a complete bibliography, the reader is requested to consult Livrea or Herter.

Ardizzoni, A. *L'Eracle Semnos del poemma di Apollonio*. Catania, 1937.

Auerbach, E. *Mimesis*. Trans. W. Trask. Princeton, 1953.

Bacon, J. R. *The Voyage of the Argonauts*. London, 1925.

Beye, C. R. "Battle Narrative and Catalogues." *Harvard Studies in Classical Philology*, 68 (1964), 345–74.

———. *The "Iliad," the "Odyssey" and the Epic Tradition*. Garden City, 1966.

———. "Jason as a Love Hero in Apollonios' *Argonautika*." *Greek, Roman and Byzantine Studies*, 10 (1969), 31–55.

———. *Ancient Greek Literature and Society*. Garden City, 1975.

Boswell, J. *Christianity, Social Tolerance and Homosexuality*. Chicago, 1980.

Brink, C. O. "Callimachus and Aristotle: An Enquiry into Callimachus' *Pros Praxinen*." *Classical Quarterly*, 40 (1946), 11–26.

Brooks, C. "The Heroic Impulse in the *Odyssey*." *Classical World*, 70 (1976–77), 455–56.

Carspecken, J. F. "Apollonius Rhodius and the Homeric Epic." *Yale Classical Studies*, 13 (1952), 33–144.

Cataudella, Q. *La Novella Greca*. Naples, 1955.

Clarke, W. M. "Achilles and Patroklos in Love." *Hermes*, 106 (1978), 381–96.

Collins, J. F. "Studies in Book One of the Argonautika of Apollonios Rhodios." Diss. Columbia Univ., 1967.

Cook, A. *The Dark Voyage and the Golden Mean*. Cambridge, Mass., 1951.

Couat, A. *Alexandrian Poetry Under the First Three Ptolemies*. Trans. J. Loeb. London, 1931.

Delage, E. *La Géographie dans les Argonautiques*. Paris, 1930.

Elderkin, G. W. "Repetition in the *Argonautika*." *American Journal of Philology*, 34 (1913), 198–201.

Erbse, H. "Homerscholien und hellenistischen Glossare bei Apollonios Rhodios." *Hermes*, 81 (1953), 163–96.

Fontenrose, J. *Python: A Study of Delphic Myth and Its Origin*. Berkeley, 1959.

Fränkel, H. "Apollonius as Narrator in *Argonautica*." *Transactions and Proceedings of the American Philological Association*, 83 (1952), 144–55.

———. "Ein Don Quixote unter den Argonauten des Apollonios." *Museum Helveticum*, 17 (1960), 1–20.

———. *Noten zu den Argonautika des Apollonios Rhodios*. Munich, 1968.

Frye, N. *Anatomy of Criticism*. Princeton, 1957.

Galinsky, G. K. *The Herakles Theme*. Princeton, 1957.

George, E. V. "Poet and Characters in Apollonius Rhodius' Lemnian Episode." *Hermes*, 100 (1972), 47–63.

Giangrande, G. *L'Humour des Alexandrins*. Amsterdam, 1975.

Graves, R. *Greek Myths*. 2 vols. Baltimore, 1955.

Guthrie, W. K. C. *Orpheus and Greek Religion*. London, 1952.

Hack, R. K. "The Doctrine of Literary Forms." *Harvard Studies in Classical Philology*, 27 (1916), 1–66.

Hadas, M. "Apollonius called the Rhodian." *Classical Weekly*, 26 (1932), 41–46, 49–54.

Händel, P. *Beobachtungen zur epischen Technik des Apollonios Rhodios*. Zetemata 7. Munich, 1954.

Harrison, J. *Prolegomena to the Study of Greek Religion*. Cambridge, 1921.

Heiserman, A. *The Novel before the Novel*. Chicago, 1977.

Herter, H. "Apollonios." Pauly-Wissowa. Supplement vol. 13, cols. 15–56.

Hurst, A. *Apollonios de Rhodes: Manière et cohérence*. Rome, 1967.

Huxley, G. L. *Greek Epic Poetry*. London, 1969.

Kirk, G. S. *The Nature of Greek Myths*. Woodstock, N.Y., 1975.

Klein, L. *Die Göttertechnik in den Argonautika*. Leipzig, 1931.

Klein, T. M. "Callimachus, Apollonius Rhodius and the Concept of the 'Big Book.'" *Eranos*, 73 (1975), 16–25.

Knox, B. M. W. "Euripidean Comedy." In *Rarer Action: Essays in Honor of Francis Ferguson*. Ed. A. Cheuse and R. Koffler. New Brunswick, 1970. Pp. 68–96.

Köhnken, A. *Apollonios Rhodios und Theokrit. Hypomnemata*, vol. 12. Göttingen, 1965.

Lang, A. *Custom and Myth*. London, 1885.

Lawall, G. "Apollonius' *Argonautica*: Jason as Antihero." *Yale Classical Studies*, 19 (1966), 119–69.

Levin, D. N. "Apollonios' Herakles." *Classical Journal*, 67 (1971), 22–28.

Lindsay, J. *Clashing Rocks*. London, 1965.

Livrea, E., ed. *Apollonii Rhodii Argonautikon Liber IV*. Florence, 1973.

Lobel, E., and D. Page. *Poetarum Lesbiorum Fragmenta*. Oxford, 1955.

Meuli, K. *Odyssee und Argonautika*. Berlin, 1921.

Mooney, G. W., ed. *The "Argonautica" of Apollonius Rhodius*. Dublin, 1912; reprint ed., Amsterdam, 1964.

Otis, B. *Virgil: A Study in Civilized Poetry*. Oxford, 1963.

Paduano, G. *Studi su Apollonio Rodio*. Rome, 1972.

Pauly-Wissowa (August von Pauly and George Wissowa). *Realenzyklopädie der klassischen Altertumswissenschaft*. 33 vols. 13 supplement vols. to date. Stuttgart, 1893–.

Perry, B. E. *The Ancient Romances*. Berkeley, 1967.

Pfeiffer, R. *History of Classical Scholarship from the Beginnings to the End of the Hellenistic Age*. Oxford, 1968.

Phinney, E. S. "Narrative Unity in the *Argonautica*: The Medea-Jason Romance." *Transactions of the American Philological Association*, 98 (1967), 327–41.

Puech, A., trans. and ed. *Pindare²*. Budé translation. 2 vols. Paris, 1931.

Rose, H. J. *Handbook of Greek Mythology*. London, 1928.

Rosenmeyer, T. G. *The Green Cabinet*. Berkeley, 1969.

Russo, J. A., and B. Simon. "Homeric Psychology and the Oral Epic Tradition." *Journal of the History of Ideas*, 29 (1968), 483–98.

Schneiderman, L. "Apsyrtos' Death." *Psychoanalytic Review*, 54 (1967), 355–72.

Scholes, R., and R. Kellog. *The Nature of Narrative*. New York, 1968.

Stanford, W. B. *The Ulysses Theme*. Oxford, 1954.

Tate, J. "Plato and Allegorical Interpretation." *Classical Quarterly*, 23 (1929), 142–54; 24, (1930), 1–10.

———. "On the History of Allegorism." *Classical Quarterly*, 28 (1934), 105–14.

Thompson, S. *Motif Index of Folk Literature*. 6 vols. Bloomington, 1955–58.

Trenkner, S. *Greek Novella in the Classical Period*. Cambridge, 1958.

Trüb, H. *Kataloge in der griechischen Dichtung*. Oberwinterthur, 1952.

Van der Valk, M. *Researches on the Text and Scholia of the "Iliad."* 2 vols. Leiden, 1963.

Vellacott, P. *"Medea" and Other Plays*. Harmondsworth, 1963.

Vian, F., ed. Apollonios de Rhodes. *Argonautiques*. Budé translation. Paris, 1974.

de la Ville de Mirmont, H. "La Navire Argo et la science nautique d'Apollonios de Rhodes." *Revue Internationale de L'Enseignement*, 30 (1895), 230–85.

Webster, T. B. L. *Studies in Later Greek Comedy*. Manchester, 1953.

———. *Studies in Menander*. 2nd ed. Manchester, 1960.

———. *Hellenistic Poetry and Art*. London, 1964.

Wendel, K. *Die Überlieferung der Scholien zu Apollonios Rhodios*. Berlin, 1932.

Whitman, C. H. *Sophocles: A Study in Heroic Humanism*. Cambridge, Mass., 1951.

Wilamowitz-Moellendorf, U. von. *Euripides Herakles erklart von Ulrich von Wilamowitz-Moellendorf*. 2 vols. Berlin, 1889.

Woodhouse, W. J. *Composition of Homer's "Odyssey."* Oxford, 1930.

Zanker, G. "The Love Theme in Apollonius Rhodius' *Argonautica*." *Wiener Studien*, NF 13 (1979), 52–75.

Ziegler, K. *Das Hellenistische Epos*. Leipzig, 1934.

Notes

Chapter 1
THE POET

1. Compare Hack, who discusses the emergence of the theory of genres and the moral urgency which became attached to the observance of them.

2. The second volume of Van der Valk is a treasure house of examples of the execution of the theory of propriety by the Hellenistic textual critics of Homer. While most lived after the time of Apollonius, they may be fairly said to represent the collective mentality of the scholars of the Museum.

3. See Pfeiffer, pp. 112–13, for a discussion of this.

4. See particularly Van der Valk, vol. I, pp. 202–302.

5. Tabulated by Erbse.

6. Compare Hurst, pp. 37–38, 150–51.

7. See Otis in the chapter "From Homer to Virgil: The Obsolescence of Epic," pp. 5–20; T. M. Klein presents the attractive idea that when Callimachus inveighed against the "big book" he was objecting to the attempt at reproducing the seriousness and hugeness of traditional epic. For the narrator's belief in the importance of his story is always evident in Homer, and apart from length the Homeric abundance of detail makes the narrative massive. Callimachus preferred instead *leptotes*, the thinness or lightness of things. Theocritus' Idyll 7.45–48 is a passage often quoted to support the notion that Callimachus and his group disapproved of what Apollonius was doing. "For the builder who tries to make a house to equal the top of Mount Oromedon is much hated by me, as are those birds of the Muses who struggle in vain to sing in competition with the singer of Chios [that is, Homer]." But Apollonius is so insistently different from Homer that one cannot imagine Theocritus to have been so dim as not to have noticed this.

8. This is the main point of Ziegler.

9. Vian lists quotations with comments in the Budé *Argonautiques*, pp. xiii–xxi.

10. Brink, pp. 16–19, conveniently sums them up.

11. Webster (1964), p. 30.

12. Which is how he chose to be remembered. The epitaph which he fashioned for himself reads: "You are walking past the tomb of Battus' son, skilled at song, at laughing along with wine, all in the proper proportion."

13. See his versified praise in fr. 27 (Pfeiffer).

14. Fr. 612 (Pfeiffer); Compare Hurst's conception of the *mode savante*, pp. 11–19 et passim.

15. Compare, for example, Otis in his chapter "The Subjective Style," pp. 141–96, who like so many others feels compelled to deride Apollonius so as to highlight his praise of Virgil.

16. Hurst, pp. 19–28 et passim.

17. Auerbach, pp. 3–23.

18. See Fränkel (1968), pp. 227–28.

19. Which Fränkel (1968) has conveniently assembled, pp. 25–26.

20. Which will be discussed in the third chapter.

21. Cross references and tabulations are to be found in Carspecken, pp. 51–52.

22. Hurst, p. 46.

23. See Russo and Simon.

24. George, pp. 49–50, discusses the way in which the poet identifies the readers with the Lemnian women bedazzled by the cloak.

25. See Carspecken, pp. 84–88; Beye (1966), pp. 36–37.

26. For a detailed psychological reading of these monologues see Paduano, pp. 9–59.

27. Scholes and Kellog, pp. 185, 200.

28. Köhnken is the most recent roasting of this old chestnut. But the matter cannot be resolved since neither the question What is imitation? nor Why imitate? can be satisfactorily answered. Compare also Otis, pp. 398–405.

29. See Carspecken's discussion of Apollonius' development of the Artemis-Medea simile (*Argonautica* 3.875–84) compared to Homer's Artemis-Medea simile (*Odyssey* 6.102–5), pp. 76, 79–80. Compare also pp. 77–79 for his identification of verbal constructs with genre painting at 1.774–80, 3.656–63, 3.969–71, 4.1062–65. Compare Webster's remarks (1964) on Apollonius' painterly vistas and lighting, pp. 69–70, 79.

30. Webster (1964), p. 76; Trenkner, p. 77, calls mockery basic to romance.

31. Compare Knox; Beye (1975), pp. 281–84.

32. For instance by Otis, pp. 62–65, who believes the poem is seriously flawed by the presentation of irreconcilable characteristics in Medea; by Paduano, pp. 63–84, who believes that Apollonius ignores Medea the witch while creating a psychologically consistent persona. See also Phinney, pp. 332–41, who argues for psychological unity specifically in refutation of Otis.

33. Odysseus is a complicated figure relative to Homer's other characterizations, as Stanford has so well demonstrated, p. 80.

34. Scholes and Kellog, p. 164.

35. Frye, p. 77.

36. Hurst, pp. 149–53, summarizes the matter of polarities and symmetries.

37. Delage, p. 12.

38. Vian, the Budé *Argonautiques*, p. xxii.

Chapter 2
THE TRADITION

1. Graves, vol. 2, p. 227; another kind of contemporary Euhemerism is to be found in Schneiderman who analyzes the myth as a story type of bringing back the totem in which there emerges the Great Mother figure who is substituted for the totem. The murder of Apsyrtus is a profane act but performed with the religious intensity of a ritual enactment. There are many interesting pages upon the religious need to commit evil.

2. See Lang, pp. 87–102, where a number of variants are collected.

3. Meuli, pp. 3–4; Bacon, p. 85.

4. Meuli, pp. 10–15; Rose, pp. 294–96.

5. Whitman, pp. 59–60.

6. Lindsay, pp. 10–11.

7. Fontenrose, pp. 485–86.

8. See the scholium at *Argonautica* 1.773.

9. Harrison, p. 659.

10. Meuli, p. 102.

11. Fontenrose, Appendix 1, pp. 477–87.

12. Vian in the Budé *Argonautiques*, p. 126.

13. See Huxley's chapter "Early Argonautika and Related Epics," especially pp. 66–67.

14. See Puech in the Budé *Pindare*, vol. 2, p. 62.

15. Heiserman, pp. 16–17.

16. Thompson, vol. 2, G5302.

17. Bacon, pp. 30–31.

18. Vellacott's translation of the *o pangkakiste* in line 465 of the play.

19. Galinsky has assembled all the evidence of a study of the extreme adaptability of this myth figure to varying cultural needs throughout the centuries.

20. Galinsky who quotes from p. 38 of Wilamowitz.

21. Compare Kirk, pp. 206–12, who discusses Heracles as a mediating figure between nature and culture.

22. This has been noticed by Brooks.

23. Compare, for example, Cook, pp. 163–72.

24. Frye, pp. 33–34.

25. Apollonius so assiduously avoids repetition that, for instance, where Homer always repeats verbatim in instructions passed on from one speaker to another, the Alexandrian allows only minimal partial repetition. The matter is discussed and the instances tabulated in Elderkin.

26. Discussed by Fränkel (1968), pp. 70–71.

27. See Beye (1966), pp. 203–5.

28. Pseudo-Demosthenes *Epitaphios* 1391.

29. Recently Heiserman who based much of what he says on Perry.

30. See Perry, pp. 44–95; 335–36, n. 65, for his discussion of this conception; on the quest see Frye, pp. 187, 316–24.

31. Frye, p. 55.

32. Scholes and Kellog, p. 12.

33. Frye, pp. 246–47.

34. Scholes and Kellog, p. 14, and objected to by Heiserman, p. 222. Epic is ideal when it is stereotypic, but the narrative line cannot share in the ideal because the epic story is, like history, peculiar and unique.

35. Frye, p. 304.

36. Scholes and Kellog, p. 14.

37. See Cataudella, pp. 17–38; Woodhouse.

38. Discussed and listed in Trenkner, pp. 110–11, 163–66.

39. Heiserman, p. 33.

40. See Rosenmeyer, pp. 128–29.

41. Couat, p. 367: "In this curious scene tragedy is mingled with comedy."

42. Webster (1953), p. 8.

Chapter 3
THE HEROES

1. Carspecken, pp. 110–25.

2. Lawall, pp. 123–48.

3. Lawall, p. 168.

4. E. M. Forster's saying (noticed by Scholes and Kellog, p. 169) that ancient narrative is "life by values" as opposed to modern narrative which is "life by time" is much less true of the *Argonautica*.

5. Carspecken lists them, p. 54.

6. Compare de la Ville de Mirmont, pp. 250–51, cited by Carspecken, p. 44.

7. Compare Fränkel (1968), p. 44, n. 50, who has gathered the references.

8. An emotional attitude common to this poem. Couat, p. 41, notices it at 1.1172 ff., 2.541 ff., 2.1001 ff., 3.291 ff., 3.656 ff., 3.744 ff., 4.106 ff.

9. See Beye (1975), pp. 288–96.

10. Lawall, p. 149–51.

11. *Hypossainōn*, certainly with that precise sense, for it is used literally at 3.883–84 ("animals . . . fawning").

12. Fränkel (1960) is excellent on Idas' anachronism.

13. Fränkel (1968) in his note on 1.338–50 suggests that Apollonius thinks Heracles too impulsive to be a leader.

14. *Iliad* 9.558 mentions that Idas had drawn his bow against Apollo. Idas and Apollo compete for the same woman, Marpessa, who chooses Idas over Apollo. Idas clearly is not to be intimidated by Idmon's pieties. It is hinted at by the scholiast. See Wendel, 42.4–5.

15. Rose, p. 202.

16. See Clarke.

17. As Vian says in the Budé *Argonautiques*, p. 41: "on a souvent noté que l'épopée, par décence, n'évoque qu'avec discretion les thèmes érotiques."

18. Giangrande, pp. 19–22, notices the possibility of a humorous double-entendre in these lines. The word "untamed" refers both to virgins and to warriors; the flowing hair describes both their virginal state and warriors' plumed helmets.

19. See Phinney, pp. 330–32.

20. The scholiast at 1.763 begins the tradition of interpreting the cloak as an allegory when he allegorizes Athena's role as its donor (which is otherwise mysterious; see Fränkel [1968] on these lines): "because the world came about through wisdom of the goddess and whatever man does in this world would not go right without her wisdom." Lawall, pp. 154–57, also employs an allegorical interpretation, claiming that the scenes are instructive of the lessons Jason learns in the first two books. Collins, pp. 65–85, and George, pp. 47–63, expand and refine the possibilities of allegorical interpretation. Because Aphrodite's glancing at herself in Ares' shield is so perfectly susceptible to allegorical interpretation, and rightly so, the other less precise images are, to my mind, forced into an equally rigid interpretation. The tendency to allegorize in antiquity began with the intellectuals, not the poets, who had been reared and steeped in the Homeric poems and who had to restructure

the Homeric view of reality so as to mean something else. The subject is well treated by Tate in his three essays.

21. George, p. 61.

22. Ardizzoni believes that this is because Apollonius makes Heracles an example of Stoic asceticism in contrast to Jason's weak passive self-indulgence. Fränkel (1968) supports this view; compare his note on *nekon* of p. 856. However that Apollonius faults Heracles while admiring him seems to me to be the better mode of interpretation, and the one suggested by Virgil whose use of Anchises seems modeled upon this Heracles figure. In the *Aeneid* Anchises, who is much prized, nonetheless mistakes the direction of the voyage and shortly thereafter dies. He is clearly out of the past whereas Aeneas must march into the future. That is the truth behind Heracles' mad dash out of this narrative and Jason's survival in it. Compare, however, Levin, pp. 22–28, who argues that Apollonius presents Heracles altogether sympathetically.

23. Phinney, p. 331. See Köhnken, p. 75, who gives some support for this point of view. Zanker chides me for making a distinction between homosexual and heterosexual love (Beye [1969]), saying, "It is pointless to differentiate between paederastic and heterosexual love. Love is seen to have the same effect." True enough, passion is passion, although we may note that Apollonius reserves his imagistic detail to describe a man's passion for a boy and a woman's passion for a man. Still what is crucial are the associations. I should say that pederastic love traditionally held more importance, was more conventional, than a grand passion for a woman. The *Symposium* seems to be testimony to this. Remember Pentheus in the *Bacchae* sneering at the disguised Dionysus (453–58) because it seems that he carried on with women. To put it into extremes in order to make my point, it would be the conventional, conservative, stuffy Colonel Blimp figure who would be gone on his teen-aged boyfriend. Levin quite ignores this aspect of Heracles which is to my mind central to understanding the poem. Herter dismisses my *GRBS* article because the idea that Jason is a lover is well-known. That is not the point. Apart from his being a heterosexual lover, Jason is described by the poet in exactly the terms used by Homer to describe a battle hero. So that insofar as epic may be said to describe the human condition and the true nature of the male, then Apollonius has *radically* redefined him.

A much-needed new perspective on the complicated and often obscure subject of ancient Greek male homosexuality is touched on by J. Boswell, pp. 3–59. His fresh analysis of the evidence sometimes contradicts what I have said in this chapter; the difficulty resides in trying to determine when homosexual acts in Greek antiquity derive from a genuine sexual need and when they derive from an acculturated response to certain social and political situations.

24. A gadfly describes Eros at 3.277; it is in any case a conventional idea

in classical literature. Perhaps, however, Apollonius came to the gadfly from *Odyssey* 22.298–301 (compare Otis, p. 400).

25. Meuli, p. 90; Vian, Budé *Argonautiques*, p. 35. Rose, p. 202, suggests that Hylas is also a vegetation figure who annually disappears and returns in the spring. The poet's identification with Hylas allows for the nuances which come from the vegetation association to be attached to the traditional hero figure, the man of adventure and war who Jason is supposed to be.

Chapter 4
THE VOYAGE

1. See Hurst, pp. 137–46, here quoting Trüb.
2. See Beye (1964), pp. 345–74.
3. See George, pp. 57–60.
4. Guthrie, pp. 171–82.
5. Lindsay explores this idea through a great body of literature.
6. Fontenrose, p. 480, calls them variants of each other.
7. Lindsay, pp. 1–74; Vian in the Budé *Argonautiques*, pp. 125–26.
8. Lawall, p. 133, lists the instances from which it might be inferred that Apollonius means to establish a thematic struggle between the Olympian and the chthonian forces. This is an attractive idea which however has its problems because Aeetes is so often identified as the son of Helios. The sun cancels out the chthonic aura.
9. Although, as the poet tells us, Jason is perfectly able to sleep through the night after killing Cyzicus (1.1080–81).
10. (1968), p. 240; "[Jason] imitiert . . . mit schwerer Ironie." It is the poet's irony, I should say.
11. Beye (1975), pp. 64–67.
12. Fränkel (1952) believes that it is impossible to decide upon Apollonius' religious convictions.
13. Lawall, p. 162.
14. The wrath of Zeus is ineffectual, essentially perfunctory, mentioned sometime after the fact to motivate the plot (4.557–58). Note how indifferent Poseidon is to the death of his son, Amycus, as compared to his continuing wrath after Odysseus kills the Cyclops. Compare L. Klein who stresses that there is no coherent relationship between divinities nor any divine purpose. There are no factions; Aeetes has no divine protector; being the son of Helios does him no good. In fact the poem is remarkable for the absence of divine hostility as a dominant motive.

Chapter 5
SWEET TALK

1. See Hurst, pp. 140–47, especially pp. 146–47, on the unity and completeness of the third book.

2. "The necessary cynical tone for the human scenes which follow," Carspecken, p. 123.

3. See Fränkel (1968), pp. 330–31, 337–40.

4. Compare Paduano, pp. 98–104, who talks of the loss of Aphrodite's power. "Ma qui se è conservato il ruolo passivo della divinità tradizionale olimpica, lo schema classico è ridicolizzato della representazione della forza superpersonale attraverso la presenza superficiale e frivole di Eros." (p. 99.)

5. Just in the dialogue between Hera and Athena, for example, at lines 11, 13, 27–28, 31, 33, 86, and 89.

6. Compare Rosenmeyer, pp. 77–85.

7. Webster (1960), p. 22.

8. Fränkel (1968), p. 339.

9. Compare Phinney, p. 333, with footnote; Paduano argues, pp. 71–72, "in realita il fatto che la magia non costitiusca una scelta necessitata per Medea costitiusce la prova migliore della sua inessenzialità come qualificazione psicologica." This approach seems unduly literal; the poet establishes associations which create an aura about Medea giving her a quality which young women do not have.

10. Compare Russo and Simon.

11. As Händel, pp. 111–12, says: "Die Rede der Krahe . . . soll das Heroische aus der Begegnung zwischen Jason und Medea auscheiden. . . . Mopsus gleicht sozusagen zwischen dem Heroischen und dem Erotischen aus, er legitimiert das Erotische."

12. See Fontenrose, pp. 306–20, who amasses all the variants of the myth which suggests what rich associations Apollonius' readers could make.

Chapter 6
LOVE AFFAIR

1. Livrea at line 26.

2. Mooney at lines 289, 319.

3. "Tale versione dovete riuscire una grossa sorpresa per i contemporanei di Apollonio," remarks Livrea at line 254, who has other good things to say about Argus' account at line 256 and at line 267.

4. To many critics Apollonius seems less successful in his execution of the

fourth book. There is awkward narrative, for instance, that two islands are conveniently vacant in the Ister (329–37), one for the Argonauts, one for the murder; or the Colchians agreeing to a truce when they far outnumber the Argonauts; the agreement to submit the decision "to the judgment of kings" (347), an unlikely group to be found in the middle of nowhere; the improbable transition of locale at Drepanē where Medea talks first to Arete, then to the crew, and then the narrator moves us into the royal bedroom for pillow talk; the peculiar apostrophe to love, 445–51, with its ambiguous concatenation of points of view and sympathies; or Jason's response to Medea just previous to the invocation which is either vague or confused. See Livrea at line 404; Fränkel (1968) at lines 394–410.

5. Fränkel (1968) at lines 202–10. See his Exkurs "Vorspiel ohne Aristie: Aristie ohne Vorspiel," pp. 469–70, which points out how Apollonius had the habit of separating the two. See Livrea at line 203 on the exhortation as an epic commonplace.

6. "Before the Argo reaches home its crew must have shed enough tears to float it." Hadas, p. 44.

7. See Livrea's comment at line 1101.

8. The tone resembles that of Theocritus' twenty-fourth Idyll, where the poet makes Amphitryon and Alcmene into typical parents. He describes baby Heracles vanquishing snakes in his crib in what is meant to be an heroic narrative scene, but which is in fact an amusing and homely vignette of parenthood. Amphitryon awakened by Alcmene rushes to the children's room; when he sees that Heracles is not hurt, like any working father whose wife and children have roused him for nothing, he plods back to bed and concentrates on sleep.

9. Jason's leadership, we may remember, has cost him many a sleepless night (compare 2.631).

10. Heiserman, pp. 22, 27–28.

11. Livrea at line 360.

12. See Livrea at line 404; Fränkel (1968) at lines 394–410.

13. Fränkel (1968) Exkurs, pp. 488–90.

14. Compare Lindsay, p. 21; Fontenrose, pp. 225–29, likens it to *Odyssey* 10.513–15, which describes the merging of the two underworld rivers.

Index

Aeetes, 104, 136; in legend, 40–44
Aitia, 27, 75, 98–100, 103, 147
Alexander, 75–76
Alexandria, 2–4, 6, 39, 60, 71; the Library in, 2–4, 6, 26; literary tastes in, 5, 18, 25, 32, 83, 100–101, 125; the Museum in, 2–3, 6
Amused tone, 31–32, 82–83, 126, 138. *See also* Irony
Antimachus of Colophon, 4, 6
Aphrodite, 41, 48, 52, 91–92, 99, 116–17, 127–28
Apollo, 13–15, 18, 113–14, 118
Apollonius, 6, 142, 151–52, 159, 172–73; ambiguity of, 107, 148; irony of, 31–32, 101, 115–16, 146; narrative style of, 13–38, 105–8, 124, 144; relationship of to Callimachus, 1, 6–7, 10; tradition in writing of, 10–11, 35–36, 64, 66–68, 133–34, 147, 158–60
Aratus: *Phainomena*, 9–10, 27
Argo story, 49, 53, 78; in Greek tradition, 41, 44–47; resemblance to Xenophon's *Anabasis*, 75–76
Argonautica, 7, 63, 79, 84–85, 95, 124; Amycus episode in, 104–5, 109–10, 112, 149–50; Apsyrtus episode in, 149–50, 153, 160, 162–64; Catalogue of Heroes in, 22–23; comedy in, 74–75, 121–24; Cyzicus episode in, 21–22, 42, 98–99,

153; fairy-tale elements in, 43–44; Hylas episode in, 16, 30, 93–97; Lemnian episode in, 27, 89–93; Phineus episode in, 104–8, 111–12, 118–19; problems of unity in, 34–38; religious attitudes in, 99, 118–19, 125–26, 155, 157. *See also* Similes
Ariadne, 42, 53, 128–129, 163
Aristeia, 8, 61, 65, 137
Aristotle, 2–5, 7
Atalanta, 41–42, 91–92, 161
Athens, 39, 49, 51, 55
Athlos, 54, 91
Auden, W. H., 101–2
Auerbach, E., 11, 12

Bacchylides: Ode Five, 148
Bacon, J., 172
Beye, C. R., 171

Callimachus, 8, 15, 31, 68, 103, 170; *Aitia*, 7; *Bath of Pallas*, 164; *Hecale*, 7–8, 138; *Hymn to Apollo*, 138; *Hymn to Artemis*, 9; *Hymn to Demeter*, 9; *Hymn to Zeus*, 14; literary principles of, 3, 7–10; quarrel with Apollonius, 1, 6–7; Tables, 3–4
Campbell, M., 175
Carspecken, J., 171–72
Catalogue, 100–102
Circe, 44–45, 49, 151–52

Clashing Rocks, 43–44. *See also* Symple-
   gades
Collins, J. F., 174
Comedy of manners, 151, 160–61. *See also*
   Meilikhïe; Politesse
Comic sensibility, 62–63, 166
Comic theater, 122–24, 151–53, 161
Cyrus, 75–76

Dante: *Inferno*, 148, 164
Delage, E., 37, 173
Diodorus Siculus, 41–42

Epic poetry, 15, 53, 68, 89, 156
Epicureanism, 59–60
Eros, 127–28
Eroticism, 122, 156–57; in Jason's meeting
   with Medea, 138–39; in Lemnian epi-
   sode, 90–93
Erotic poetry, 146, 163–64, 172
Euripides: *Alcestis*, 56, 145; *Electra*, 32, 34,
   83; *Helen*, 70–71; *Heracles*, 56; *Ion*, 32;
   Iphigenia at Aulis, 34, 50; *Iphigenia at
   Tauris*, 70–71; *Medea*, 34, 49–53, 131;
   Orestes, 17–18, 83

Fleece, 155–57
Fränkel, 28, 84, 108, 113, 130, 163, 171,
   173–74
Fraser, P. M., 174
Free will, 141–42
Frye, N., 34, 63, 71–72, 170

George, E. V., 174
Giangrande, G., 172
Gilgamesh, 44, 61–62

Händel, P., 172
Harrison, J., 44
Hecate, 44, 139
Heiserman, A., 173
Hellenistic attitudes, 6, 14, 130, 147
Heracles, 149, 171, 184; as a foil to Jason,
   83–84, 93–98; as a theme, 117–18; in
   the tradition, 53–56
Hero: *aristeia* of, 139–41; concept of, 57–
   62, 137; Homeric version of, 48, 81, 171
Herodotus, 3, 57, 69
Herter, H., 175
Hesiod, 3, 7, 10, 16, 68, 103–4

Heterosexual love, 73–74, 89–90, 93–94,
   96, 171, 184
Hippodameia, 42
Homer: Catalogue of Ships, 12, 22, 65, 80;
   Iliad, 7, 11, 62–63; *Odyssey*, 7, 44–45,
   61–62, 68, 72, 121–22; Phaiacian epi-
   sode, 154–55
Homeric poems, 49, 99, 119–20; manner of
   narration, 5, 11–13, 57, 64–66, 83–84;
   in relation to the *Argonautica*, 16, 19–20,
   23–25, 27, 34–36, 38, 63–64, 66–68,
   87, 100, 172
Homosexual love, 73, 94–96, 171, 184
Hübscher, A., 175
Humor, 98, 105, 117, 131, 133; in Lem-
   nian episode, 82–83, 90–93
Hurst, A., 23, 36, 103, 174
Huxley, G. L., 46
Hymns, 13–14, 19. *See also* Callimachus,
   hymns

Idas, 85–86, 140, 171–72
Idmon, 45–47, 113
Irony, 31, 82–83, 90–94, 103, 115–16,
   128–29, 131, 163–64

Jaeger, W., 60
Jason, 63, 64, 75–76, 78, 81, 84; as anti-
   hero, 170–71; *aristeia* of, 139–41; cen-
   trality of to poem, 77–78; as love hero,
   93, 171; lust of for fleece, 155–57; made
   ridiculous, 31–33, 82–84; modest role of
   in second and fourth books, 114–16,
   148–49; as naïve, 130–31; in tradition,
   40–43

Kellog, R., 71
Klein, T. M., 174
Köhnken, A., 174
Kurtz, J. G., 124

Lawall, G., 170
Levin, D. N., 171, 173
Lindsay, J., 43
Livrea, E., 172
Love, 97, 99, 120–21, 134–35, 150, 159–
   60, 171; described on Jason's cloak, 91–
   92; in Euripides' *Medea*, 51–52; as Jason's
   athlos, 116–17; in romance and New
   Comedy, 72–75; symbolized by Aphrodite

scene, 125–28
Lykophron, 6
Lysippus, 21

MacKail, J. W., 170
Margolies, M., 174
Medea, 82, 145–46, 155–57, 166, 169,
    175; as ambivalent figure, 33–34, 133–
    35, 144–46; character evolution of, 157–
    60; compared to Nausicaa, 64, 129, 137–
    38; as hero, 135, 143–45; monologues of,
    28–29, 135–36; in the tradition, 42, 49,
    50–51, 63, 132–34
Meilikhiē, 120–21, 131, 162. *See also*
    Comedy of manners; Politesse
Melancholia, 81–82, 149, 155
Menander, 74–75
Meuli, K., 44
Mimnermus, 46
Mooney, G. W., 173
Muse, 15–17, 35–36

Nagler, M., 65
Naïve sensibility, 11, 22, 69, 103, 174
Narrator, 105–8
New Comedy, 70, 74–75, 122
Nicander, 27
Nostos, 148
Novel, 72, 122, 152, 173

Odysseus, 50, 62, 82
Orpheus, 18–19, 45, 86
Otis, B., 151, 175

Paduano, G., 175
Parry, M., 65
Pederasty, 95–96, 171. *See also* Homosexual
    love
Perry, B. E., 173
Pfeiffer, R., 174
Phineus, 18, 44–45, 113, 146
Phinney, E. S., 175
Pindar: *Fourth Pythian Ode*, 16, 43–44, 47–
    49, 158–59
Pirsig, R., 60
Politesse, 48, 52, 82, 84–85, 89, 93, 98,
    117, 122. *See also* Comedy of manners;
    Meilikhiē

Rhianus, 10, 74
Rieu, E. V., 175
Romance, 71–73
Rose, H. J., 40

Sainte-Beuve, C. A., 169–70
Sappho, 138
Scholes, R., 71
Seneca: *Medea*, 49
Similes, 10, 25–26, 32, 48, 81–82, 88, 94,
    108, 110, 121, 123, 136–38, 141, 146,
    148, 150, 154, 160, 172
Sophocles: *Trachinian Women*, 55
Stoicism, 59–60, 119
Strabo, 42
Suidas, 42
Symplegades, 104, 110–11. *See also* Clashing
    Rocks

Telemachus, 119
Theocritus, 15, 56, 60, 73–74, 126, 174–
    75; Idyll One, 91; Idyll Two, 134; Idyll
    Thirteen, 30, 47, 93; Idyll Fifteen, 32,
    127; Idyll Twenty-two, 15, 109
Thucydides, 3, 19, 26, 57, 69–70
Tiphys, 45, 113
Tragic sensibility, 58, 62–63

Underworld, 44–45, 112–14, 165–66

Virgil: *Aeneid*, 10, 83, 90, 92, 148, 159,
    170

Wandering Rocks, 104
Webster, T. B. L., 8, 31
Wit, 82–83. *See also* Amused tone; Humor;
    Irony
Wordsworth, J. C., 170

Xenophon: *Anabasis*, 75–76; *The Education of
    Cyrus*, 72–73

Youth, 109, 112, 119; of *Argo* crew, 80–81;
    as a theme, 111–12

Zanker, G., 171
Zenodotus, 4, 5

CHARLES ROWAN BEYE is Professor of Classics, Boston University. He has also taught at Harvard (where he acquired his Ph.D. degree), Yale, Stanford, and Wheaton College. Among his books are The "Iliad," the "Odyssey" and the Epic Tradition and Ancient Greek Literature and Society. He has been awarded the Olivia James Traveling Fellowship and a Senior Fellowship from the National Endowment for the Humanities.

JOHN GARDNER, critically acclaimed best-selling author, is Professor of English, State University of New York at Binghamton. He has treated the Argonautica theme in his epic poem Jason and Medeia. Most widely known as a novelist and poet, he has also published children's fiction, essays, innumerable scholarly articles, and several scholarly books.